# THE HEART
# OF HUMAN RIGHTS

# THE HEART OF HUMAN RIGHTS

ALLEN BUCHANAN

OXFORD
UNIVERSITY PRESS

# OXFORD

UNIVERSITY PRESS

Oxford University Press is a department of the University of Oxford.
It furthers the University's objective of excellence in research,
scholarship, and education by publishing worldwide.

Oxford   New York

Auckland   Cape Town   Dar es Salaam   Hong Kong   Karachi
Kuala Lumpur   Madrid   Melbourne   Mexico City   Nairobi
New Delhi   Shanghai   Taipei   Toronto

With offices in

Argentina   Austria   Brazil   Chile   Czech Republic   France   Greece
Guatemala   Hungary   Italy   Japan   Poland   Portugal   Singapore
South Korea   Switzerland   Thailand   Turkey   Ukraine   Vietnam

Oxford is a registered trademark of Oxford University Press
in the UK and certain other countries.

Published in the United States of America by
Oxford University Press
198 Madison Avenue, New York, NY 10016

Library of Congress Cataloging-in-Publication Data
Buchanan, Allen E., 1948–
The heart of human rights / Allen Buchanan.
pages cm.
Includes index.
ISBN 978-0-19-932538-2 (hardback : alk. paper)—ISBN 978-0-19-932539-9 (updf)—
ISBN 978-0-19-932540-5 (epub)
1. Human rights. 2. Law—Philosophy. I. Title.
K3240.B79   2013
323.01—dc23      2013003211

3 5 7 9 8 6 4

Printed in the United States of America
on acid-free paper

# CONTENTS

# PREFACE

By the time I had finished writing *Secession: The Morality of Political Divorce* I had begun to think about state-breaking not just in two-party terms—taking account only of the rights and interests of the secessionists and of the state—but also in terms of the rights and interests of third parties, especially other states. This led me to think about the morality of the state system. The result of my first effort to do this was *Justice, Legitimacy, and Self-Determination: Moral Foundations for International Law*. Soon after the publication of that book I became convinced that I needed to think harder about legitimacy and about human rights.

The present book took shape as I came to focus on what I believe to be the most neglected topic in the theory of global justice and perhaps in the philosophy of international law as well: the moral foundations of the system of international legal human rights. Thinking about the system of international legal human rights, which includes norms and institutions, led me, I hope, to a better understanding of institutional legitimacy. It also led to my questioning the implicit assumptions of current philosophical theories of human rights.

There has already been much valuable philosophical work on the theory of human rights, but the focus has been almost exclusively on moral human rights, not on international legal human rights. Even philosophers who espouse Practical or Political theories of human rights have not acknowledged the centrality of human rights law in human rights practice. Those who favor Orthodox or Moral theories of human rights have tended to talk almost exclusively about moral human rights while assuming that what they say has clear implications for human rights practice. That practice, however, is largely anchored in international human rights law. *Human rights law, not any philosophical or "folk" theory of moral human rights, is the authoritative lingua franca of modern human rights practice.*

While ignoring the actual character of international human rights law, philosophers have uncritically assumed that the major work in theorizing human rights will be done when a theory of moral human rights is produced and defended. They have not considered the full range of options concerning the relationship between moral human rights and legal human rights. Instead, they have tended to proceed as if it is obvious that the function of international human rights law is to realize a set of moral human rights. I argue that this is a mistaken assumption.

Some philosophers contend that human rights imply the existence of a state system because these rights serve to limit state sovereignty; others deny this, pointing out that it would make sense to talk of human rights if there were no states or a single world state. Each group assumes, without so much as a sketch of an argument, that there is one concept of human rights (theirs). Practical or Political theorists don't just assert that their concept of human rights is the one predominantly used in modern human rights practice; they make the stronger claim that *human rights are rights that limit state sovereignty*. Orthodox or Moral theorists don't just say that there is a concept of human rights that does not presuppose the existence of a state system; they say that *human rights do not presuppose a state system*. Each group is guilty of conceptual imperialism, failing to consider the possibility that there is more than one concept of human rights or to put the same point differently, that the phrase 'human rights' is used in at least two different ways: to refer to rights that function (among other things) to limit sovereignty against the backdrop of the state system and to refer to moral rights that all human beings have simply by virtue of their humanity.

My hope is that this book will do two things (beyond avoiding conceptual imperialism): direct the energies of philosophers toward the moral assessment of international human rights law in both its doctrinal and its institutional aspects, and contribute to the growing awareness of the importance of the philosophy of international law. If this book succeeds in shifting philosophical attention toward the morality of international human rights law in the way *Secession* focused attention on the morality of state-breaking, I shall be very pleased.

# ACKNOWLEDGMENTS

For whatever is valuable in this book, I am indebted to many people—too many to thank here, even if my memory were up to the task. Above all, I am grateful to Samantha Besson and James Nickel, for their outstanding work on human rights. They have been patient and generous in explaining matters on which I am much less well versed and in providing detailed comments on my work in progress. They are both role models for me, combining philosophical acuity with solid knowledge of international law. And unlike the vast majority of thinkers preoccupied with human rights, they appreciate the central role of human rights law in modern human rights practice. In my judgment, Nickel's book *Making Sense of Human Rights*, the first version of which was published in 1987 at a time at which few philosophers were thinking about the topic, is still the best available general treatment of the subject. I will be very happy if this book makes a contribution that even approximates that of Jim's book. Samantha's articles on human rights and equality and on the connection between human rights and democracy are exemplary. I am confident that her forthcoming book *A Legal Theory of Human Rights* will be pathbreaking (and will no doubt make more effectively some of the points I try to make in this volume).

Like everyone else working on human rights, I owe a debt to Henry Shue for his pioneering work on the subject. I have also benefitted greatly from more recent theorizing by John Tasioulas and Charles Beitz. I hope that John and Chuck will forgive me for spending more energy in this book on my disagreements with them than on emphasizing how much I have learned from them.

I must also thank my colleague Gopal Sreenivasan. It was his work on the right to health that spurred me to refine my thinking about the dubiousness of the assumption that international legal human rights mirror moral human rights, a major theme of this volume.

I have also profited greatly from the work and collegial generosity of many other scholars, including especially Carl Wellman, James Griffin, Hans Morsink, Joseph Raz, and William Talbott.

Julian Culp, Kristen Hessler, Robert O. Keohane, Jim Nickel, Steven Ratner, Bas Van der Vossen, and Kit Wellman provided extremely valuable comments on drafts of all of the chapters of this book. Finally, anyone who is familiar with the way I used to do philosophy before I began collaborating with Robert O. Keohane will immediately see his institutionalist influence on my thinking in this book.

I also want to express my gratitude to the leaders of three outstanding research institutions. Much of the work for this book was done during my time at the Forschungs-Kolleg Humanwissenshaften in Bad Homburg, Germany, and at the Center for the Philosophy of Freedom at the University of Arizona in Tucson. I am grateful to Rainer Forst and Stephan Gosepath for inviting me to spend a rewarding six weeks in Bad Homburg and to David Schmidtz for appointing me as an annual visiting professor at the Freedom Center. Finally, I want to thank the chair of Duke's Department of Philosophy, Alex Rosenberg, Dean Laurie Patton, and Provost Peter Lange of Duke for helping to create and sustain an environment that is so conducive to serious scholarship.

# THE HEART
# OF HUMAN RIGHTS

# CHAPTER 1

---

# Introduction

## I. *The Subject of This Book*

Human rights are an increasingly potent force in our world. They are not just an important factor in world politics; they have also become embedded in the very structure of the international order. With greater power comes greater liability to scrutiny. Thus, unsurprisingly, human rights theory and practice are the target of a number of criticisms. Some contend that the very idea of setting universal standards for the behavior of states is flawed because it ignores the fact that there is plurality of valid or at least reasonable moralities. Others argue that the practice presupposes a theory of moral rights that no one has succeeded in providing, or that it lacks adequate moral foundations of any kind, or that human rights are a weapon wielded by strong states to pursue their own interests, or that the institutions through which human rights are asserted and implemented lack legitimacy because they are not democratic. Still others claim that international human rights law undermines federalism and threatens domestic constitutions or violates the collective right of political self-determination.

Any attempt to evaluate these criticisms must take into account a crucial fact: *International human rights law is central to human rights practice.* Therefore, *any assessment of the moral status of human rights practice must acknowledge the importance of international human rights law in the practice.* That is the primary methodological thesis of this book.

Taking the international legality of human rights seriously requires a different approach to philosophical theorizing about human rights than has hitherto been the norm. Unfortunately, philosophers have for the most part either failed to notice the centrality of international human rights law to the practice or have not appreciated the implications of this fact for what a philosophical theory of human rights should do if it is to shed light on the practice of human rights.[1]

---

[1] Perhaps the clearest exceptions to the generalization that this literature has neglected the centrality of international human rights law to human rights practice are Samantha Besson, Kristen Hessler, and myself. Besson is about to publish a book entitled *A Legal Theory of Human Rights*, which I am sure will be a major contribution. Hessler has developed an important component of a philosophical theory of the right sort in her work on the proper division of labor between states and international institutions in the interpretation of international legal human rights norms. James Nickel is also an exception. He states that the human rights of today are "the rights of the lawyers, not the philosophers," and he too recognizes that international legal human rights need not mirror preexisting moral human rights. However, in my judgment he does not focus sufficiently on the question of what it would take to justify having an international legal human rights system, where this includes an account of why there is a need for individual rights at the international in addition to the domestic constitutional level and an examination of the legitimacy of international legal human rights institutions. Nonetheless, much of what I say in this book is consonant with Nickel's approach. In particular, I agree with and expand upon his comment that it is a mistake to assume that human rights (and by this I think he means international legal human rights) norms must all be rights norms strictly speaking. I go farther, arguing that norms included in international human rights law needn't be rights norms in any sense. I note the magnitude of my debt to both Besson and Nickel in the acknowledgments. Carl Wellman's fine recent book, *The Moral Dimension of Human Rights*, also stands out from the theorists whose approach I criticize in several respects. Unlike many, he clearly distinguishes between moral and legal human rights. He also holds that some international legal human rights may not correspond to moral human rights. However, he does not appreciate how independent the basic idea of a system of international legal human rights is from the notion of moral rights. Further, and more importantly, he does not see that, as I shall argue, many international legal human rights have a scope (or content) that is much greater than that of the corresponding moral human rights. By 'scope' (or 'content') here, I mean the range of correlative duties. Nor does Wellman address the central theme of this book, the justification of a system of international legal human rights. He is correct to note that the founders of the international legal human rights system thought that the rights it contains presuppose corresponding moral rights, but from that it does not follow that the best reconstruction of the system will retain that assumption. My sense is that he, like others, overestimates how far a theory of moral human rights would take us toward the goal of justifying the system. See Kristen Hessler, "Resolving Interpretive Conflicts in International Human Rights Law," *Journal of Political Philosophy*, 13:1, (2009): 29–52; Carl Wellman, *The Moral Dimension of Human* Rights (Oxford: Oxford University Press, 2005); and James W. Nickel, *Making Sense of Human Rights*, revised edition (Malden, MA: Wiley, 2007).

Of course, some might deny that a philosophical theory of human rights *should* shed light on the practice. True enough: There is nothing wrong with attempting to theorize moral human rights, where these are conceived simply as moral rights that all human beings have by virtue of being human, with no pretense of engaging with human rights practice.

Indeed, there is a concept of moral human rights that antedates modern human rights practice and that makes no reference to international law or even to the existence of a system of states. This concept was employed in the nineteenth century in the struggle to abolish slavery and by feminists, though its origins are much earlier. James Griffin provides a succinct interpretation of the historical development of this concept, which I shall call the concept of *moral human rights*.[2] If one's only concern is with that concept of human rights, then one need not show how it makes sense of or provides a basis for criticizing modern human rights practice.

My aim, in contrast, is to try to make sense of the practice, and especially of its international legal core, and to do so in a critical way. So, when I examine the views of contemporary philosophers who work on human rights I will do so with an eye to whether they shed light on the practice and especially on the system of international legal human rights. In most cases, at least, I do not think this will be unfair, because I think it is clear that the philosophers in question do think they are saying something relevant to the evaluation of the practice.

## The Importance of International Legal Human Rights in the Practice

The practice of human rights, or, for brevity, simply the Practice, is enormously variegated. It includes all of the following and more: the processes by which human rights declarations and treaties are drafted and ratified, the processes by which human rights norms enter international customary law, the activities of international organizations that monitor compliance with the treaties (Treaty Bodies), the actions of international and regional courts when they make reference to human rights in their decisions, the work of

---

[2] James Griffin, *On Human Rights* (New York: Oxford University Press, 2009).

human rights nongovernmental organizations (NGOs), the efforts of individual citizens, various civil society groups, and "whistle-blowing" government officials to hold their states accountable for their human rights obligations under international law, the recourse to international human rights law by judges in domestic courts, the creation or amendment of domestic constitutions to reflect international legal human rights obligations, efforts by legislatures to bring domestic law into compliance with human rights treaty obligations, policies that make a state's membership in multilateral organizations or access to loans and credits conditional on human rights performance, the imposition of sanctions on states by the UN Security Council in response to human rights violations, the appeal to massive violations of basic human rights violations as justification for military interventions, and the recourse to human rights norms by domestic, regional, and international organizations in formulating their policies, goals, and missions.

My focus in this volume is on *the international legal human rights system* because of the central role it plays in the Practice. By 'the international legal human rights system' (or 'the system of international legal human rights') I mean UN-based human rights law and the institutions that support it. From time to time I will refer to regional human rights systems, and in particular the European legal human rights system, but my main focus will be on the UN-based system.

The Practice has a conceptual-discursive dimension, the single most important element of which is a set of documents that contain canonical formulations of rights. These include, at minimum, the Universal Declaration of Human Rights (UDHR), the International Covenant on Civil and Political Rights (ICCPR), the International Covenant on Economic, Social, and Cultural Rights (ICESCR), and the Genocide Convention.[3] Because its highly developed jurisprudence influences

[3] Given the potentially far-reaching consequences of its implementation, one might also include among the core documents the Statute of the International Criminal Court. The ICC transforms the human rights landscape because it provides for international enforcement of human rights norms without Security Council authorization. However, its reach is limited by the fact that the human rights violations it is allowed to prosecute are limited by the Statute and by the fact that any permanent member of the Security Council can block a prosecution. I will focus in this volume on features of the international legal human rights system that have broad application to all or most of the international human rights.

the interpretation of international legal human rights worldwide, the European Convention on Human Rights (ECHR) may also be included in the list of core documents.

Although the UDHR is not a legally binding document—it is a declaration, not a treaty—according to some theorists it is nonetheless international law. Whether or not the notion of nonbinding law makes sense here (or elsewhere) is a complex issue. Regardless of how that issue is resolved, however, a preponderance of international legal opinion holds that at least some, and perhaps many, of the rights listed in the UDHR are now norms of international customary law. So, even if the UDHR itself is not binding law, some of the norms contained in it are.

It has been said that human rights are a global moral lingua franca. More accurately, international human rights law is the universally accessible *authoritative* version of the global moral lingua franca. This branch of international law is not just employed as a powerful instrument for realizing moral values; in addition, compliance with its norms is widely thought to be morally obligatory. Especially in its embodiment in the core documents, international human rights law provides a uniquely salient global standard to which various parties—from international and domestic judges to NGO workers to protestors against tyrannical governments or opponents of the rapacity of global corporations—can appeal.

There is no "folk" (that is, widely held, pretheoretical) conception of moral human rights nor any philosophical theory of moral human rights that enjoys this authoritative status in the Practice. A widespread consensus that individuals' international legal human rights should be realized appears to have developed without being preceded by a widespread consensus on what moral human rights there are. This phenomenon is puzzling, if not inexplicable, if one assumes that international legal human rights are attempts to realize preexisting moral human rights, but perfectly understandable if one rejects that assumption. I shall argue that one should reject it.

In all the aspects of the Practice listed above, appeals to international legal human rights facilitate morally coordinated action; they provide focal points around which to organize efforts to achieve moral ends. To say that much and no more, however, would still be to underestimate the unique role of international law in the Practice. Unlike natural languages, the authoritative global moral lingua franca that is international human rights law includes public, institutionalized, rule-governed practices for its own deliberate, self-conscious formation and revision over time. International human rights law creates organizations and processes that provide structured venues for scrutinizing, contesting, and revising its own content—and, I shall argue, even its own purposes. Both the perception that it is the authoritative formulation of human rights norms in the Practice and the effectiveness of the Practice's reliance on it depend greatly upon the fact that international human rights law, like law generally, is an institutionalized form of practical reasoning that serves moral values while at the same time managing moral disagreement by constraining the types of reasons and evidence it admits as relevant and that has the resources for improving itself over time.[4]

Further, international human rights law, qua law, has the potential for enforcement; and there is evidence of a trend toward greater enforceability overall.[5] Where there is enforcement, or the likelihood of it, international human rights law can help solve or at least mitigate collective action problems that otherwise would remain intractable. It can change the incentives so as to avoid free-riding and provide assurance of reciprocity to those who do not wish to free-ride but who are willing to comply if, but only if, others reciprocate.

Finally, international legal human rights have a great advantage over *direct* appeals to morality, when it comes to influencing the behavior of states. When I asked him for his view about the moral foundations of human rights, an officer of one of the world's most powerful human rights NGOs told me: We don't have to talk about morality; we can say to government officials, "You are legally obligated to do this, because you ratified the treaty." Of course, that kind of reminder would have no effect if international legality didn't matter to states, but there is evidence that it does.[6] Whether or not it matters because state leaders are sincerely committed to the rule of law (or to doing what they have committed themselves to doing) is

---

[4] Samantha Besson, *The Morality of Conflict: Reasonable Disagreement and the Law* (Portland, Oregon: Hart Publishing, 2005).

[5] Kathryn Sikkink, *The Justice Cascade: How Human Rights are Changing World Politics* (New York: Norton, 2011).

[6] Beth A. Simmons, *Mobilizing for Human Rights: International Law in Domestic Politics* (Cambridge: Cambridge University Press, 2009).

another matter. In the case of "liberal" states at least, leaders may take legality seriously because they think that powerful domestic constituencies do and expect them to do so as well.[7] And even those states that are least responsive to the preferences of their own people typically care about their reputation in the society of states, especially when a bad reputation can deprive them of tangible benefits that other states can confer. What matters is that the fact that they are legally obligated can and apparently often does carry some weight in their decisions.

The point of the NGO officer's remark was not that law is a substitute for morality, nor that law's efficacy does not depend on moral motivation. Instead, he was calling attention to the fact that once a state acknowledges that it has obligations under human rights law, it is not necessary to argue the moral issues from the ground up. The fact of legality narrows the space for debates about what morality requires; the more basic moral issues are, in effect, taken off the table. A state that has incurred legal human rights obligations cannot evade them simply by denying that morality requires it to treat its citizens in certain ways. This is a significant advantage of legal discourse; it enables us to make appeals to moral motivation without having to engage in foundational controversies or justify substantive moral norms, including rights-norms, from the ground up.

Given the centrality of international human rights law to the Practice, any philosophical theory of human rights that purports to provide a comprehensive evaluation of the moral status of the Practice must include a moral assessment of the international legal human rights system. One of the most important aspects of such an assessment is to determine whether the system of international legal human rights is morally justified.

## Philosophical Theories

Of late there has been a remarkable surge of interest in human rights on the part of philosophers. As philosophers, their characteristic response to the growing power of human rights and the

---

[7] Anne-Marie Slaughter and Jose E. Alvarez, "A Liberal Theory of International Law," *American Society of International Law: Proceedings of the Annual Meeting* (2000), pp. 240–53.

criticism it has provoked has been to try to develop theories of human rights.[8]

In my judgment, contemporary philosophical work on human rights suffers from two major deficiencies. First, it has not focused squarely on the moral evaluation of the system of international legal human rights and, more specifically, has not taken up the task of determining whether the system is morally justifiable. If international human rights law is central to the Practice, then the fact that philosophical theories of human rights have not addressed the question of whether there is a sound justification for having a system of international legal human rights is a serious omission, at least for those theories purport to shed light on the Practice.[9] Second, most philosophers have been conceptual imperialists when it comes to human rights. They have assumed, without argument, that there is only one concept of human rights (namely, theirs). Political or Practical theorists assert that human rights *are* rights that serve to limit sovereignty in the context of the state system. Orthodox or Moral theorists assert that human rights *are* rights that people have simply by virtue of their humanity and conclude that human rights do not presuppose a state system. They are both right and both wrong. Sometimes the phrase 'human rights' is used to refer to moral rights people have simply by virtue of their humanity (as it was by the abolitionists and early feminists before there was an international human rights law), and this concept makes no reference to the state system. Sometimes the phrase 'human rights' is used to refer

---

[8] For the most part, the literature I engage in this volume includes works by what might be called mainstream Anglo-American philosophical theorists of human rights who have produced books on the subject, along with the responses to their work. The list of participants in this literature includes William Talbott, Henry Shue, James Nickel, James Griffin, John Tasioulas, Joseph Raz, Ronald Dworkin, Charles Beitz, David Miller, Carl Wellman, Christopher Wellman, and Andrew Altman.

[9] As I shall explain in more detail, later, Charles Beitz does provide an historical explanation of the origins of modern human rights practice. He says that it arose as a response to the perception—which became widespread in the aftermath of the destruction wrought by World War II and the Holocaust—that people needed to be protected from harms inflicted on them by their own states. However, he does not explain why the protective response took the form of international law or why it took the form of a new body of international law that recognized rights of individuals.

to international legal human rights (or, perhaps less frequently, to legal rights that ought to be included in international human rights law), and these rights do presuppose the state system. It is equally implausible either to assert that the latter usage has completely replaced the latter (so that there no longer exists a concept of human rights that does not presuppose the state system) or to assert that only the former usage is correct.

Nor will it do to say that the concept of human rights as rights that people have simply by virtue of their humanity is the primary or focal sense of the term and that the concept of human rights as limits on sovereignty is secondary or peripheral. No one has given us reason to crown one or the other of these two senses as primary or focal. One might think that the concept of moral human rights is primary or focal if one thought that international legal human rights are the legal embodiment of a subset of moral human rights. If that were true, then the concept of moral human rights would be primary or focal and the concept of international legal human rights would be secondary or peripheral in the sense that the latter could be explained in terms of the former but not vice versa. But if one thought that, as I shall argue, one would be wrong: International legal human rights are not the legal embodiments of a subset of moral human rights. Rather, *they are what they are: legal rights; and legal rights need not be embodiments of corresponding moral rights. Nor need legal rights be justified by appealing to moral rights.* Legal rights, as instrumental human creations, can serve a number of different purposes and can be justified by appeal to a number of different kinds of moral considerations, of which moral rights are only one.

Philosophers who have written extensively on human rights, including myself in previous works, have not even addressed the prior task of unpacking what 'justify' would mean in this context. To justify *a particular international legal human right* could mean to show that it is not impermissible (not wrong) to enact it—that is, to include it in a system of international legal human rights—or that there is sufficient reason to include it, all things considered, or that it is morally obligatory to enact it. Similarly, to justify *an international legal human rights system* could mean either showing that having such a system is permissible or that there is sufficient reason, all things considered, or a moral obligation, to create such a system or to sustain it if it already exists. Even if having *such* a system is justified in the latter, strong sense, an important question would remain: Is the *actual* international legal system justified and if so, in which sense(s)?

Further, the goal should be a genuinely moral justification, not a mere modus vivendi justification.[10] By the latter I mean a case for having or sustaining an international legal system that is grounded solely in the self-interest of various parties and, more specifically, in each believing that they are too weak to be likely to impose and sustain their own preferred alternative. The chief worry about mere modus vivendi justifications thus understood is that they are unacceptably fragile: If the balance of power is upset—or even if some actors erroneously believe they are now in a position to impose their own preferred alternative—the system may collapse. A moral justification can sustain support for the system even when supporting it and doing what is in a particular party's best interest diverge. Further, a moral justification, if it is widely accepted, can reduce the system's reliance on coercion.

In addition to lack of attention to the problem of whether the international legal human rights system is justified, there is another feature of the philosophical literature on human rights that is quite striking: Philosophers routinely use the phrase 'human rights' without making it clear whether they are talking about moral human rights or international legal human rights. This is unhelpful, especially if one of the goals of a philosophical theorizing is to explain the relationship between moral and international legal human rights.

Here is one example of the problems that can arise when one uses the phrase 'human rights' without being clear about whether it refers to moral or legal rights. John Tasioulas, a vigorous defender of the Moral or Orthodox approach, criticizes Charles Beitz, the leading proponent of the Political or Practical approach as follows. He notes that advocates of the latter approach are committed to the view that the concept of human rights applies only where there are states (and a state system), because they think that it is part of the very concept that human rights can be invoked by other states to criticize the behavior of states toward those under their jurisdiction. Tasioulas

---

[10] I thank Julian Culp for emphasizing this point.

says this is wrong, because the concept of human rights, which he thinks are rights we all have by virtue of our humanity, would be applicable in a world without states (where there was either complete anarchy or a single, world government).[11]

Practical or Political theorists like Beitz can handily rebut this objection by conceding that there is a concept of moral human rights that does not presuppose states, namely, what I have called the concept of moral human rights, and then go on to emphasize that this is not the concept of human rights they are concerned with. Instead, their focus is on the concept of human rights that is dominant in the Practice, and that is the concept of rights that play the role of limiting sovereignty in the context of the state system. In other words, they can simply distinguish between Tasioulas's concept of moral human rights and the concept of human rights as those rights that are central to the Practice, on the understanding that the latter are international legal human rights. The Political or Practical theorist can also acknowledge that the dominant use of the phrase 'human rights' in the Practice sometimes refers not just to those legal rights that are part of current international human rights law, but also to those that should be. In either case, the relevant concept of human rights implies the existence of the state system.

Not distinguishing between international legal human rights and moral human rights obscures the fact that Tasioulas's objection is off-target. Unfortunately, Beitz encourages Tasioulas's objection, by proceeding as if he is illuminating *the* concept of human rights. That is, Beitz writes as if the only legitimate object of a philosophical theory is the concept that is deployed in contemporary practice. He prescribes a method for philosophical theorizing about *human rights*—not just for theorizing that can shed light on the Practice—saying that the theorist of human rights must begin with the Practice. In doing so he wrongly implies that it is a mistake to focus on the earlier concept of moral human rights and try to understand it in its own right, independently of any connection it may have to the Practice.[12] If Beitz had stopped after saying that the dominant use of

[11] John Tasioulas, "Human Rights, Universality, and the Values of Personhood: Retracing Griffin's Steps," *European Journal of Philosophy* 10:1 (2002): 79–100.

[12] I made this same mistake—that is, assuming that a theory of human rights must exhibit "fidelity" to the Practice. Allen Buchanan, "The Egalitarianism of Human Rights," *Ethics*, 120 (2010): 679–710.

the term 'human rights' in the Practice presupposes the state system, he would have been on solid ground. Unfortunately, he went further, making a claim about the proper way to theorize *human rights*, assuming, without warrant, that there is only one proper or philosophically interesting concept of human rights. (Recall that the title of his book is *The Idea of Human Rights*, not *The Predominant Idea of Human Rights in Human Rights Practice*.) In other words, he proceeds as if the earlier concept of moral human rights as rights that people have simply by virtue of their humanity no longer exists, having been replaced by a concept that presupposes the state system.

## The Mirroring View

Just because philosophers have not explicitly addressed the question of whether there is a sound justification for the system of international legal human rights does not mean that they lack opinions on the matter. Some philosophers, when offering theories of moral human rights, make statements that strongly suggest that they hold a particular—and, I shall argue, inadequately unsupported—assumption about what is typically necessary for justifying the inclusion of a particular right in the system of international legal human rights, namely, that there must be a corresponding, antecedently existing moral human right. I call this assumption the Mirroring View. A number of philosophers, including Joseph Raz and Hans Morsink, hold the Mirroring View, as did I and Kristen Hessler in previous work.[13] It is difficult to determine conclusively which philosophers hold the Mirroring View, for two reasons: the tendency not to address explicitly the question of the justification of international legal human rights, and the tendency to use the phrase 'human rights' without saying whether one is talking about moral or legal rights.

According to Raz, human rights are a subset of general moral rights. By this he appears to mean that international legal human rights, when they are justified, are legal embodiments of a subset of

---

[13] Allen Buchanan and Kristen Hessler, "Equality, Democracy, and the Human Right to Health Care," *Medicine and Social Justice: Essays on the Distribution of Health Care*, 2nd ed. Eds. Margaret Battin, Rosamand Rhodes, and Anita Silvers (New York: Oxford University Press), pp. 231–45, 2012.

moral rights that all human beings have, that is, moral human rights.[14] The subset of moral rights in question are those that properly limit sovereignty. On this view, international legal human rights are the international legal counterparts of those moral human rights that properly limit sovereignty. His view, then, apparently is that being the legal embodiment of a moral human right (a moral right that properly limits sovereignty) is a necessary condition for being a justified international legal human right.

That is the only interpretation, so far as I can tell, that makes sense of three features of Raz's view. First, there is his claim that human rights are a subset of moral human rights. Given his assertion that human rights serve to limit sovereignty *and his insistence that he is focusing on the political function of human rights in the Practice*, this first claim strongly suggests that he thinks that international legal human rights, when they are justified, mirror moral human rights. For in the Practice, it is international legal human rights that serve to limit sovereignty, not the rights of any "folk" or philosophical theory of moral human rights. No folk or philosophical theory of moral human rights is determinate enough or widely accepted enough to play the roles in the Practice that international legal human rights play. Second, there is the following passage.

"The ethical doctrine of human rights should articulate standards by which the practice of human rights can be judged, standards which will indicate what human rights we have."[15] No moral theory of human rights is needed to help us identify which international legal human rights we have; that can be determined by consulting international law. If, instead, the task is to determine which international legal human rights we should have, then knowing which moral human rights we have would be essential, *if* international legal human rights are supposed to mirror moral human rights. In other words, *if* one assumed that international legal human rights are supposed to mirror moral human rights, then one would quite naturally think that a theory of moral human rights (or, in Raz's terms, the ethical doctrine of human rights) would guide the Practice by telling

[14] Joseph Raz, "Human Rights without Foundations," *The Philosophy of International Law*, eds. Samantha Besson and John Tasioulas (New York: Oxford University Press, 2010), pp. 321–37.
[15] Ibid., p. 322.

us which rights should be included in international human rights law. Third, Raz criticizes several Orthodox or Moral theorists, including Griffin, for not properly identifying what is characteristic of moral human rights (namely, their sovereignty-limiting function) and then concludes that this prevents them from providing guidance for the Practice.[16] That way of proceeding makes perfectly good sense on the assumption that international legal rights should mirror moral human rights. Raz never considers the possibility that international legal human rights could properly perform the function of limiting sovereignty even if they did not mirror moral human rights.

Raz, like Beitz, is a conceptual imperialist when it comes to human rights. He doesn't just say that those, like Griffin, who espouse a concept of human rights that makes no reference to the state system are not engaging with the concept of human rights employed in the Practice; he also says that Griffin is wrong about what human rights are. That is, according to Raz, human rights are rights that function to limit sovereignty, not rights that serve to protect normative agency. That is why Raz says that Griffin's understanding of human rights is irrelevant to the Practice. If Raz had stopped after asserting that Griffin's concept of human rights sheds no light on the Practice because the concept of human rights predominantly used in the Practice is that of rights that properly limit sovereignty and presupposes the state system, he would have said something plausible. In going further to make the claim that human rights are rights that function to limit sovereignty (and therefore presuppose the state system) he says something wrong—he implies that there is no legitimate concept of human rights that makes no reference to sovereignty and the state system.

Hans Morsink holds that the international legal human rights documents are attempts to give legal form to "inherent" rights of all human individuals, that is, moral human rights.[17] Unlike Raz, he does not overlook the possibility that there are two or more different, equally legitimate concepts of human rights, but like Raz he

[16] Ibid., pp. 323–27.

[17] See Johannes Morsink, *The Universal Declaration of Human Rights: Origins, Drafting and Intent* (University of Pennsylvania Press, 1999), and Johannes Morsink, *Inherent Human Rights: Philosophical Roots of the Universal Declaration* (Philadelphia: University of Pennsylvania Press, 2009).

assumes that international legal human rights are the legal embodiment of moral human rights.

The Mirroring View holds that to justify an international legal human right typically involves defending the claim that a corresponding moral human right exists. The qualifier 'typically' is designed to accommodate the fact that some who hold this view acknowledge that in some cases a justified international legal right does not mirror a moral human right, but rather is either (a) a specification of a moral human right (as the right to freedom of the press is a specification of the right to freedom of expression), or (b) something that is instrumentally valuable for realizing a moral human right (as some think that an international legal right to democratic government is instrumentally valuable for realizing some important moral human rights, even if there is no moral human right to democratic government). Andrew Altman and and Christopher Wellman, for example, deny that there is a moral human right to democratic government, but allow that it may be appropriate to include a right to democratic government among the international legal human rights.[18] Similarly, most theorists would presumably acknowledge that a list of legal rights may include specifications of more abstract moral rights. What makes the term 'Mirroring View' appropriate, despite these qualifications ((a) and (b)) is that the kind of view I use it to refer to assumes that typically—or, one might say, standardly—justifying an international legal human right involves showing that there is a corresponding moral human right. If one thinks that the chief purpose of international human rights law is to realize in international law a list of moral human rights, this view about how to justify international legal human rights seems natural enough.

James Griffin also appears to assume the Mirroring View. He complains that the idea of human rights is unacceptably indeterminate and suggests that the philosopher can perform a service of practical value by providing a theory that achieves greater determinacy.[19] He then sets out a theory based on the idea that human rights (by which he must mean moral human rights) serve to protect normative agency. Having done that, he uses his account of moral human rights

---

[18] Andrew Altman and Christopher Wellman, *A Liberal Theory of International Justice* (New York: Oxford University Press, 2011).

[19] James Griffin, *On Human Rights* (New York: Oxford University Press 2009).

to argue that items in international human rights law, including the right to work and the right to periodic holidays with pay, should not be there, because they can't be justified as protections of normative agency.[20]

As the following passage shows, Griffin assumes—without argument—that there is only one concept of human rights, namely, the concept of moral human rights that he is attempting to analyze, *and* that international human rights documents are attempts to list moral human rights: "The Universal Declaration contains a right to periodic holidays with pay, to which the overwhelming and cheering reaction has been that, whatever that supposed entitlement is, it is certainly not a human right."[21]

What has happened here? Griffin has shifted from making assertions about moral human rights (namely that they protect normative agency) to assertions about international legal human rights (namely, that the inclusion of the right to work and the right to periodic holidays with pay among them is a mistake because these rights are not needed to protect normative agency)—and he has not marked the transition by distinguishing clearly between moral and international legal human rights. In other words, he assumes that the phrase 'human rights' is used univocally when we speak of moral human rights and when we point to rights included in international human rights law. Similarly, in a paper on "discrepancies" between the best theory of moral human rights (his) and international human rights law, Griffin issues report cards on various other international legal human rights, saying that some are "unacceptable" (i.e., should not be part of this body of law) because there is no such moral right. He assumes—not argues—that differences between what he thinks is the most defensible list of moral human rights and the lists found in international legal documents are discrepancies because he assumes the Mirroring View.

Griffin simply assumes that international legal human rights documents are attempts to give legal embodiment to moral human rights; that is, he assumes that international legal human rights are simply moral human rights in legal dress. That is why he slips from the assertion that there is no moral human right to periodic holidays

---

[20] Ibid., pp. 207–8, 5, 16, 86.
[21] Ibid., p. 5.

with pay to the conclusion that it is a mistake to include this right in international human rights documents. In other words, he simply assumes the Mirroring View.

The mere fact that the phrase 'human rights' is used both to refer to moral human rights and to refer to international legal human rights is clearly not a sufficient reason to believe that international legal human rights are simply moral human rights in legal dress. Nor is it a sufficient reason to assume that an international legal human right is justifiable only if there is a corresponding moral human right. International legal human rights, like legal rights generally, need not be legal embodiments of corresponding moral rights and they can be justified by appealing to a variety of moral considerations.

So, without a defense of the Mirroring View, Griffin's rejection of some international legal human rights as unacceptable is wholly unwarranted. If international legal human rights need not mirror moral human rights, then the fact that there is no moral human right to periodic holidays with pay and no moral right to work does not imply that these rights are mistakenly included in international human rights law. I will argue that the Mirroring View is indefensible.

There is another interesting feature of Griffin's way of proceeding. He complains that the idea of human rights has remained indeterminate for hundreds of years. This may be true of the concept of moral human rights. But it is off-target if 'human rights' refers to international legal rights (and not just because the latter are of more recent vintage). As with other legal rights, international legal human rights have become significantly more determinate over time, through legal processes. For example, the European Court of Human Rights has ruled in well over 10,000 cases. In addition, the various international treaty bodies have made hundreds of rulings as to the content of various rights listed in their respective treaties.

Griffin's point must be, rather, that the concept of *moral* human rights is seriously indeterminate. That may well be the case, but it leaves entirely open the question of how damaging this indeterminacy is to the international legal human rights enterprise. If one assumes the Mirroring View, then one will naturally be concerned that the supposed indeterminacy of moral human rights will carry over to international legal human rights. But if one doesn't hold the

Mirroring View, then one can admit that the indeterminacy of moral human rights is a major problem for moral theory, but point out that it is not necessarily a problem for international legal human rights or the practice that is anchored in it. Griffin says far too little about why he thinks that the indeterminacy of the idea of 'human rights' is such a big problem, but if he means it is a practical, as opposed to a purely theoretical problem—a problem for human rights practice, including its legal dimension—then he seems to be assuming that international human rights law should mirror the landscape of moral human rights and that if the idea of moral human rights is indeterminate this will somehow hinder the law and the Practice built upon it.

My conclusion, then, is that Griffin (sometimes at least) implicitly holds the Mirroring View: He assumes, without argument, that the function of the system of international legal human rights is to realize a set of corresponding preexisting moral human rights. He does not first investigate the system to try to determine what its functions are; nor does he explicitly address the question of what its functions should be. Even if he were correct in holding that moral human rights serve to protect normative agency, there is no reason to assume that this is the function, or the only function of international legal human rights.

Kristen Hessler has suggested an alternative interpretation of Griffin.[22] She thinks that his goal is simply to point out that there are differences between the best interpretation of the notion of moral human rights, on the one hand, and some aspects of international human rights law, on the other, and then to assert that where this is the case the notion of moral human rights cannot be invoked to justify international human rights law (or aspects of the Practice based on it). On this interpretation, Griffin is not assuming that in order to justify international legal human rights one must show that they are needed to realize moral human rights. He is only making the weaker claim that *if* one must show that, then some international legal human rights are not justifiable.

If that is Griffin's view, then it is odd that he did not state it and odder still that he does nothing to subject to critical scrutiny the antecedent of the conditional—the assumption that to justify an international legal human right one must show that are needed to

---

[22] Kristen Hessler, personal communication to the author, August 15, 2012.

realize antecedently existing moral human rights. Moreover, his procedure of rejecting as unacceptable those international legal human rights that are not found on his list of moral human rights goes far beyond the conditional view Hessler charitably attributes to him: It commits him to the Mirroring View. Griffin is not alone; many philosophers assume the Mirroring View and none argues for it.

In their defense, it should be emphasized that it is quite natural to assume the Mirroring View, because the justificatory rhetoric of the most important international human rights documents suggests it. The UDHR, ICCPR, and ICESCR all feature preambular language that refers to rights that we are "born with" and, if taken literally, this can only mean moral human rights.[23] This language suggests that the function of the documents is to specify international legal analogs of a set of preexisting moral human rights, or perhaps to do that and also in some cases to formulate legal rights that are instrumentally valuable for realizing preexisting moral rights.

In chapter 2, I shall argue that the best interpretation of the international legal human rights system—the interpretation that achieves the best balancing of fidelity to the content of that law and the strongest justification for it—will reject this suggestion. I will show that if international human rights law is to perform its distinctively valuable functions then some and most likely many international legal human rights will not be legal counterparts of moral human rights, nor specifications of them, nor valuable instruments for realizing them. I will show that appealing to an antecedently existing moral human right is not necessary for justifying international legal human rights and that, in the case of a number of important international legal human rights, appealing to a preexisting moral human right is not sufficient to justify the legal right. For now, I only want to emphasize how understandable it is, given the preambular rhetoric of the key documents, that one would assume the Mirroring View or the Complex Mirroring View.

Instead of proceeding to theorize on the basis of the unexamined Mirroring View, the better course would be to first try to determine,

---

[23] Universal Declaration of Human Rights (UDHR), International Covenant on Civil and Political Rights (ICCPR), and International Covenant on Economic, Social and Cultural Rights (ICESCR).

on the basis of an understanding of the characteristics of the system of international legal human rights, what functions it fulfills, and then assess the moral propriety of those functions, the system's efficacy in performing them, and the means by which it does so. If the task, at least in part, is to illuminate the Practice, then in this regard I whole-heartedly concur with Charles Beitz's assertion that philosophers should begin with an examination of the Practice, and, I would add, in particular, its legal core, rather than first developing a theory of human rights without regard to it and then trying to determine whether reality measures up to the theory.

If, as I suspect, the Mirroring View is something that is widely assumed among philosophers writing about human rights, this would explain the absence of explicit attention in the philosophical literature to the problem of whether the international legal human rights system is justified. If one assumes the purpose of the system is to create a set of international legal rights that realizes a set of preexisting moral human rights, then one will conclude that the task of the philosopher is largely accomplished if he or she produces a sound theory of moral human rights. Once such a theory is in hand, the main question will be this: Which international legal human rights are needed to realize the proper set of moral human rights? Answering the latter question, one might think, is a relatively minor affair when compared with the task of developing a theory of moral human rights. Hence the virtually exclusive focus in philosophical theorizing on providing an account of moral human rights and the near total neglect of any explicit attention to the problem of justifying international legal human rights.

I will show that even if it is true that the justification of international legal human rights must rest to some extent on claims about corresponding moral human rights, the development of a theory of moral human rights would only be the first, small step in the task of justifying the international legal human rights system. There would be much more to do than to determine which moral human rights are suitable candidates for being realized in international law. For one thing, justifying the international legal human rights system requires justifying having the sorts of institutions that are included in it and, beyond that, showing that the actual institutions are legitimate. It would also require showing why having a system of *international legal* human rights (rather than a collection of domestic or regional legal human rights systems) is the best way to realize certain moral human rights.

In chapter 2, I will offer a systematic critique of the Mirroring View. That critique will begin by identifying functions the existing system of international legal human rights performs, and then proceed to ask whether they make good moral sense. For now I want to concentrate on beginning to convey just how complex the task of justifying the international legal system is, emphasizing that a justification of the existing system, or any system similar to it, must take into account its distinctive features, including, above all, the functions that the system of rights is supposed to fulfill.

## II. *Key Features of the International Legal Human Rights System: A Preliminary Characterization*

### *Limiting Sovereignty*

It is sometimes said that the most distinctive feature of international legal human rights is that they function to limit the exercise of sovereignty or that they limit the exercise of sovereignty within a state's own jurisdiction. Neither characterization fully captures what is distinctive about international human rights law, however. International law before the advent of human rights law limited sovereignty, sometimes even within the state's own jurisdiction. What is distinctive about international human rights law is that it limits sovereignty, even in its internal exercise, for a new purpose. *The innovation of international human rights law is that it serves to limit state sovereignty, even within the state's own jurisdiction, for the sake of individuals themselves.* Traditional international law sometimes provided protection for individuals, as in the case of diplomatic immunity — but it did so to serve the interests of states, not individuals.

The phrase 'limiting sovereignty' is ambiguous: It can mean either the international *legal* limitation of sovereignty, that is, limitations on the international legal rights, privileges, powers, or immunities of states; or it can mean *effective constraints* on what states actually can do. The distinction is important, because states sometimes are able to do what they are prohibited from doing by international human rights law.

Although the question of how effectively international human rights law actually constrains states is debatable and although there are different accounts of how it achieves constraint when it does, I think it is now clear that the empirical literature shows that significant constraint does occur.[24] However, at this juncture, my point is simply that, within the Practice, international legal human rights are conceived as providing international legal constraints on sovereignty and with the expectation that these legal constraints will actually affect the behavior of states. Whether or to what extent actual constraint is achieved will be relevant, of course, to whether the system of international legal human rights is justified. If, for example, it turned out that the system provides no effective constraints on sovereignty but nonetheless has significant moral costs—for example, because appeals to human rights violations can be used by powerful states as a weapon to pursue their own geopolitical aims—then that would count heavily against the system's being justified.

## The Ascription of Duties

In addition to the sovereignty-limiting function, another important feature of the existing international legal human rights system is that the legal duties that correspond to individual international legal rights, at least in the case of rights created by human rights conventions, are generally understood to have three distinctive characteristics: (1) they are ascribed primarily or exclusively to states,[25] (2) for the most part, a particular state only has these duties regarding individuals who are under its jurisdiction, and (3) when a state is unable or unwilling to fulfill these duties, other states may have some sort of responsibility to achieve their fulfillment, but this responsibility usually does not rise to the level of a full-fledged legal duty.[26]

---

[24] See, for instance, Kathryn Sikkink and Thomas Risse, *The Power of Human Rights: International Norms and Domestic Change* (Cambridge: Cambridge University Press, 1999). Also, Beth A. Simmons, *Mobilizing for Human Rights: International Law in Domestic Politics* (Cambridge: Cambridge University Press, 2009).

[25] This may be changing. Some would argue that for some international legal human rights, international law is beginning to recognize that the corresponding legal duties also fall on individuals, as when a man's physical abuse of his spouse or a soldier's participation in a pattern of mass rapes during armed conflicts is regarded as a violation of human rights.

[26] See Charles Beitz, *The Idea of Human Rights* (New York: Oxford University Press, 2009).

In principle, a system of international legal human rights could be quite different—and perhaps morally better for being so. It might assign primary duties rights not only to states, but also to international organizations and/or global corporations. Alternatively, it might assign full-fledged, determinate duties, not mere responsibilities, to states or to alliances of states (regional or otherwise) to secure human rights when a state fails to fulfill its duties. More radically, it might unambiguously assign to states substantial primary legal duties (not just default responsibilities) toward those who are not under their jurisdiction.

There is evidence that the existing system is already moving in the direction of the some of these changes—though whether it will achieve them is another matter. A number of anticorruption and environmental treaties impose duties on corporations that can have a positive impact on international legal human rights, whether the treaties in question are regarded as human rights treaties or not.[27] Further, even when international human rights law does not assign duties to corporations, political action to make corporations respect international legal human rights is sometimes effective. For example, the recently formulated *Guiding Principles on Business and Human Rights* utilize the lingua franca of international human rights law, even though they are not legally binding, and this document may become a focal point for effective political action.[28] The Responsibility to Protect (R2P) doctrine can be seen as an attempt to steer the system in the direction of genuine default duties for states, though it stops short of that goal at present.

The *Guiding Principles* are only one example of many in which international legal human rights can have a significant effect, but in an indirect way. In such cases the effect of the existence of international legal human rights exceeds the scope of the corresponding legal duties. Similarly, even if the legal duties that states have under international human rights law are primarily only to those under their jurisdiction, various actors attempt, with some success, to pressure states to conform to the standards that law prescribes in their behavior toward those not under their jurisdiction. The form this pressure

[27] Steven R. Ratner, "Business," *The Oxford Handbook of International Environmental Law*, ed. Daniel Bodansky, Jutta Brunnée, and Ellen Hey (New York: Oxford University Press, 2007), pp. 807–28.
[28] UN Office of the High Commissioner for Human Rights, *Guiding Principles on Business and Human Rights* (Geneva: 2011).

can take ranges from public criticism and protest, to sanctions, to withholding of foreign aid, to freezing a state's financial assets, to exclusion from desirable trade regimes and alliances, to armed humanitarian intervention.

The crucial point here is that *the efficacy of international human rights law exceeds its legal reach*. In other words, because of its saliency, its relative determinateness, and the prestige it enjoys, international human rights law serves as a moral standard that can be employed for political mobilization to change the behavior of states, corporations, and other agents, even in cases where it does not impose clear legal duties on them. It is an interesting question, nonetheless, whether international human rights law will—and should— develop further in the direction of ascribing robust, full-fledged legal duties to corporations, more extensive duties on the part of states regarding their behavior to people who are not under their jurisdiction, and genuine default duties, as opposed to responsibilities. I return to this question in the final chapter.

## The Claim to Supremacy

The existing international legal human rights system has another distinctive feature: It exists within a context of legal pluralism with respect to its own status vis-à-vis the authority of domestic law. Different states have different constitutional arrangements and political practices for incorporating international law into their own domestic legal systems and for responding to conflicts between domestic law, including constitutional law, and international law. For some states, ratification of a human rights treaty is not sufficient to give the treaty obligations domestic legal effect; a special legislative or executive act is required.

An arrangement according to which ratification had immediate domestic legal effect for all states would be quite different from the existing one—and would endow international human rights with a more robust legality than they now possess. In the existing system, only a few states include in their constitutions the stipulation that when the scope of a particular right is broader under international law than it is under domestic law, domestic courts are bound to interpret the right as having the broader scope. A system in which all states acknowledged the supremacy of international human rights law in this way would differ significantly from the status quo.

A more radical change is worth considering: One can conceive of an international legal system in which the duties that correspond to the legal rights in human rights conventions are legally binding even on states that do not ratify the conventions, if a supermajority of legitimate states ratify them. Such an arrangement would, of course, be a major departure from the status quo (even though it would be a mistake to say that all existing international law is binding on states only if they have consented to it).[29]

My aim at this point is not to pass judgment on whether any or all of these changes would be progressive; it is only to make clear the vacuity of any inquiry into the justification of international legal human rights that is not indexed to the distinctive features of the system to be justified. Because several different types of systems might qualify as an international legal human rights system, a generic justification would be rather uninformative.

## The Basic Idea of the System

I shall argue that the basic idea of the system of international legal human rights is *to develop a regime of international law whose primary function is to provide universal standards for regulating the behavior of states toward those under their jurisdiction, for the sake of those individuals themselves, conceived as social beings.*[30] If I am correct in thinking that the existing international legal human rights system is best construed as instantiating this idea, then any justification for the existing system must show that this basic idea is morally cogent.

---

[29] Jus cogens norms (e.g., against slavery and torture) are binding on states independently of their treaty commitments and norms of customary international law that developed before a state came into being are binding on it nonetheless. The ICC is another exception to voluntariness: The ICC Statute makes nonconsenting states subject to the Court's jurisdiction and to the enforcement of its verdicts.

[30] Although I will not always repeat the qualifying phrase 'as social beings' I include it here to forestall an objection, namely, that because of its ascription of rights to individual on the basis of the assumption that individuals count morally in their own right (independently of their contribution to society, usefulness to the nation, etc.), the system of international legal human rights is somehow parochially individualistic. As I emphasize later, the Universal Declaration of Human Rights and the human rights treaties that followed it make it very clear that human beings are social by nature and go out of their way to repudiate any notion that humans are "atomistic individuals."

The case for this formulation of the basic idea of the system will unfold in stages, as this book progresses, and more determinate content for it will emerge. In a nutshell, I will argue that this formulation is apt because it best fits the most accurate information about what the system is like and about its origins, while at the same time construing the system in a morally attractive way.

It is crucial to understand that the basic idea of the system as I have just formulated it is noncommittal on two key issues. First, it does not speak to whether such regulation is to be achieved voluntarily, that is, through the consent of all states subject to it, or otherwise. It may be true that at the founding of the system of international human rights law, there was no practical alternative to reliance on the consent of states, that is, to create this law primarily through the making of treaties. But if circumstances changed sufficiently, it might become feasible to take a less voluntary approach. And it would be a mistake to assume that doing so would be morally unacceptable or deprive international human rights law of legitimacy. Second, the basic idea leaves open the question of whether, or to what extent, the standards must take the form of norms that assert individual legal rights. The point here is that other types of norms—for example mere duty norms—might be capable of performing the distinctive function of this type of law.

## The Status Egalitarian Function

Another feature of the existing system deserves emphasis: *It exhibits a robust commitment to affirming and protecting the equal basic moral status of all individuals.* There are at least five aspects of the existing international legal human rights system that are central to its performing this function. (1) Inclusive (or universal) ascription of rights (international legal human rights are ascribed not just to men, or whites, or so-called civilized peoples, or to believers, or to those who contribute to society, etc., but to all people).[31] (2) Equality of

---

[31] UN General Assembly, *Universal Declaration of Human Rights*, December 10, 1948, 217 A (III). Article 2 of the UDHR states: "Everyone is entitled to all the rights and freedoms set forth in this Declaration, without any distinction of any kind, such as race, colour, sex, language, religion, political or other opinion, national or social origin, property, birth or other status. Furthermore, no distinction shall be made on the basis of the political, jurisdictional or international status of the country or territory to which a person belongs, whether it be independent, trust,

rights for all (the *same* rights are ascribed to all in a very strong sense: They are understood to have (a) the same *content* (including the same correlative duties), (b) the same *weight*, and (c) the same conditions of abrogation, that is the factors that allow abrogation do not discriminate among persons. (3) States are obligated to make *everyone's* rights effective, that is, they are not allowed to make any distinctions among persons that would disadvantage anyone with regard to the effectiveness of their rights.[32] (4) Robust equality before the law (including an extensive set of *equal* due process rights and the requirement that governments are to ensure that domestic

---

nonself-governing or under any other limitation of sovereignty." The standard interpretation (and the most reasonable interpretation, given the overall character of the document) of the phrase "without distinction . . . of any kind" is that it refers not just to the ascription of rights (i.e., they are ascribed to all "members of the human family"), but also to the content and weight of the rights (i.e., that they are the same for all). The major documents include provisions, under exceptional circumstances, for the restriction of some rights, but there are no provisions for restricting the rights of some people for reasons that do not justify restrictions on the rights of all, see UN General Assembly, *International Covenant on Civil and Political Rights (ICCPR)*, December 16, 1966, Article 22 (2). The clear implication is that the content and weight of the rights listed, and their conditions of abrogation, are the same for all. This conclusion is reinforced by the provision that "all are equal before the law and are entitled without any discrimination to equal protection of the law," found in both UN General Assembly, *ICCPR and* UN General Assembly, *International Covenant on Economic, Social and Cultural Rights*, December 16, 1966, Article 7. Further, the requirement that "everyone has the right to an effective remedy" for violations of the rights listed (also repeated in the UN General Assembly, *ICCPR*, Article 8 and UN General Assembly, *ICESCR*, Article 8) rules our any differences in available remedies that would render some people's rights less effective. In addition, articles in the major documents that ascribe a right to all for remedies for rights-violations contain no suggestion that inequality in access to remedies or in the nature of remedies is permissible. Finally, ICCPR, Article 3 provides further confirmation by stating that "the States Parties to the present Covenant undertake to ensure the equal right of men and women to the enjoyment of all civil and political rights set forth in the present Covenant."

[32] UN General Assembly, *ICCPR*, Article 14 (1), requires that "all persons shall be equal before the courts and tribunals." Article 14(3), requires that "in the determination of any criminal charge against him, everyone shall be entitled to the following minimum guarantees, *in full equality*: (A) to be informed promptly and in detail in a language which he understands of the nature and cause of the charge against him" (italics added). UN General Assembly, *ICESCR*, Article 3 states that "the States Parties . . . undertake to ensure the equal right of men and women to the enjoyment of all economic, social and cultural rights set forth in the present Covenant." In all of these cases, the documents go beyond ascribing certain rights to all — where this is compatible with unequal weights, contents, and access to remedies — to

legal systems provide effective legal remedies for all when the rights are violated, with no allowance for discrimination among persons as to the legal remedies to be made available).[33] And (5) the inclusion of strong rights against discrimination on grounds of race or gender (where this includes both formal legal discrimination and informal practices of discrimination in the public and private sectors). 'Strong rights against discrimination' here means rights against any form of discrimination, whether public or private, and not just discrimination that rises to the level of serious harms or undercuts an individual's opportunity for leading a minimally good life or decent life or prevents the fulfillment of her "basic needs."[34] The clearest example of such rights is the right to equal pay for equal work. This right is included not just in the Convention on Eliminating All Forms of Discrimination Against Women (CEDAW), but also in the UDHR, the ICCPR, and the ICESCR.

Taking these five features together, we can say that the existing system of international legal human rights has a robust *status egalitarian* aspect. The modifier 'status' here is intended to signal that what is at stake is not distributive equality (equality in the distribution of resources or opportunities or outcomes), but something more basic, namely, a notion of equal standing.

It is easy to fail to appreciate the status egalitarian elements of the system of international legal human rights. It is tempting to focus simply on the fact that a set of rights is ascribed to all and then note that the realization of these rights serves certain important interests that all humans typically have, thus helping to ensure that all have the

---

embrace a more robust egalitarianism. Finally, it is worth emphasizing that when international or regional courts and human rights treaty bodies interpret and apply international legal human rights there is no suggestion that these rights have different weights or contents for different individuals. Yet as I explain above, there is nothing incoherent in the idea of a legal system that ascribes a set of rights to all, but discriminates among various groups as to the content or scope of certain rights or the weights that are accorded to certain rights. Indeed such systems have existed in societies exhibiting institutionalized racism or sexism and in caste societies.

[33] The UDHR and the ICCPR contain detailed provisions designed to ensure due process and equality before the law for all. See, for example the UDHR, Articles 6, 7, 8, 9, 10, and 11; the ICCPR, Articles 2(1), 3(a), (b), and (c), 3, 6, 9, 14 (1,2,3), and 16 (1,2).

[34] Samantha Besson, "Evolutions in Non-Discrimination Law within the ECHR and ESC Systems: It Takes Two to Tango in the Council of Europe," *American Journal of Comparative Law*, 60:1 (2012): 147–80.

opportunity for a minimally good or decent life. That is the standard line on human rights one finds among philosophers, but it fails to take into account the fact that the international legal human rights system and decent domestic legal systems do much more than that: They also include the other status egalitarian elements and thereby prohibit various forms of discrimination in the system of legal rights itself. In brief, they prohibit various practices that would relegate some individuals to an inferior position in spite of the fact that they are accorded the same list of rights. In doing so, they do more than help ensure that all have a minimally good or decent life. That more modest goal could be achieved by a system of legal rights that was not so thoroughly egalitarian, one that varied significantly in the extent to which it protected the interests of different classes of individuals.

It is a sign of how far the idea of equal status has penetrated our assumptions about what counts as a decent legal system that we do not appreciate the fact that a legal system can—as many have done in the past—assign the same rights to all, and thereby provide some significant protection to the basic interests of all, and yet bestow quite different statuses on different individuals, depending on whether their rights are treated as having exactly the same content as those of others, as being subject to the same conditions of abrogation, and as having the same the weight as the rights of others, and upon whether all have access to the effective remedies—the same remedies—for violations of them. Because we now take for granted the status egalitarian aspects of decent domestic legal systems, we may fail to notice that the international legal human rights system exhibits a robust commitment to equal basic status. Focusing only on the fact that this system uses a set of rights ascribed to all to protect the basic interests of all, we may overlook the fact that it does much more than that. The key point is that a legal system, whether domestic or international, can provide protection for the basic interests of all or ensure that all have the opportunity for a minimally good or decent life, without exhibiting the status egalitarian features of the system of international legal human rights.

## The Well-Being Function

To appreciate fully the status egalitarian function of the system, it is useful to distinguish it carefully from the other main function of the system, the well-being function. From the very beginning of the post-World War II modern human rights era, during the discussions leading up to the drafting of the UDHR, it was assumed that international legal human rights would do more than protect people from the worst harms that their states could inflict on them and from abuses of state power. From the outset, the major documents, beginning with the UDHR, included rights whose realization requires states to provide positive benefits to those under their jurisdiction—to contribute to their well-being in ways that go beyond refraining from harm and abuse. In other words, the system of international human rights and the Practice that is anchored on it have from the outset proceeded on the assumption that the responsibilities of states include *basic welfare state functions*—provisions for public health and medical insurance, protection against unemployment, public education, and so on. Articles 22–28 of the founding document, the UDHR, list a number of social and economic rights, including rights to "social security"; to rest and leisure; to an adequate standard of living understood as including food, shelter, clothing, education, healthcare, and social services—in brief, all the rights we now associate with the modern welfare state.[35] As Glendon shows, the consensus that the new international law should require all states to be welfare states extended even to the United States, though that country has to this day refrained from ratifying the International Covenant on Economic, Social, and Cultural Rights, the treaty in which the commitment to social and economic rights became most robust and unequivocal.[36] In addition to affirming and protecting equal basic status for all, then, the system has a two-pronged well-being function: It protects people from harms and abuses inflicted by their own states and it requires all states to provide the goods and services characteristic of the modern welfare state.

The crucial point I wish to make at this juncture is that a system of legal rights (whether international or domestic) that was limited to the two-pronged well-being function would fall short of the robust commitment to equal basic status that the existing system of international legal human rights exhibits. It could ascribe an abstract

---

[35] UN General Assembly, *UDHR*.
[36] Mary Ann Glendon, *A World Made New: Eleanor Roosevelt and the Universal Declaration of Human Rights* (New York: Random House, 2002), pp. 4–45.

set of rights to all, and include both rights that protect against harms and abuses and rights distinctive of the modern welfare state, but allow for departures from equality in the specification of the content, weight, conditions of abrogation of some or all rights, or availability of remedies for violations, depending upon to whom the particular rights are ascribed. For example, a system might ascribe a right of freedom of expression to all, but restrict the content of the right (the set of correlative duties) in the case of some minority. Or, it might ascribe a set of rights to all, and stipulate that the content is the same for all, but give greater weight to the rights of some in cases in which the right conflicted with other rights or with considerations of the public good. Or, it might discriminate among persons as to the conditions of abrogation. Or, it might ascribe the same rights, with the same content and weight to all and the same conditions of abrogation for all, but restrict the range of effective remedies for violations in the case of some persons. Finally, a legal system could ascribe to all the same rights, with the same content and weight, with the same conditions of abrogation for all and the same availability of remedies for violations, but not include rights against discrimination on grounds of race or gender that prohibit subtler forms of social, as opposed to formal legal discrimination.

Legal systems under apartheid and Jim Crow (institutionalized racism in the Southern United States after the abolition of slavery), as well as customary law systems in caste societies, have lacked one or more of these five elements of the robust commitment to equal basic status that the system of international legal rights exhibits. The current Iranian legal system, to take only one contemporary example, accords a right of due process to all citizens, but restricts this right in the case of women, by according women's testimony in court much less weight than that of men. In so doing, it renders women's recourse to legal remedies for violations of their rights less effective than those available to men. Such legal systems may ascribe certain rights to all individuals and the realization of these rights may provide some significant protection to all against standard threats to basic interests we all typically have—in other words, they may help ensure that all have a minimally good or decent life—but they do not affirm equality of basic status in the way that decent domestic legal systems and the international legal human rights system do.

I believe that standard philosophical discussions of human rights have not taken the robust status egalitarian feature of the system seriously enough, when they have noticed it at all. A number of prominent philosophers continue to assert that the justifying function of human rights is to protect the conditions for a minimally good or decent life or to satisfy basic needs.[37] For brevity, let us call such views *minimal well-being only* conceptions of the function of human rights.[38] What those who hold these views typically do not acknowledge is that their conception of the function of human rights is at odds with some of the most basic features of human rights as they are understood in the Practice and embodied in international human rights law. If advocates of the minimal well-being only view protest that they are only referring to the function of moral human rights, this move has a price: Nothing follows about whether the function of international legal human rights should be similarly restricted to securing minimal well-being, unless one adds the Mirroring View as a premise.

To repeat: A system of international legal human rights could protect the conditions for leading a minimally good human life or decent life or ensure that everyone's basic needs are satisfied and yet not be as robustly status-egalitarian as the existing system. One can easily imagine conditions under which a system of rights could help ensure that all have a minimally good or decent life, even if it lacked one or more of the five status egalitarian elements listed above. For example, in a society in which gender or racial discrimination were restricted to the private sphere and were not engaged in by public

---

[37] This includes Nickel, Wellman and Altman, Shue, Miller, and myself in earlier work.

[38] James Nickel holds a version of what I call the minimal welfare only view. His concern is primarily with international legal human rights and he holds that when realized they help ensure that individuals have the opportunity for a decent or minimally good life, where this includes the ability "to lead a life," that is, some modicum of autonomy. My understanding of what the minimal welfare only view encompasses can accommodate this—that is, it can acknowledge that (many) international legal human rights, if realized, help individuals to promote their own welfare on their own terms. Nonetheless, it is one thing to say that the system of international legal human rights functions only to help secure minimal welfare thus understood and another to say they do that and also to affirm and protect equality of basic moral status. My view is that the best interpretation of the existing system portrays it as serving both functions. See James Nickel, *Making Sense of Human Rights* (Malden, MA: Wiley-Blackwell, 2007).

officials, or where official discrimination was relatively mild, women and people of color might well be able to live minimally good or decent lives or have their basic needs satisfied. Yet under international human rights law their rights would be violated.

So what are we to conclude from this? It appears that there are only two alternatives. Either the existing international legal human rights system goes beyond the minimal well-being function to ensuring equal basic status, considered as something of independent value, or the system is predicated on the problematic assumption that the only way reliably to ensure that all have an opportunity to lead a minimally good or decent life is to include all the robust status egalitarian features noted above. On the latter interpretation, the status egalitarian features, or at least some of them, are not included in the system because equal basis status is an independent value the system is designed to realize, but only because they are instrumentally necessary for securing the opportunity for a minimally good or decent life for all.

There is no use in trying to discern the purposes of the founders of the system as to this matter. The question is not what they thought the role of the five status egalitarian features is, but rather how they are to be understood on the best construal of the system. My surmise is that it would be hard going to try to justify all five of the status egalitarian features as being necessary for reliably ensuring that the minimal welfare function is achieved, that is, to make a convincing case that they are instrumentally necessary in order to ensure that all have an opportunity for a minimally good or decent life (or to satisfy basic needs). In other words, understanding the status egalitarian features as being mere instruments for achieving the minimal well-being function does not provide a cogent justification for including them in the system of international legal human rights.

If that is the case, then one is left with two options. One must either show that including the status egalitarian features in the system is justified because equal basic status is of sufficient moral importance in its own right, independent of its instrumental role in promoting the minimal well-being function; or one must take the path of revisionism and argue—not assume—that their inclusion is a mistake. And, I would emphasize, this would be no minor revision. It would amount to arguing that the international legal human rights system, unlike decent domestic legal systems, should allow various forms of discrimination in the implementation of the rights it contains. In effect, one would have to argue that international human rights law would be quite alright if it allowed systematic, legally sanctioned sexist or racist discrimination in the application of international legal human rights.

When philosophers characterize the function of human rights as ensuring the opportunity for a minimally good or decent human life or satisfying basic needs (the minimal well-being only view), they might just be referring to moral human rights, not international legal human rights. But if they are saying that international legal human rights, if they are justified, only serve the minimal well-being function, then they are in effect advocating a sweeping revision of the existing international legal human rights system, namely, rejection of its robust status egalitarian aspect of the system.

### Description Versus Prescription

I conclude, then, that those theorists who assert that 'human rights' (note the fatal ambiguity!) serve only the minimal well-being function must either abandon this view as failing to be faithful to the legal character of the Practice or they must argue for their revisionist proposal, showing why international legal human rights should not be as robustly status egalitarian as it is. So far, they have done neither.[39] Later, in chapter 4, I will argue that it is appropriate for the system to include a status egalitarian element that is more

---

[39]  This criticism applies to Joshua Cohen's view of human rights, even though he characterizes the function of human rights differently, as specifying conditions for membership in political communities. Cohen's conception of membership requires only that each individual's good be taken into account in the public order, but this is compatible with systematic inequality of status. In a caste system or a system of institutionalized gender or racial discrimination, the good of each might count but the good of some would count much less than that of others. So, although he says that his view exhibits the virtue of fidelity to the Practice, it clearly does not, because it omits the prominent status egalitarian elements of the practice embodied in international human rights law. In addition, he cites no evidence from human rights documents or discourse to support his claim that human rights are understood in the Practice as conditions for membership in his thin sense, where membership is understood to be compatible with systematic inequalities in status reflected in the domestic law, as with unequal rights for women or people of color. Joshua Cohen, "Minimalism about Human Rights: The Most We Can Hope For," *Journal of Political Philosophy*, 13: 2 (2004): 190–213.

robust than anything that could be justified on purely instrumental grounds, that is, as being conducive to the reliable achievement of the well-being function. Even if I fail to pull that off, I think I will have made an important point by showing that there is a discrepancy between the widely held minimal well-being only view and the legal content of the Practice and by making it clear that the tacit revisionism of the minimal well-being only view needs argumentative support.

My discussion of the robust status egalitarian function has a more general upshot: A justification for having a system of international legal human rights must specify the particular features of the system to be justified and then show that having a system with these features—all of them, or at least all of the most important ones—is justified. To do this, it will be necessary to first make the case that the system is supposed to perform certain functions—for example, constraining sovereignty in order to affirm and protect equal basic status and to ensure that all have the opportunity to lead a minimally good or decent life—and then show how its having these particular features contributes to performing those functions. Whether an adequate characterization of all or any of these functions requires reference to moral human rights should remain an open question.

In this chapter, I am concerned with description, not prescription. My contention is that most of the rights included in the various human rights treaties can be seen as either affirming and protecting equal basic status of all individuals, or as helping to ensure that all individuals have the opportunity to lead a minimally good or decent life. There are two different kinds of threats to the opportunity to lead a minimally good or decent life against which international legal human rights provide protections: harms, including restrictions on liberties needed for autonomy, and lack of resources broadly understood (food, shelter, education, etc.). Some international legal human rights function primarily to protect against harms inflicted by the state; others contribute to well-being in a positive way by providing valuable resources. For example, the bulk of the rights in the ICCPR function primarily to protect individuals from harms inflicted by their state (or with the complicity of the state). The various welfare rights that are more prominent in the ICESCR function primarily to contribute to well-being in more positive way by ensuring access to important goods and resources. Rights fulfilling both of these functions are included in the UDHR.

The standards whose realization is intended to achieve the well-being and status egalitarian functions are prominently, though far from exclusively, formulated in terms of individual legal rights. Nonetheless, it is important to understand that the main idea of the system can be stated without stipulating that the standard is to take the form of a list of individual legal rights.

## III.  *The Dimensions of the Justification Problem*

The task of justification would not end if one could make the case that there are good reasons for having a system of international law that serves the well-being and status egalitarian functions, however. It also requires showing that the institutions through which these legal rights are created, interpreted, and implemented are legitimate. Doing this would require, inter alia, an account of the sort of legitimacy that is appropriate for these kinds of institutions and an account of the proper division of labor between domestic, regional, and international institutions with regard to the formulation, interpretation, and implementation of international legal human rights.[40]

### *Two Justificatory Strategies*

There are two quite different ways, then, in which one might approach the justification of a particular international legal human right. First, one could hold constant the distinctive features of the actual system of international legal human rights and then argue, against this set of background assumptions, that a particular right ought to be or may rightly be included in that system or one similar to it. This way of proceeding would not engage the deeper question of whether having a system of that sort is justified. Alternatively, and more ambitiously, one could first argue in favor of having an international legal system of individual human rights of a certain type—perhaps one that is significantly different from the existing

---

[40] Kristen Hessler provides a valuable exploration of the question of the division of labor. See Kristen Hessler, "Resolving Interpretive Conflicts in International Human Rights Law."

system—and then argue that various particular rights ought to be or may rightly be included among its norms. Both approaches require a prior characterization of the nature of the system in which the particular rights to be justified are situated, a characterization that specifies the features and functions of the rights and the sort of authority they will have.

## Justification and History

To appreciate just how neglected the justification of international legal human rights is in the current philosophical literature, consider a recent valuable book, *The Idea of Human Rights*, by Charles Beitz, perhaps the foremost proponent of the Political or Practical approach. To his credit, Beitz forcefully makes the case that if philosophical theorizing about human rights is to be useful for assessing the Practice, it should focus on the Practice and begin with an accurate characterization of it. Further, he insists that the theorist should not assume that the moral foundations for the Practice lie in a conception of human rights that is independent of it—in particular, a concept of human rights that makes no reference to the state system.

Beitz offers a hypothesis as to why the Practice (at least in its modern, post-1945 form) arose. He sees the Practice as a response to the widespread perception, amid the smoldering ruins of World War II and the unspeakable horrors of the Holocaust, of the need to remedy a fault of the international order: the vulnerability of individuals to "mistreatment" inflicted on them by their own states, which was due in part to the virtually unlimited internal sovereignty that the norms of the international order confer on all states.[41] He uses this hypothesis about how the Practice arose to suggest an understanding of what the Practice is: It is an attempt to remedy this flaw of the international order. The Practice, he suggests, is an ex post facto modification of the international order designed to curb the mistreatment of people by their own states that results from the sovereign powers that the order confers on states.

The problem with Beitz's historical explanatory hypothesis is that it does not explain why the remedy for vulnerability took the form

---

[41] See Charles Beitz, *The Idea of Human Rights* (New York: Oxford University Press, 2009), pp. 128–29.

of *individual* rights, much less a system of *international legal* individual rights. There were in fact several alternatives for reducing the vulnerability of individuals to mistreatment by their own states. Here are some of the more obvious ones: (1) the imposition of a new set of duties on states (without correlative rights of individuals); (2) the international recognition of group rights (at first blush, this makes sense, given that the Holocaust and other major atrocities in the Second World War were perpetrated against individuals qua members of groups); (3) a modification of international law that lowered the barriers against intervention when states abuse their citizens, thus allowing third parties to aid the oppressed in their efforts to protect themselves from their state; and (4) international efforts (not necessarily utilizing international law), led by powerful democratic states, to encourage states to provide effective domestic constitutional guarantees of basic rights for their citizens.

Notice, with respect to option (1), that the actual system of international human rights law does include duties on states that are not formulated as correlatives of rights. The Universal Declaration of Human Rights (UDHR) and various human rights treaties include a number of nonrights items that appear to be simply imputations of duties to states.[42] To indicate how extensive nonrights norms are in international human rights documents, I have included an appendix on Nonrights Norms in Human Rights Documents (appendix 1).

The question arises, then, as to why the actual system features a prominent role for rights rather than simply duties. Beitz does not answer or even pose this question, and his historically based characterization of what the Practice is obscures it. Nor does his later assertion that human rights protect urgent interests remedy this deficiency, since interests, urgent or otherwise, can be protected by mere duties, without rights. What is lacking is an account of when interests have the right sort of character and moral weight to ground rights. Not all important interests ground duties and not all interests that ground duties ground rights.

So, simply saying that the Practice arose in response to a perceived threat posed by states to their own peoples is clearly insufficient to

---

[42] See appendix 1 for a long a list of some 'nonrights' provisions of several major human rights conventions.

explain the fact that *individual rights* are central to the Practice. Nor does it explain why the founders of the Practice agreed that the response to the problem of vulnerability to "mistreatment" by states should rely heavily on *international law*, rather than on some other legal or informal normative practice, whether international, regional, or domestic. (Note that Beitz's characterization of the point of the Practice includes no mention of international law. Yet as I have emphasized, a characterization of the Practice that omits reference to the fact that it was grounded on the idea that *international law* is to be used to regulate the behavior of states is clearly inadequate, given the centrality of international law to the Practice.)

### A More Accurate Characterization of What Requires Justifying

In terms of *justifying* the system, as opposed to explaining how it arose or characterizing what it is, the gap is equally wide. It is one thing to say that there was a need for some sort of protection for individuals against the depredations of their own states, quite another to make the case that the protection should take the form of a body of international law, and yet another to show that the needed system should have the features we see in the existing system, including the substantial role it assigns to individual legal rights.

Beitz's reference to the "mistreatment" that states are able to inflict on their people might suggest that the problem for which the system of international legal human rights is the proposed solution is limited to harmful or abusive state behavior. But that would be to characterize the point of the enterprise, as well as the function of international legal human rights, too narrowly. It would overlook the fact that the system promotes well-being in a positive way, not just by preventing harms and abuses, but also by requiring all states to be modern welfare states. It may be that the recognition of a need to protect people from harms or abuses by their own states was a crucial causal factor in the founding of the modern human rights practice. This is plausible, given that it was founded in the aftermath of World War II and the Holocaust. Nonetheless, as Beitz himself stresses, it is clear that the system of international legal human rights functions, and was designed to function, to achieve much more than that.

## IV. *The Strategy of This Book*

Given how complex—and how neglected—the task of justifying the international legal core of human rights practice is, I cannot hope to complete it in this book. My goal is more modest: to provide a framework for tackling the problem of the justification for having a system of international legal human rights and to take the first steps toward determining whether it is likely that a convincing justification can be constructed. I shall argue that in spite of the various moral criticisms of the existing system, there is good reason—for now at least—for a wide range of actors, public and private, to support it on moral grounds and good reason for all states to participate in it.

My ultimate goal is to improve the quality of philosophical theorizing that is relevant to the Practice, not by delivering a full-blown theory, but by setting an agenda for more productive enquiry and stimulating others to produce work that exceeds what I am able to accomplish. Nonetheless, I will take a clear position on some of the most important issues. By way of preview, in the remainder of this introduction, I will outline the chapters of the book.

### Chapter Summaries

Chapter 2 examines alternative philosophical methodologies regarding human rights in the light of their ability to help answer the question of whether the existing international legal human rights system is morally justified. There I articulate and criticize what I believe to be a widely held, though usually implicit assumption about the justification that has shaped much philosophical theorizing: the Mirroring View, according to which the typical or standard way to justify an international legal right requires making the case for the existence of an antecedently existing, corresponding moral human right, which the international legal right is to help realize.[43]

My aim in this second chapter is to show that an inquiry into the justification of international legal human rights should not proceed on the basis of the Mirroring View, but instead should exhibit the virtue of open-mindedness, adopting a pluralistic justificatory

---

[43] In earlier work, I referred to this as the Grounding View, but I now think Mirroring View is more illuminating, because it makes apparent the assumption of correspondence between moral and legal human rights.

methodology, at least provisionally. A pluralistic justificatory methodology allows for the possibility that in some, perhaps many cases international legal human rights can be justified without appealing to corresponding, preexisting moral rights, but instead by appealing to other moral considerations; and it also acknowledges the fact that not all of the standards that international human rights law imposes on the conduct of states must take the form of individual legal rights. More radically, a pluralistic approach allows for the possibility that justifications for international legal human rights can be moral individualistic justifications without appealing to moral human rights at all. In other words, it refuses to assume that moral rights are the only sufficiently sturdy building blocks for satisfactory justifications of international legal human rights.

Chapter 2 contrasts the Mirroring View with a Pluralistic Justificatory Strategy and makes the case that, provisionally at least, philosophical theorizing about human rights, if it is to be relevant to the moral assessment of the Practice, should reject the former and adopt the latter. The reason for rejecting the Mirroring View is not simply that major human rights documents contain a large number of mere duties, rather than rights, and a number of exhortations to action that may fall short of being statements of duties, though that in itself should give pause to proponents of the Mirroring View. (See Appendix 1: Nonrights Norms in International Human Rights Documents.) My stronger point will be that even in the case of items that are formulated as individual legal rights, it is a mistake to assume that their inclusion in human rights law is justified only if there are corresponding, antecedently existing moral rights or the legal right is a specification of such a moral right or instrumentally valuable for realizing it. I will argue that in a number of prominent cases there is no need to appeal to any moral right, much less a corresponding moral right, in order to justify an international legal right *and that in some prominent cases a justification of an international legal right cannot succeed if it appeals to a corresponding moral right.* In other words, I will argue that the existence of corresponding moral rights is neither necessary nor sufficient for justifying international legal human rights.[44] Once we see that

---

[44] This part of chapter 2 draws heavily on Allen Buchanan and Gopal Sreenivasan, "Taking Legality Seriously: A Methodology for Human Rights," unpublished paper.

this is the case and abandon the Mirroring View, the path is clear for a more open-minded justificatory approach, one that allows for justifications that do not appeal to corresponding moral rights. We can keep an open mind toward the question of the functions of the international legal human rights system, acknowledging that there is no reason to assume that the sole function (or even the chief function) is to use international legal norms to realize antecedently existing, corresponding moral rights.

Chapter 3 fills out the sketch of what justification requires that was provided in chapters 1 and 2. It distinguishes three stages in the task of justifying international legal human rights: (1) characterizing the system type, that is, specifying a type of system of international legal rights of individuals and making a moral case for having such a system (or for supporting a system of this sort if it already exists), where this includes a specification of the functions the system is to serve, a characterization of the types of norms the system includes (rights norms only or rights norms and mere duties, etc.), the function that appeals to the norms perform in political discourse, and the type of legal authority claimed on behalf of the norms; (2) articulating arguments for the conclusion that various particular rights ought to be, or may permissibly be, included in a system of that type; and (3) showing that a system of that type, including those rights, can be legitimately institutionalized.

Chapter 4 traverses the first two stages of justification, postponing stage (3) until chapter 5. With respect to the first stage of justification, I articulate three distinct arguments. The first explains the benefits, for a wide range of parties both public and private, of having a system of international legal human rights that has the basic contours of the existing system and then concludes that these benefits are substantial enough to constitute strong reasons for having such a system. The second argument shows that the system is justified in a stronger sense: Having a system of international legal human rights is a necessary condition for the existing international order to be justifiable, because without a system of international legal human rights the strong rights of sovereignty that the international order confers on states would be morally unacceptable. According to the second argument, the international order prior to the development of a system of international legal human rights was so deeply flawed as to be unjustifiable. The flaw was that it bestowed strong rights of sovereignty on all states, regardless of how they treated those under their jurisdiction. By bestowing these rights on all states, the international legal system erected formidable obstacles to third parties supporting people in their efforts to combat oppression by their own state and thereby increased their vulnerability, but also made it possible for states to resist the legitimate demand that they perform welfare state functions.

The third argument shows that having a system of this sort is morally obligatory *for states and hence for the governments that are their agents*, because it is they that are responsible for the creation and maintenance of the existing international legal order and because they are the chief beneficiaries of the strong rights of sovereignty it confers. Since the international legal system is primarily constituted by the actions of states and was designed to benefit them, states and the governments that act on their behalf had an obligation to modify the system so as to correct this flaw and, once the modification was made, an obligation to sustain it.[45]

The case for having an international legal human rights system similar to the one that exists can only be prima facie at this point, for two reasons. First, the question of whether or to what extent the institutional apparatus of the Practice is legitimate has not yet been addressed. This third stage of justification requires answering that question. Second, perhaps the most potentially serious moral criticism of the existing system, the allegation that what are supposed to be universal rights are in fact expressions of a parochial moral point of view and that the quest for universal normative standards is doomed because of the fact that there is a plurality of reasonable moralities—what I shall call the Reasonable Ethical Pluralism Objection—has not yet been evaluated.

With respect to the second stage of justification, I do not attempt to provide arguments for all the rights that should be, or permissibly may be, included in the sort of system specified at the first stage of

[45] Charles Beitz hints as this second argument, when he says that the Practice can be seen as an attempt, after the fact, to remedy a flaw of the international order. However, he presents this either as a remark about the actual history of the rise of the Practice or perhaps as part of his characterization of what the Practice is. He does not frame it as a justification for the system. Nor does he say that the vulnerability created by the international order's strong commitment to sovereignty obligated states to remedy this flaw by creating a system of international legal human rights. Charles Beitz, *The Idea of Human Rights*, pp. 128–29.

justification. Instead, I provide fairly detailed outlines of arguments for rights from each of several major classes of international legal human rights, showing how they are compatible with the system in which they are included performing the function of constraining sovereignty for the sake of protecting human dignity, where this encompasses both affirming and promoting equal basic status (the status egalitarian function) and ensuring that all have access to the conditions for a minimally good or decent human life (the well-being function). This should be enough to establish the feasibility of the Pluralistic Justificatory Strategy.

A key conclusion of chapter 4 is that moral human rights often have a much narrower scope—a less extensive set of corresponding duties—than international legal human rights, because in the former case, but not the latter, the corresponding duties must be grounded exclusively in some aspect of the individual right-holder. The crucial point is that with moral rights the corresponding duties are owed, morally speaking, to the right-holder. This means that there must be something about the right-holder herself of sufficient moral importance to ground the duties. This is not the case with legal rights. There can be a number of different kinds of reasons for making a legal duty owed (legally speaking) to the right-holder. In other words, the grounds of the correlative directed duty need not be restricted to morally important features of the individual right-holder. Instead, because the duties that correlate with legal rights are often grounded at least in part in the interests of large numbers of people, legal rights typically have greater scope, that is, a more extensive set of correlative duties. This simple fact has large consequences for the task of justifying international legal human rights that have hitherto gone unnoticed.

Chapter 5 addresses the third, institutional stage of the task of justification. I begin with a statement of the chief challenges to the legitimacy of international legal human rights institutions: (i) the charge that, due to vast inequalities in power among states, the implementation of human rights norms is bound to violate appropriate standards of impartiality; and (ii) the complaint that the institutions of the international human rights system lack crucial features that confer legitimacy on domestic legal systems, namely, a representative legislative process and an independent judiciary capable of ensuring the fidelity of legislation to reasonable constitutional requirements. My response to challenges to the legitimacy of international legal human rights institutions comes in three steps. First, I offer a general account of institutional legitimacy, what I call the Metacoordination View, and then apply it to some of the key international (UN-based) institutions that create, interpret, and implement international legal human rights. I argue that the "legitimacy deficit" these institutions are said to suffer looks much less serious once we recognize two facts about how they operate: (i) They contribute to the legitimacy of states in several distinct ways, and their playing this role contributes to their own legitimacy; and (ii) they outsource key functions, including legislation, adjudication, and enforcement, to states an increasingly larger proportion of which are constitutional democracies. Once this outsourcing becomes well-entrenched, it makes sense to view the institutional capacity of the international legal human rights system in a more favorable light. Just as philosophers speak of the Extended Mind to capture the fact that human beings now rely heavily in their cognitive lives on items that lie outside the brain, such as computers, so we can speak of the Extended Legal-Institutional Order, to do justice to the fact that the international legal human rights system relies on institutional resources that lie beyond the boundaries of international institutions narrowly conceived. Second, I show that for these international human rights institutions to be legitimate, they need not be democratic.

The basic idea of this chapter is that institutional legitimacy, properly understood, is an *ecological* notion: The legitimacy of a particular institution cannot be judged in isolation and, more specifically, is not determined solely by the relationship between it and those to whom its rules are addressed, but also depends upon its relationships with other institutions. I argue that the key to assessing the legitimacy of the institutional aspect of the international legal human rights system is an appreciation of the phenomenon of reciprocal legitimation in an extended legal-institutional order.

Chapter 6 completes the treatment of institutional legitimacy begun in chapter 4 by sorting out and critically evaluating a set of related concerns that arise because of assertions of the supremacy of international human rights law vis-à-vis domestic law, including constitutional law. A striking feature of the Practice is that it includes robust claims of legal authority vis-à-vis domestic law even in the case of the most admirable, rights-respecting constitutional democracies with the most highly developed legal systems. I argue that there is good reason to be concerned about the impact of international legal human rights law on domestic constitutional structures, even though there is no incompatibility in principle between a firm commitment to constitutionalism and an acknowledgment of the supremacy of international human rights law. I also argue, however, that *how* a domestic legal order incorporates international human rights law makes a great deal of difference as to whether it doing so infringes the collective right of political self-determination. I argue for the following principle: Where the acceptance of the supremacy of a norm or body of international law by a constitutional democracy can be reasonably expected to result in important changes in the nature of the polity—significant alterations in constitutional structures or significant diminution of political self-determination or both—then, as with significant constitutional changes generally (such as consensual secession, accession to a federation, or devolution from a centralized state to a federal or consociational one), there is a strong presumption that some robust form of democratic authorization is required. The basic idea here is that if recognizing the supremacy of international law will produce something as momentous as constitutional change or a significant diminution of collective self-determination, then ordinary treaty-making as usual is not sufficient. A more robustly democratic means of incorporating international law into domestic legal systems is required.

Chapter 7 carefully formulates and then evaluates perhaps the most fundamental challenge to the very idea of international human rights, so far as this includes the project of developing *universal* standards for the evaluation of the behavior of states: the Ethical Pluralism Objection. The focus is on the most plausible form of this objection, the claim that a system of international legal rights of individuals gives short shrift to reasonable collectivistic moralities. I argue that this is not the case. If the Mirroring View were true, then the Ethical Pluralism Objection would be fatal: A system of international legal human rights could not be justified to those who adhere to reasonable collectivist moralities, or at least not to those instances of this type of morality that reject the idea of individual moral rights or that deny that there are universal individual moral human rights. But if we abandon the Mirroring View and adopt the Pluralistic Justificatory

Strategy, then the way is clear for making the case that those who espouse collectivistic moralities have good reason to accept and even to support a system of international legal human rights, at least if the system has resources for mitigating whatever individualistic biases it presently contains. I also emphasize that the existing system is designed, from the standpoint of its key institutions, to mitigate cultural or ideological biases that have the potential to undermine the project of establishing global legal standards in the form of individual legal rights. The chapter concludes with a defense of the thesis that a proper acknowledgment of Reasonable Ethical Pluralism is compatible with the project of using international law to affirm and protect the equal basic status of all individuals.

Chapter 8, Conclusions, restates the core methodological ideas of the book, summarizes the chief results of the inquiry, identifies the major challenges for the system of international legal human rights and the broader human rights practice that it supports, and indicates the path for future research. I make the case for pursuing a research agenda that will require philosophers to draw more heavily on the study of international human rights law, considered from an empirically informed, institutional perspective. I argue that a sound philosophical theory of human rights that engages the Practice will be more philosophy of law and less pure moral theory than many thinkers have assumed, but that the kind of philosophy of law that is needed is one that is much more institutionally-oriented and factually grounded than traditional analytic philosophy of law.

Finally, in light of the book's account of the strengths of the international legal human rights system, I revisit the charge that the inequality of power among states undercuts the justifications for having the system and place it in a quite different perspective. I show how the admittedly limited but nonetheless impressive success of the system has depended on historical contingencies and that future changes in distribution of power among states (and in particular, the continued rise of a China that repudiates the basic idea of the Practice) may reverse the progress that has been achieved. Contemplation of the unpleasant possibility that we may be living in the golden age of human rights and on the cusp of its decline reinforces the conclusion of chapter 4 that a world in which powerful states are not restrained by international human rights law is almost certainly worse than one in which the application of the law is less than impartial.

# CHAPTER 2

———

# A Pluralistic Justificatory Methodology
# for Human Rights

This chapter has two aims: to focus attention more closely on the strangely neglected problem identified in chapter 1—the justification of the international legal human rights system—and to establish the proper methodology for addressing it. Philosophical theories of human rights are proliferating, but they have had little to say about the system of international legal human rights. There are two possible sources of this neglect. Philosophers may have failed to appreciate how central international human rights law is to the practice of human rights; or, they appreciate it, but hold a simplistic conception of what the law is and does, relegating it to the philosophically uninteresting task of merely providing legal form to antecedently existing moral rights whose grounding and content can be understood without thinking about legalization. On this simplistic conception, law is merely an instrument for realizing preexisting moral rights that we can know simply by the power of individual moral reasoning, without relying on the collective, institutionally structured practical reasoning that law supplies. If that is how one conceives of the relationship between the morality of human rights and the law, then it is not surprising that one's theorizing about human rights would have little to say about the law, as has been the case with the majority of contemporary philosophers writing about human rights.

It appears that at least some theorists who take the so-called Moral or Orthodox approach to theorizing human rights have tended to assume what I referred to in chapter 1 as the Mirroring View: that the standard or typical justification for an international legal human right must appeal to an antecedently existing, corresponding moral human right (while allowing for the possibility that some justified international legal human rights are specifications of more abstract moral human rights or valuable instruments for realizing moral human rights). The hypothesis that they hold the Mirroring View would explain their almost exclusive focus on the question of how to justify assertions about the existence of moral human rights, to the neglect of other, at least equally daunting questions relevant to the justification of a practice anchored in a system of international legal human rights. Perhaps the Mirroring View has inclined them toward the trivializing view of the law characterized above, and toward proceeding as if the main philosophical task will be completed if a sound theory of moral human rights is produced.

It is worth emphasizing, however, that even if the Mirroring View were true, things look quite different if one has a richer view of what the law is and does. Even if international legal human rights (to the extent that they are justified) often mirror preexisting moral human rights, legal processes can provide greater determinateness, with the result that the effort to realize moral human rights in law actually changes our understanding of the content of the moral human rights. If that were the case, then Griffin would be mistaken in his apparent assumption that giving more determinateness to the idea of moral human rights is a task largely reserved for the philosopher.

I shall argue that there are two problems with a methodological approach that assumes the Mirroring View and focuses primarily or exclusively on the justification of statements about the existence of moral human rights. First, the Mirroring View is assumed, not argued for, and false to boot. Second, even if the Mirroring View were true, producing a theory of moral human rights would, for reasons I will specify shortly, only be one necessary condition for justifying international legal human rights; the bulk of the work of justification would still have to be done. Justifying assertions about the existence of certain moral rights is one thing; justifying an institutionalized system of international law designed to realize them is quite another.

Advocates of the so-called Political approach to theorizing human rights, who say that we should attend to the actual practice of human rights and not assume that it must have philosophical foundations that are, as it were, antecedent and external to it, have also neglected to provide either a justification for having an international legal system of individual human rights or anything approaching a satisfactory account of how to justify the inclusion of any particular right within it. If we assume that philosophical theories of human rights are supposed to shed light on the practice of human rights (or restrict our attention to those that purport to do so), then this failure to engage the justification of international legal human rights is a major shortcoming, given how central that law is to the Practice.

The main conclusions of this chapter can be previewed as follows: (1) It is a mistake to begin philosophical theorizing of human rights with the assumption that the purpose of human rights practice is to realize a set of preexisting corresponding moral human rights;[1] indeed, once we appreciate the instrumental character of legal rights, it is a mistake to assume that to justify an international legal human right one must appeal to any moral human right. Instead, it may be possible to provide an adequate grounding for international legal human rights in other kinds of moral considerations, for example, moral duties which are not the correlates of individual moral rights. (2) Given the main functions and key features of the international legal human rights system, the existence of preexisting, corresponding moral human rights is neither necessary nor sufficient for justifying international legal human rights. (3) Some prominent international legal human rights, including rights to freedom of expression, health, to democratic government, and rights to due process, cannot be justified by appeal to corresponding moral rights, because there are no moral rights that have the extensive scope of these legal rights. (By 'scope' here I mean the set of duties that correlate with the right; one might also call this the content.) Nonetheless, there are cogent moral justifications for all of these international legal rights. (4) The

---

[1] It might be thought that Charles Beitz has already made this point in *The Idea of Human Rights*. In my judgment, he has not. He does not clearly articulate the Mirroring View. And his arguments against what he calls "naturalistic" theories of human rights are directed mainly against strawmen and do not engage more plausible versions of the Mirroring View. To put the same point differently: Not all Mirroring View proponents are naturalistic theorists in his sense; they need not and do not all hold, if any of them hold, that moral human rights are timeless and pre-institutional. See Charles Beitz, *The Idea of Human Rights* (New York, New York: Oxford University Press, 2011).

argumentative distance between identifying the basic moral values or moral rights on which a system of international legal human rights is most securely based and providing a sound justification for such a system is much greater than philosophical theorists have assumed. It is one thing to make the case for certain values or certain moral human rights, another to show that they should be realized through law, and yet another to establish that they should be realized through international law and, more specifically, through international law that constrains state sovereignty even in its exercise over domestic matters and has the other features that the existing system exhibits. By concentrating almost exclusively on the development of an account of moral human rights, philosophical theorists have not only proceeded with an unduly constrained conception of the moral considerations that ground international legal human rights; they have also failed to appreciate how complex and daunting the task of justification is.

## I. *Why Corresponding Moral Human Rights Aren't Necessary*

At least some of the most prominent international legal human rights, as well as their domestic law counterparts, can be justified without appealing to corresponding moral rights. Indeed, it appears that they can be adequately justified without appealing to moral human rights at all. Consider the legal right to health, whether in a domestic or regional or international legal system. This legal right admits of a powerful pluralistic justification that does not include an appeal to an antecedently existing moral right to healthcare. A legal entitlement to goods, services, and conditions that are conducive to health, which include but are not limited to healthcare, can promote social utility, contribute to social solidarity, help to realize the ideal of a decent or a humane society, increase productivity and to that extent contribute to the general welfare, and provide an efficient and coordinated way for individuals to fulfill their obligations of beneficence.[2] Taken together, these distinct lines of justification, none of which appeals to an antecedently existing moral right to health, make a strong case for having a legal right to health.

---

[2] Allen Buchanan, "The Right to a 'Decent Minimum' of Health Care," *Philosophy & Public Affairs*, 13:1 (1984): 55–78.

*Justifying Legal Rights Without Premises About Moral Rights*

Further, it is not at all clear that these arguments need to invoke premises asserting the existence of moral rights of any kind. Instead, it appears that these arguments only require an appeal to some rather uncontroversial values and can achieve the desired conclusion by invoking mere duties to promote or protect them, without recourse to rights. Once we appreciate the instrumental character of legal rights, it becomes clear that there is nothing inconsistent about justifying a legal claim-right by showing that, if enacted and implemented, it would help realize important values or fulfill important moral duties, even though the duties are not correlatives of rights. In other words, it can be beneficial, and even morally mandatory, to create a legal right, where this means a legal duty that is owed to the legal right-holder, in order to fulfill a (mere) moral duty.

Similarly, legal rights that promote physical security—rights against assault, arbitrary killing, torture, and so on—can be justified by appeal to a number of moral considerations, without recourse to antecedently existing corresponding moral rights. Legal physical security rights serve several important values, including individual autonomy, peaceful and productive social cooperation, social utility, the protection of minority groups, and the protection of property rights (by shielding individuals from coercive expropriation of their property).

Once such a pluralistic justification for physical security rights is provided, it can serve as the basis for justifying other legal rights, such as the right to democratic governance and the various rights of legal due process, on the grounds that these latter rights are needed to make the legal physical security rights effective.[3] At no stage does the argument require reference to corresponding moral rights.[4]

---

[3] Thomas Christiano critically presents impressive empirical evidence that democratic governance provides important protections for the right to physical security. See Thomas Christiano, "An Instrumental Argument for a Human Right to Democracy," *Philosophy & Public Affairs*, 13:1 2 (2011): 142–76.

[4] Whether there is an international legal right to democratic governance is disputable. The ICCPR includes a right to periodic elections, but that falls short of what is generally meant by democracy. In chapter 4 I consider arguments for including a right to democratic government in the system of international legal human rights.

Further, as with the right to health, one should not assume that these justifications for the legal right are sound only if they rely on premises about the existence of moral rights, as opposed to (mere) moral duties.

## Legal Rights: Instruments to Serve a Variety of Purposes

The fundamental and quite general point is that legal rights, whether domestic or international, do not presuppose corresponding moral rights. This should be no surprise, given that individual legal human rights are instruments that can serve a number of purposes, including moral ones of various types. The moral purposes for which individual legal rights are instrumentally valuable are not restricted to the realization of antecedently existing individual moral rights. Consequently, one should not assume that if a legal right is morally justified, there must be a corresponding moral right that it serves to realize. The fact that law is an instrument capable of serving quite diverse purposes, including the realization of a diversity of moral concerns, including the fulfillment of mere duties, should make one skeptical about the assumption that to justify international legal human rights one must show that they are grounded in corresponding moral human rights.

## Avoiding Confusion About Enforcement and Rights

One might assume that a system of legal individual rights is justifiable only if there are corresponding moral human rights, if one made two further assumptions: first, that if something is to be a legal right, it must be justifiable to enforce it; and second, that only duties that are the correlates of moral rights may be justifiably enforced. For my purposes, it is not necessary to take a position on the first assumption; I will remain agnostic on whether there is such a tight connection between legality and enforceability. The second assumption, however, is clearly false. It can be justifiable to enforce legal rights even if there is no corresponding moral right. Although some libertarian philosophers have uncritically assumed it, it is not the case that duties may justifiably be enforced only if they are correlates of moral rights. For example, in some cases, it is morally justifiable to enforce duties the fulfillment of which is necessary for securing morally important public goods, but its being justifiable does not depend on the implausible claim that each individual has an antecedently existing moral right to the public good.[5] Justifying a legal right may require justifying the enforcement of the correlative legal duties, but the enforcement of legal duties does not require correlative moral rights. If the existence of a moral right is not necessary for the justified enforcement of duties, then one should not assume that if the duties that correspond to international legal human rights are to be justifiably enforceable, they must be grounded in moral human rights. Hence, even if one assumes that to justify an international legal human right one must show that it is justifiable to enforce the duty the right entails, it does not follow that an international legal right is justified only if it is necessary for realizing an antecedently existing moral human.

## II.  *Why Moral Rights Are Not Sufficient*

### *Some Moral Rights Are Not Plausible Candidates for Legalization*

Thus far, I have shown that justifying claims about the existence of corresponding moral rights, or any rights at all, is not necessary for justifying legal rights, international or otherwise. It should be obvious that, generally speaking, the existence of a moral right is not a sufficient reason for establishing a corresponding legal right either. Sometimes the attempt to enforce a moral right would be require dangerously high levels of coercive capacity on the part of the state. In other cases, even if enforcement would not require excessive coercive capacity, the content of a particular moral right is such that enforcing it would be inappropriate. One might argue that this is so with the rights generated by promises (as opposed to contracts) and the right to be treated with respect, among others.

In brief, as the literature on the relationship between law and morality has long acknowledged, not all moral rights are suitable candidates for legalization, whether domestic or international. On the face of it, it seems that the same sorts of considerations that can

---

[5] Allen Buchanan, "Justice and Charity," *Ethics*, 97:3 (1987): 558–75. Also, Allen Buchanan, "What's So Special About Rights?" *Social Philosophy and Policy*, 2:1 (1984): 61–88.

make it inadvisable to legalize some moral rights generally apply to some moral human rights. If this is so, then we shouldn't expect that all moral human rights are appropriate for international legalization.

The right to be treated with respect is, on some views, a moral human right; but it would not be a good idea to make it a legal right, assuming that being treated with respect includes ways of being treated, especially in personal relationships, that are not the proper business of law. Some might deny that the right to respect, understood in this way, is a moral human right, however, because they think that moral human rights are, by definition, rights that are suitable for international legalization. That is not a promising line of thought, given that the notion of moral human rights, as it was invoked by philosophers at least as early as the seventeenth and eighteenth centuries made no reference to international legalization. Restricting the term 'moral human rights' to moral rights that may rightly be included in international law seems arbitrarily stipulative, given the long history of the notion of moral human rights that antedated even the proposal for an international legal human rights system. But even if we accept the stipulation, all that follows is the trivial assertion that all moral human rights in this special, stipulated sense, may rightly be made international legal rights. It does not follow that being a moral human right is sufficient for being included among international legal human rights, because there is a quite respectable usage of the term 'moral human right,' as I have noted, that does not refer to international legalization.

Quite apart from the familiar considerations that sometimes speak against legalizing moral rights, whether a particular moral human right ought to be given international legal embodiment will depend upon the functions that the system of international legal human rights is supposed to serve. Not all moral human rights may be relevant to those functions and including legal counterparts of some of them might actually detract from the system's ability to perform them. In particular, there is no reason to assume that every moral human right is important enough to play a role in a system of international law designed to limit sovereignty, given the important values, including collective self-determination, that sovereignty protects and promotes.

*Some Plausible Legal Rights Cannot Be Grounded in*
*Corresponding Moral Rights*

I now want to articulate a less obvious reason why a strong correspondence between international legal rights and moral rights should
not be assumed. A sound theory of the moral rights of individuals
will not include counterparts of some important individual legal
rights, including the right to health, the right to democratic government, and rights of legal due process. Therefore, even if philosophers could produce a comprehensive and sound moral theory of
human rights, this would be inadequate for justifying some of the
most important international legal human rights. The problem is
that many international legal human rights have a much broader
scope or content—a more extensive set of correlative duties—than
the moral human rights that go by the same name.

Moral human rights are typically claim-rights in Hohfeld's sense
(though as Carl Wellman has shown they may also have other Hohfeldian features as well).[6] In the case of moral claim-rights generally, including moral human rights, the correlative duties are morally owed
to the right-holder, or as is sometimes said, they are directed duties.

What must be true if these duties are to be owed, morally speaking,
to the right-holder? The only cogent answer, so far as I can tell, is
that there must be something about the right-holder that is of sufficient moral importance to ground the duties and it is because this is
so that the duties are owed to him or her. Or, to put the same point
in different terms, in the case of a moral claim-right, the right-holder
is morally entitled to the performance of the correlative duties and
this can only be the case if there is something about the right-holder
that makes him or her so entitled.

Joseph Raz appears to acknowledge this point about moral claim-
rights when he says that A has a right only if there is some aspect of A's
interest that is sufficient to ground the correlative duties.[7] This makes
sense if Raz is referring to moral claim-rights, rights with directed correlative duties. For the correlative duties to be owed, morally speaking,
to A or for A to be morally entitled to the performance of those duties,

---

[6] Carl Wellman, *The Moral Dimensions of Human Rights* (New York: Oxford
University Press, 2010).

[7] Joseph Raz, *The Morality of Freedom* (New York: Oxford University Press,
1988).

there must be something about A that is of sufficient moral importance to justify the claim, not only that someone has those duties, but that they owe them to A. Raz uses the notion of interests to capture this something.

To highlight this feature of moral claim-rights, let us say that the correlative duties, as directed duties, are *solely subject-grounded*. But let us remain agnostic as to whether that something is always an interest (leaving open the possibility that it might also be something else—perhaps the moral status of the right-holder or some capacity of the right-holder that confers moral status). The key point is that to justify the assertion that A has a moral claim-right R, it is not enough to show that someone has a duty or even that someone has a duty regarding A; one must show that that duty is owed, morally speaking, to A or that A is morally entitled to the performance of that duty; and to show that one must identify something about A that is sufficient to ground the directed duty.

Notice that while Raz's assertion is plausible if it refers to moral claim-rights, it is not if it refers to legal claim-rights. To say that someone has a legal right to R is only to say that the corresponding duties are owed, legally speaking, to the right-holder, where this means only that the right-holder has legal standing to demand that the duty be fulfilled, is eligible for compensation or restitution, and so on. There is no assumption that the right-holder is morally entitled to the performance of the duties, nor that the only way to justify having the correlative duties owed, legally speaking, to the right-holder is to identify some feature of the right-holder that is of sufficient moral importance to ground the legal duties.

Raz notes that with some genuine rights the moral importance of the right-holder's interests is not sufficient to ground the correlative duties.[8] He tries to accommodate this fact by abandoning his original assertion about what is necessary to justify duties and hence correlative rights. He says that the grounding of the correlative duties can rest on the importance of the interests of large numbers of people, not just those of the right-holder, so long as the former are served by the protection of the right-holder's interests. In other words, he backtracks on his original claim that there must be some aspect of the right-holder's interest that is sufficient to ground the duties.

---

[8] Ibid.

This move seems to me (as it has to many others) to be wholly ad hoc. Further, and more importantly for present purposes, it cannot explain why, morally speaking, the duties are owed to the right-holder. Why would the fact that the correlative duties happen to serve the interests of others via serving my interests show that the duties are owed, morally speaking, to me?

If Raz restricted his revised view to legal claim-rights, it would be more plausible. With respect to legal claim-rights, one need not show that, morally speaking, the correlative duties are owed to the right-holder. One need only provide a sound justification for having the duties owed, legally speaking to the right-holder, and such a justification can quite properly appeal to the interests of persons other than the right-holder.

In the case of a legal right, the corresponding duty can be (legally) owed to the right-holder simply by virtue of the fact that the law confers that (legal) standing on her. There can be sound instrumental reasons for giving individuals this sort of legal standing, even in cases in which there is nothing about the individual that is in itself of sufficient moral importance to justify the duties in question. For one thing, by conferring legal standing on individuals, it may be possible to achieve more effective compliance with the duties, at least when the right-holders have appropriate incentives for advancing claims on the basis of the right.[9] Further, it is perfectly appropriate to justify making certain duties owed, legally speaking, to an individual, if that is needed to promote the interests of large numbers of other people. The failure to appreciate this fundamental difference between moral and legal rights has done much mischief in philosophical theorizing about human rights, as I shall show.[10]

[9] Buchanan, "What's So Special About Rights?," 61–88.

[10] The same conclusions follow if one adopts, instead of Raz's Interest Theory, the Will Theory of Rights. As I understand Carl Wellman's Will Theory, unlike Raz's interest Theory, it is not an attempt to identify the conditions for justifying assertions about the existence of rights, but rather a view about what rights are. Be that as it may, Wellman holds that if A has a claim-right to R, then A "controls" the correlative duties. Perhaps the idea is that the duties could be controlled by A only if they were owed to A (not somebody else). If that is so, then we need an account of why they are owed to A if we are to understand why A controls them. But as I have already suggested, it is hard to see how the duties could be owed, morally speaking, to A (and hence how A could control them) unless there were something about A that made this so. Once again, however, this only applies to moral rights. The law can grant A control over a set of legal duties (can legally empower A to invoke or waive the duties, etc.), for any number of reasons, including the fact that doing so promotes public interests of the right sort.

In the case of the rights to health, to democratic government, and to due process no individual's interests alone could justify the imposition of the corresponding duties that are reasonably associated with them as legal rights, whether domestic or international. In each case, the scope or content of the legal rights is very broad: The range of corresponding duties includes duties to ensure that various large-scale social arrangements are created and sustained. For example, in the case of rights of due process, the duties include the training and supervision of the police, appropriate processes for selecting an able and independent judiciary, and the establishment and maintenance of courts.

The same is true with regard to the right to health, if we grant the now widely accepted and empirically well-supported assumption that the individual's health depends significantly on various social-structural and environmental factors.[11] If this assumption is valid, then, as Gopal Sreenivasan has argued, protecting and promoting an individual's interest in health will require large-scale social investment for the provision of public goods such as "herd-immunity" to infectious diseases through vaccination programs and, given the negative effects on health that certain social inequalities appear to produce, most likely large-scale social reforms as well.[12] Further, such policies will involve restrictions on the liberty of many individuals. No individual's interest in health is morally sufficient to justify the great costs that such large-scale policies entail and the significant restrictions on many individuals' liberty that they would inevitably require. If there is a moral right to health, it is narrower in scope—it has a less extensive set of correlative duties—than a reasonable legal right to health.

Similarly for the right to democratic government: Fulfilling the corresponding duties requires not only large outlays of social resources but also extensive control over large numbers of individuals, where this involves significant restrictions on their liberty. The duties that correlate with the right to democratic government, as an international legal right, include more than just the duty not to interfere with a citizen's attempts to vote or to run for office. The scope of the right also includes duties on the part of the state to

---

[11] Gopal Sreenivasan, "A Human Right to Health? Some Inconclusive Skepticism," *Aristotelian Society Supplementary Volume*, 86:1 (2012): 239–65.
[12] Ibid.

arrange and conduct fair elections, where this includes expending resources to prevent coercion or fraud from distorting the electoral process, and ensuring that the logistics for voting are in place.

One could also develop the same point for the right to freedom of expression. The interest of the right-holder herself may not be sufficient to justify such a right, at least if we think of it as being fairly robust in the protection for expressive activities it provides. But assigning such a legal right to the individual may be justifiable, because doing so serves the interests of large numbers of people, including their interest in keeping government under control.

With regard to all of these rights, it only because the fulfillment of the correlative duties positively impacts the interests of a large number of people that ascription of such extensive, expensive, and liberty-limiting duties is reasonable. But if that is so, then the interests of the individual cannot justify the ascription of the right to him or her, because the right implies the corresponding directed duties. The point is that while the contribution to any particular individual's interest that fulfillment of the duties that correlate with these rights makes would not warrant the costs and burdens that fulfilling the duties requires, the consequences of the fulfillment of the duties for the population as a whole may be sufficiently good to justify the costs and burdens and hence the imposition of the duties.

The results of the analysis can now be formulated as an argument.

1. Many important international legal human rights have corresponding duties the fulfillment of which requires large-scale social investment and limitations on the liberty of large numbers of people.
2. Such duties, and hence the corresponding rights, are justifiable only because their fulfillment would positively impact the interests (or autonomy, etc.) of large numbers of people.
3. In the case of moral rights, the corresponding duties must be justifiable by appealing solely to some morally important aspect of the individual to whom the right is ascribed, because the duties are supposed to be owed, morally speaking, to the individual to whom the right is ascribed. (In contrast, in the case of legal rights, the fact that the correlative duties are owed,

legally speaking, to the individual right-holder does not imply that they are grounded solely in the moral importance of some aspect of the right-holder.)

4. (Therefore), there are no moral rights that correspond to (i.e., have the same content as) many important international legal human rights.

5. If there are no moral rights that correspond to many international legal human rights, then for many international legal human rights, it is not possible to justify them by appealing to corresponding moral human rights.

6. Yet many international legal human rights that cannot be justified by appealing to corresponding moral human rights are justifiable—they are suitable for inclusion in a system of international legal rights, given the functions such a system is supposed to perform and given the moral appropriateness of those functions.

7. (Therefore), in the case of many justifiable international legal human rights, showing that the legal right helps to realize a corresponding moral human right will not fully justify the legal right, not because there would be unacceptable consequences of legally realizing the moral right (as with the case of the right to be treated with respect), but because the moral right has a narrower scope than the legal right.

Argument 1 through 7 relies on a fundamental difference between moral and legal claim-rights that, so far as I can tell, has gone unappreciated in the philosophical literature on rights. Because the point is unfamiliar, it may be useful to elaborate on it. The core idea is this: Because the duties that correspond to moral claim-rights are directed, that is, morally owed to the right-holder, they must be solely subject-grounded. That is, to establish the existence of the directed duties and hence of the right it is necessary to make the case that there is something about the right-holder that justifies the assertion that the duties are owed, morally speaking, to him or her. But neither the interests nor the autonomy, nor any other feature of any particular individual is of sufficient moral importance to justify the ascription of the extensive and expensive duties that are correlates of many legal rights, whether domestic or international. To put the point bluntly: No matter who you are, you are not important enough to justify a set of duties that correlate with the panoply of legal rights that constitute the modern rights-respecting welfare state, much less important enough to justify a system of international human rights law that serves to support the welfare state's system of rights. But the interests and autonomy of large numbers of people like you are important enough. That is why legal rights, whether at the domestic or international level, often do not mirror moral rights. Legal rights can be and are much more expansive in their content than moral rights and the fact that this is so requires a radical transformation of the way philosophers have tended to think about human rights.

## III. *Appealing to the Interests of Many, Without Embracing Consequentialism*

It is crucial to emphasize that by acknowledging that the justification for legal human rights can appeal to the interests, not just of the right-holder, but also of large numbers of other people, I am not endorsing nor am I committed to a consequentialist justification for these legal rights. One can appeal to the interests of many people without holding that legal rights are simply instruments for maximizing aggregate utility. Recall that on my view the international legal human rights system expresses a commitment to affirming equal basic status for all; that is, affirming and protecting the equal basic status of all individuals is one of its chief functions. The commitment to equal basic status constrains the appeal to the interests of the many: Appeals to the maximization of aggregate interests that sacrifice the interest of some are ruled out. In other words, on my view, the justification for any particular international legal human right proceeds in the context of the commitment to status egalitarianism. In particular, the background assumption is that each right will be ascribed to all human individuals, with the same general content, that it will have the same weight for all to whom it is ascribed, the same conditions of abrogation (if any), and that each will have an equal right to remedies for its violation. Accordingly, the kind of justification I am exploring allows one to escape the narrow confines of a solely subject-centered grounding for international legal human rights without collapsing into consequentialism. In my judgment, this is an impressive virtue of it.

## IV. *Taking the Distinction Between Legal and Moral Rights Seriously*

Thus far, I have shown (1) that plausible justifications for some of the more prominent international legal rights need not appeal to moral rights, whether corresponding or otherwise, and (2) that for some prominent international legal human rights, including the right to health, rights of due process, the right to freedom of expression, and the right to democratic government, arguing that the legal right realizes a corresponding, preexisting moral right is not sufficient to justify the legal right, because the moral right has a much narrower scope than the legal right.

In chapter 1, I defined the Mirroring View as holding that to justify an international legal human right one typically must show that it mirrors an antecedently existing moral human right while allowing for the possibility that in some cases the legal right is a specification of such a right (as the right to freedom of the press is a specification of the right to freedom of expression), or that it is instrumentally valuable for realizing a moral human right (as the legal right to democracy is said to be instrumental for realizing the moral human right to physical security). It is worth pointing out that my reflections on the difference between legal and moral rights show that some international legal human rights cannot be seen as specifications of moral human rights. Specification is a matter of the determinateness of the object of the right (for example, a right to freedom of the press is more determinate than a right to freedom of expression). The broader scope of international legal human rights is a matter of more extensive duties, understood as means for realizing the object of the right, not a matter of difference in the specification of the object of the right.

I now want to take the argument a big step farther. If it is true that a moral right exists only if the interests or some other aspect of the right-holder are sufficient to justify the corresponding duty of the right-holder, then (general) moral rights have a narrower scope—that is, have much leaner corresponding duties—than is usually assumed. The reason for this is simple: The duty-justifying grounds of moral rights are much narrower than those of legal rights; the former are limited to morally significant aspects of the individual right-holder, the latter are not. In other words, if moral rights are solely subject-grounded, but legal rights are not, then, other things being equal, legal rights have a broader scope—a wider range of justifiable duties—than moral rights.

### Moral Rights Versus Legal Rights: The Distribution of the Costs of Fulfilling Duties

There is another reason why a system of international legal human rights should not mirror a list of moral human rights. Generally speaking, it is easier to justify a legal right than to justify the corresponding moral right, at least so far as legal rights are enforceable. To justify a moral right, one must show that the corresponding duties exist, that is, that someone has the duties in question or, on some theories of rights, one must at least show that it would be justifiable to impose the duties on someone. But whether an individual, A, has a moral duty, D, to do X, and whether it is justifiable to require A to do X (to impose the duty on him) can depend on whether A has reasonable assurance that others are going to fulfill that duty. Without this assurance, it may be unfair to require A to do X. If D is merely a moral duty, then A may not have this assurance, in which case he will not have the duty and it will not be justifiable to impose the duty on him; consequently, there will be no duty and hence no right. But if D is a legal duty and enforceable as such, then A will have the needed assurance and hence it will be justifiable to require him to do X. What one has a duty to do, absent reciprocity on the part of others, can be less than what one has a duty to do, given reasonable assurance of their reciprocating. Because the law can provide reasonable assurance of reciprocity, legal duties, and hence legal rights, can be more robust than moral rights. That is another reason why the law can be a more effective mechanism for achieving moral ends if it does not restrict itself to giving legal form and enforcement to preexisting moral rights.

If these conclusions are correct, then it is a mistake to assume that a theory of moral human rights will carry us very far toward the goal of providing a critical perspective on the modern human rights practice. That is a mistaken assumption, given that the system of international legal human rights is central to the Practice. For there is no good reason to assume that a system of international legal human rights must be grounded on a corresponding set of moral human rights and good reason to assume that some important international legal human rights cannot be justified in that fashion but are nonetheless justifiable. Nor is it obvious that a sound justification for legal human rights must show that they all help realize some moral human right or other. International legal human rights, like other legal rights, can be justified by appeal to considerations other than the need to realize moral rights, such as the need to fulfill mere duties.

So, we ought to reject the Mirroring View. A more reasonable methodology is to keep an open mind and proceed on the assumption that the justification of international legal human rights may well be more pluralistic in nature. Whether or to what extent the justification of international legal human rights will rest on assertions about the existence of moral rights should remain an open question.

## V. *Constraints on a Pluralistic Justificatory Methodology*

I have argued that recognition of the fact that legal rights can serve a number of moral functions, as well as the fact that international human rights law contains more than lists of rights, suggests a pluralistic strategy for justifying international legal human rights—one that allows appealing to a broader range of moral considerations. At this point it is important to emphasize, however, that it is not enough to show that some sort of international legal individual rights could be justified without grounding them on preexisting corresponding moral rights: The ultimate task, rather, is to justify international legal rights that can function in the way that international legal human rights actually function in the existing system and that have the key characteristics that rights in the existing system have. In other words, any justification for international legal human rights must satisfy certain constraints of "fit," if it is to succeed as a justification for international legal human rights of the right sort—the sort that are relevant to a critical evaluation of the existing system.[13] If a justification only worked for international legal rights that were quite different in their characteristics or functions they serve or roles they play than existing international legal human rights, it would fail to shed much light on the normative status of the existing system.

---

[13] I thank Miriam Ronzoni for pressing me on this point.

In the next chapter, I sketch pluralistic justifications for items from each of four major categories of international legal human rights. Here I want only to show that there is no good reason to adopt a justificatory methodology that assumes that appeals to moral human rights play an ineliminable role in sound justifications for international legal human rights similar to those that now exist. To do this, we need a clear idea of the constraints that a justification would have to satisfy in order to justify legal rights of that sort.

## Chief Functions of the Existing International Legal Human Rights System

The most important constraints, in my judgment, are that international legal human rights constrain sovereignty for the purposes of affirming and promoting the equal basic status of all people (the status egalitarian function) and helping to ensure that all have the opportunity to lead a minimally good or decent life by providing protections and resources that are generally needed for such a life (the well-being function). Some might object that international legal human rights can serve these functions only if they are grounded in some preexisting moral right or rights. I now want to show that this is not the case.

As I observed in chapter 1, among the most important roles of rights in the existing international legal human rights system is to constrain the exercise of sovereignty in the domestic sphere—to articulate legal norms that specify how a state is to treat those under its jurisdiction. In addition, violations of some basic international legal rights, at least if they occur on a large scale, can serve as an important premise in justifications for armed humanitarian military intervention. Finally, respect for some of the most basic international legal human rights is sometimes regarded as a necessary condition for proper recognition of a state's legitimacy, in the case of new states created by secession from existing ones, and as a necessary condition for the legitimacy of governments in some cases.

If they are to play these sovereignty-limiting roles, existing international legal human rights must be justified in ways that make it plausible for them to do so. It is not enough to produce considerations that justify some sort of individual legal right or other; one must show that individual legal rights having the potency that is distinctive of international legal human rights are justified. The fact that international legal human rights constrain sovereignty in these ways restricts what will count as a sound justification for having a system of international legal human rights that has this feature.

Assuming that there are weighty moral reasons for a presumption that sovereignty is to be respected, the justification for having a system of international legal rights that constrains sovereignty in these ways will have to be comparably robust. Arguments that might suffice to justify a legal right in a domestic system, where there is no attempt to constrain the sovereignty of other states, may not be adequate to justify a corresponding international legal human right.

Here it is important to avoid the error of thinking that only moral rights could provide sufficient weight. There is nothing in the concept of a right, or a claim-right, that guarantees exceptional weight and nothing in the concept of a (mere) duty that precludes exceptional weight. Nor is it a self-evident fact about morality that only moral rights, as opposed to (mere) duties, have sufficient weight to ground legal rights that can perform the functions that international legal human rights do.

In addition to grounding the sovereignty-constraining roles, a justification must also be consistent with a striking feature of the existing international legal human rights system noted earlier: the fact that, taken as a whole, this system of rights expresses a strong commitment to equality of basic status for all people. Fidelity to the status-egalitarianism of the system significantly also constrains the sorts of justifications that can be offered. For example, justifications that are limited to the claim that international legal rights serve to protect individuals from the harms that can undermine the opportunity for leading a minimally good life or provide resources needed for such a life will not be adequate because they will not be sufficient to justify the strong rights against discrimination that are characteristic of the existing international legal human rights system. A system of rights could protect individuals against state inflicted harms and provide resources for a minimally good or decent life for everyone and yet be compatible with arbitrary discrimination along gender, racial, or ethnic lines, so long as this discrimination did not rise to the level of gross harm or undermine the prospects for a minimally good life. Similarly, as I have already shown, the status-egalitarian feature rules out a justificatory strategy that relies solely on utilitarian justifications that appeal to the aggregation and maximization of benefits across individuals, to the extent that such a consequentialist procedure gives short shrift to a recognition of the "separateness" and independent worth of persons that status-egalitarianism implies and the constraints on utility-maximization that it entails.

It is crucial to emphasize that fidelity to status-egalitarianism is a requirement for justification at the system level. It is not necessary that every right in the system be grounded in the commitment to recognizing and protecting equal basic status for all. Instead, every justification must be compatible with that commitment and the system as a whole must exhibit that commitment.

The second primary function, that of ensuring that all have the opportunity to lead a minimally good or decent human life, introduces an additional constraint on justification. A system of legal rights might protect all from discrimination, but not require even the most minimal well-being promoting measures. (Absence of discrimination means only that there are no arbitrary differences in the treatment of different people; it is compatible with not providing needed resources to anyone.) So, a justification for the system of international legal rights must be adequate to capture this second function as well.

To make a prima facie case for the claim that justifications for international legal human rights can satisfy these constraints without appealing to antecedently existing moral human rights, I will fill out the justification, offered early, for one especially important international legal right, the right against arbitrary deprivation of life, one of the most important rights of physical security, and show that it can satisfy the key criteria for adequacy without appealing to an antecedently existing moral right to physical security. My aim is not to provide a conclusive justification for this international legal right at this point, but rather to outline one in sufficient detail to show that it is consonant with this right serving as a constraint on sovereignty, with it contributing to the affirmation and protection of basic moral status, and with it helping to ensure that all have the opportunity to lead a decent or minimally good life. The arguments I give for this legal right will not appeal to any moral human right; they can be formulated strictly in terms of (mere) moral duties.

The justification for having an international legal right against arbitrary deprivation of life for all individuals, and one that is understood to provide a constraint on sovereignty, is, to put it mildly, overdetermined. Physical security is generally a necessary condition for the enjoyment of a wide range of other legal rights, and the lack of physical security threatens all that is worthwhile in human life. Without physical security, the opportunities for autonomous living, for reaping the fruits of our labors, and for engaging in collective projects that make life meaningful, are all threatened. Even if individuals do not actually suffer violent death, being vulnerable to arbitrary killing can greatly decrease the quality of human life. Given that one of the greatest threats to physical security has historically been an individual's own state—often through abuses of the domestic legal system—there is a strong case for an international legal right against arbitrary deprivation of life, and one that is understood to constrain exercises of sovereignty that threaten it. Moreover, the case for providing international legal protection for our interest in physical security is so compelling and broadly grounded that first inferring that this interest grounds a moral right to physical security and then arguing from that moral right to the conclusion that there ought to be a legal right seems to be an unhelpful detour. Nor is it at all obvious that to explain the aptness of a legal right to physical security one must appeal to some supposedly more basic moral right, such as a right to equal concern and respect or a right to justification. Instead, the language of basic values or of fundamental goods, cashed out in terms of (mere) duties, seems wholly adequate. I suspect that the tendency to overlook this simple point is an indication that many of us at least have come to assume, without good reason, that moral rights are the only really serious or weighty items in the moral universe. The fact that legal rights are so distinctively valuable, along with carelessness about the distinction between moral and legal rights, encourages that delusion.

Justifying an international legal human right against arbitrary deprivation of life along these lines, without appealing to an antecedently existing moral right, also clearly satisfies the second key criterion of adequacy. One of the most important ways of affirming and protecting the equal basic moral status of individuals is to provide them with equal protection from threats to their physical security. A legal right against arbitrary deprivation of life, ascribed to all persons, helps to achieve this end. Further, affirming and protecting equal moral status is of sufficient moral importance to justify endowing this legal right with the authority to constrain sovereignty. A justification for this legal right that appeals to the notion of equal moral status need not move from equal status to a moral right to physical security and then to a legal right. It can proceed more directly. A person who did not have the concept of a moral human right or who had it but believed that no such rights existed could produce a compelling justification for a legal right to physical security.

Of course, one might formulate the commitment to equal basic status in rights-terms: One might assume that the robust commitment to equal basic status that the system of international legal rights embodies is best understood as an attempt to realize a moral right to equal basic status. But it is not clear that the notion of a right is doing any necessary work here. One could just as well say that the affirmation and protection of equal basic status for all is a fundamental moral value, one that grounds a very high-priority (mere) moral duty.

Finally, a legal right against arbitrary deprivation of life is also extremely valuable form the standpoint of helping ensure the opportunity to lead a minimally good or decent life. Generally speaking, physical security is necessary for such a life or, to put the point negatively, lack of physical security seriously diminishes one's prospects for a minimally good or decent life or at least renders them unacceptably insecure. As with the status egalitarian function, it is not clear that formulating it in terms of a moral right to minimal well-being is necessary; framing it in terms of basic moral values and a (mere) moral duty to promote and protect them suffices.

### Is the Mirroring View Part of the Modern Conception of Human Rights?

At this point it might be objected that the preambular rhetoric of some international human rights documents, including the Universal Declaration of Human Rights (UDHR) and several of the most general conventions, strongly suggests that international legal rights are conceived as the embodiment in international law of antecedently existing, corresponding moral rights. In other words, the language of these documents at the very least suggests the Mirroring View. For example, the UDHR begins with the assertion that it is important to recognize the "equal and inalienable rights of all members of the human family." These can only be natural or moral rights. So, if the goal is to justify a system of international legal rights that is like the one that exists, we should assume the Mirroring View.

Suppose it is true that, according to an important strand in the discourse of human rights practice, international legal human rights are conceived as the counterparts of antecedently existing moral rights. It does not follow that this is the best way to conceive of the system from the standpoint of justifying it. On the best interpretation of the system, a more pluralistic mode of justification—one that does not assume the Mirroring View—may be appropriate.

I noted in chapter 1 that from the very beginning the core documents of the system have included items that are neither individual rights norms, nor explications of duties corresponding to such norms, nor instructions for setting up institutions for monitoring compliance with such norms. So, if the founders intended the purpose of these documents to be limited to giving international legal form to antecedently existing moral rights, they failed. Be that as it may, my surmise is that even if the founders of the modern international legal human rights system conceived of it as an effort to give international legal effect to antecedently existing, corresponding moral rights and this only, the system has developed in ways that do not recognize that constraint. My arguments in this chapter suggest that such development may best be regarded as progressive, rather than degenerate.

### Simply by Virtue of Their Humanity

Another objection can be anticipated: One might reasonably require that any justification for the system of international legal human rights must make sense of the idea, which appears to be deeply embedded in the Practice, that international legal rights are ascribable to individuals simply by virtue of their humanity—and one might assume that this requirement can only be satisfied if international legal rights are grounded on corresponding moral rights of individuals. It is not the case, however, that the assumption that international legal human rights are grounded in corresponding moral rights is necessary for making sense of the idea that international legal human rights are ascribable to individuals simply by virtue of their humanity. The phrase 'simply by virtue of their humanity' can reasonably be interpreted as conveying two ideas, neither of which implies that justifiable international legal human rights are grounded in corresponding moral human rights.

The first is purely negative; it is the idea that one's having these international legal rights does not depend on any characteristics that only some human beings have, such as being a member of a particular race, or being socially productive, or being male, or being a citizen of some state or other. The second is more positive; it is the idea that these legal rights are ascribable to human beings on their own account, an idea that is also conveyed by the frequent references to human dignity that are found in the Universal Declaration of Human Rights and the conventions that followed it. The idea that every human being has worth on her own account (rather than derivatively, by virtue of God's will or their membership in a nation or their ability to make a net contribution to social cooperation, etc.) and that this worth requires some sort of recognition in international law, is compatible with a number of different kinds of moral justifications for having a system of international legal human rights, so long as justifications that appeal ultimately to the moral importance of the well-being and freedom of individuals are included. A justification for having an international legal right to health or to freedom of expression that appeals to the beneficial consequences of the implementation of these rights for human beings generally, where each individual is recognized to be of moral importance on his own account, and which does not depend on the assumption that the interest of any particular individual is sufficient to ground the corresponding duties fits that description. As such, it is compatible with the idea that individuals ought to have these legal rights by virtue of their humanity.

## VI. *Advantages of Taking Legalization Seriously*

I now want to explain the advantages that accrue to the pluralistic justificatory methodological strategy. The essence of that strategy is to take the legality of human rights in the Practice seriously, where this means abandoning the dogma that justified international legal human rights typically mirror antecedently existing moral human rights or serve only to realize some moral human right or other and embracing instead an open-minded approach to the question of whether the international legal system can be morally justified. Adopting a pluralistic approach to justification makes the existing system more coherent and defensible in several respects. It also enables us to avoid certain mistakes.

## A Less Dogmatic Perspective on Rights Inflation

First, if one adopts my approach, the supposed truism that there is human rights inflation looks to be less obviously true. Many philosophers believe that there is human rights inflation—that the standard lists found in some of the major human rights conventions include items that are not plausibly regarded as human rights. As I noted earlier, a perennial target of philosophical derision is the right to periodic holidays with pay. The point cannot be that these are not genuine international legal human rights, because their inclusion in these international legal documents (along with the legal practice that has developed around them) ensures that they are. Instead, the claim must be that there is no corresponding moral human right. But the fact that there is no corresponding moral human right would show that there is rights inflation only if the existence of such a moral right were a necessary condition for the justification of the legal right. As I have just argued, however, that assumption is not warranted: Legal rights can be justified even if there is no corresponding, antecedently existing moral right, and this is true of several prominent international legal human rights. So, contrary to what philosophers have assumed, simply invoking the intuition that there is no moral right to R is not sufficient to show that the existence of an international legal right to R is an instance of rights inflation.

Those who decry rights inflation might deny that they are assuming that a justified international legal human right presupposes a corresponding moral human right. But then the charge of inflation looks problematic. Is it so obvious, for example, that international law shouldn't include a right to periodic holidays with pay? International law regarding labor standards has evolved through a complex process in which a plurality of justifications have been adduced, and it would be highly implausible to claim that for every item in this body of law the justification depends on the existence of a corresponding moral right. Perhaps in the end the right to periodic holidays with pay will not prove to be a plausible candidate for being an international legal right, but whether or not it is can only be determined by argument informed by an accurate characterization of the proper purposes of international human rights law, not by appealing to raw intuitions about what is or is not a human right morally speaking. Moreover, the sort of argument needed for deciding this matter will be quite complex, appealing not only to moral values (not all of which are moral rights), but also to assumptions about the appropriateness of realizing moral values through the law and more specifically through international law that has the authority of existing international legal human rights law.[14] Most importantly, it will require making and defending assumptions about what the proper functions of international legal human rights law are, without the constraining dogma that they are simply to realize corresponding, antecedently existing moral rights or realizing moral human rights. If one abandons these assumptions and adopts a methodology of pluralistic justification, there is a better prospect of justifying a larger portion of the human rights that are currently recognized in international law—and the so-called problem of human rights inflation may be less serious than would otherwise appear. At least for those of us who are largely—though hardly unreservedly—sympathetic to modern human rights practice and the law that undergirds it, this is an advantage.

Earlier in this chapter, I argued that there are no corresponding moral rights on the basis of which to ground some prominent international legal human rights, including the rights to due process, the rights to health, freedom of expression, and to democratic government. If

[14] One might think that an international legal right to periodic holidays with pay cannot be justified if one assumed that international legal human rights—all of them—provide grounds for intervention. But as Charles Beitz and others have pointed out, that is an indefensible assumption. It might be true that the violation of some international legal human rights supplies a prima facie reason for intervention, but there is nothing in the current understanding of international legal human rights that supports the assumption that the violation of any international legal human right, no matter what its relevant importance, provides even a prima facie reason for intervention, must less a permission to intervene. See Beitz, *The Idea of Human Rights*.

this is the case, then the shoe is on the other foot: Instead of complaining that the international legal human rights system is bloated, we should conclude that a theory of moral human rights is too slender a basis for developing a satisfactory justification for the system of international legal human rights.

### Disarming the Parochialism Objection

Second, my justificatory strategy provides an effective response to the perennial complaint that human rights are parochial, not universal, because there are some reasonable moralities that cannot accommodate the concept of individual moral rights. If the Mirroring View were correct, this would be a serious problem for the international legal human rights system; but as I have argued, the Mirroring View is false. Whether or not one's morality recognizes moral human rights, one can appreciate the benefits of having an international legal rights system, to the extent that it serves other important purposes than the realization of individual moral human rights. (In chapter 7, I elaborate this point and take up other forms of the challenge to the universalism of human rights, when I consider the Ethical Pluralism Objection.)

### Avoiding Mistaken Claims About Incoherence

Third, some features of the existing system of international human rights look anomalous if we assume that the function of international legal human rights is to realize individual moral human rights, but are quite unproblematic if we reject it and acknowledge that other kinds of justifications for legal rights are possible. The first feature is the fact that some of the most important international human rights documents include a right to political self-determination and a right of peoples to resources, which can only be sensibly understood as group rights, not individual rights. The second feature is the Genocide Convention, which is not framed in terms of individual rights, but is commonly thought to be a crucial element of the system of legal international human rights. If the function of the system is to realize moral human rights, standardly understood as moral rights of individuals, this is an anomaly, but not so, according to the pluralistic justificatory methodology.

## VII.  *What a Philosophical Theory Should Do*

Thus far, I have tried to clear the way for a reasonable approach to justifying international legal human rights by criticizing unwarranted assumptions about the relationship between moral human rights and legal human rights, and identified several significant advantages of taking a more open-minded methodological approach. My aim in this part of the chapter is not to develop a philosophical justification for having a system of international legal human rights, much less a justification for the particular system that now exists. Instead, it is to begin to set an agenda—to lay out the daunting range of questions that a philosophical theory of would have to answer in addressing the issue of justification. Doing this will make abundantly clear how mistaken it is to assume that the major philosophical work will have been done if a sound theory of moral human rights is produced. It will also set the itinerary for the next chapter.

### *The Complexity of Justification*

First, it is necessary to provide an account of what sorts of international legal human rights there should be and to do so without the constraining assumption that these will be limited to those that have moral counterparts. This will require being very clear on exactly what the function or functions of the international legal human rights system should be. Should a central function be to affirm and protect equal basic status for all individuals, as I have argued the existing system aims to do, or should it instead have the more modest aim of ensuring the opportunity for a minimally good or decent life by protecting all from the serious harms states can inflict and providing all with basic resources for living? If the system's functions include a well-being component, is it best characterized as the provision of the opportunity for a minimally good or decent human life or in some other way? Further, should the violation of the rights the system contains or of some of them (and if so, which ones) play a significant role in the justification for humanitarian military intervention or other interferences with what would otherwise be regarded as the proper domain of state sovereignty? In the design of the system of individual international legal rights, how much weight should be given to preserving peace among states as opposed to other values?

Second, also of crucial importance is an explanation of why an international system of rights ascribed to all individuals is needed. In other words, an account of why the specified purposes could not or should not be achieved by the constitutional entrenchment of individual rights in domestic legal systems, without recourse to international law and institutions.[15]

Third, a justification of the international legal human rights system would also have to engage the question of whether the distinctive features of international law as it now exists—including the absence of some key features of well-developed domestic legal systems, such as representative legislatures and a hierarchy of courts with compulsory jurisdiction that are thought to be important for the rule of law—are an obstacle to the justification of a system of international legal human rights or at least significantly constrain the sort of system that can be justified.

Fourth, it is necessary to determine the extent, if any, to which the best justification for the current system of international legal human rights should appeal to antecedently existing moral rights and to what extent to other moral considerations, including an account of which moral rights should and which should not have international legal counterparts. (Nothing I have said so far suggests that there will be no role for the appeal to moral rights in the justification of a system of international legal rights.)

Fifth, it makes no sense to try to justify a system of international legal human rights without first specifying the kind of authority that such a system would claim vis-à-vis domestic legal systems. Presumably, a system that claims an unqualified supremacy over domestic law, including the domestic constitutional law of reasonably democratic, rights respecting states, would be harder to justify, other things, being equal, than one that did not. Although few philosophers have participated in it and many seem unaware of its existence and importance for philosophical theorizing about human rights, there is a vigorous debate among international and constitutional lawyers about whether international human rights law is or should enjoy supremacy over domestic law, including domestic

---

[15] Allen Buchanan, "Why *International Legal* Human Rights?" *Foundations of Human Rights*, eds. Rowland Cruft, Matthew Liao, and Massimo Renzo (Oxford: Oxford University Press, forthcoming 2014).

constitutional law.[16] The issue of supremacy is complicated by the question of whether the international legal human rights system should recognize a hierarchy of rights, with more robust legal implications, including greater weight, for items at the top of the hierarchy, and by the question of what the division of labor should be between domestic institutions and international institutions regarding the authority to interpret international legal human rights norms.[17]

Finally, to justify a system of international legal human rights requires not only providing sound moral arguments for various rights-norms, but also an account of the legitimacy of the institutions in which the norms are formulated, interpreted, and implemented. To put the point most forcefully, a system of international legal norms ascribing rights to all individuals might be strongly justified in principle, but it might turn out that, under current and foreseeable conditions, efforts to institutionalize the norms would be extremely problematic, due to the weakness of international institutions and/or their tendency to be disproportionately shaped and controlled by a handful of the most powerful states and the global corporate interests that exert considerable influence over those states. In brief, a philosophical theory of the international legal human rights system must go far beyond providing an in principle moral justification for having such a system and must include both a theory of institutional legitimacy and an empirically-informed judgment about whether legitimate institutions are likely to be obtainable.

Even if the justification for international legal rights includes a more prominent role for moral human rights than my argument thus far suggests is likely to be the case, the preceding list of theoretical desiderata makes it clear that having a serviceable theory of moral human rights would only be one component of a comprehensive justification. That is a point worth emphasizing, given how much attention philosophers have paid to developing an account of moral

---

[16] Allen Buchanan and Russell Powell, "Constitutional Democracy and International Law: Are They Compatible?" *Journal of Political Philosophy*, 16:3 (2008): 326–49.

[17] See Kristen Hessler, "Resolving Interpretive Conflicts in International Human Rights Law," *Journal of Political Philosophy*, 13:1 (2005): 29–52.

human rights and how little they have had to say about most of the issues that would have to be addressed to construct a cogent justification for the system of international legal human rights.

## VII. *Moral or Political?*

I can now draw the implications of my analysis so far for the debate between so-called moral and political theories of human rights. First, as I observed in chapter 1, this debate has been greatly impaired by a failure to distinguish between international legal human rights and moral human rights and by the unwarranted assumption that there is only one concept of human rights. Like most other philosophers (including myself until recently), both groups habitually use the ambiguous phrase 'human rights' without making it clear when they are referring to moral human rights and when they are referring to international legal human rights.[18] Arguing about whether *the* concept of human rights includes reference to the existence of a system of states or whether human rights are essentially constraints on sovereignty wrongly assumes that there is only one concept of human rights. More importantly, it overlooks the possibility that the dominant use of the term nowadays refers to international legal human rights or to rights that ought to be included in international human rights law (and hence implies the existence of a system of states), even if it is descended from a usage of the term 'human rights' that does not presuppose a system of states.

Second, and more important, my justificatory methodology is more sympathetic to political theories than to moral ones, but only in this limited sense: I believe that understanding and exploring possible justifications for existing international human rights practice, and for the system of international legal rights that is central to it, should be the focus of philosophical theorizing, if one's concern is with the moral status of the practice of human rights, and I believe that one

---

[18] If the Mirroring View were true, then theorists such as Tasioulas would be on stronger ground in claiming that the noninstitutional, purely moral concept of human rights is "focal" and that the institutional concept of international human rights is somehow derivative or of secondary importance, or the latter must be explained in terms of the former. But as we have argued, neither he nor anyone else has made the case for the Mirroring View.

should not approach this topic by assuming that international legal human rights are simply the legal embodiment of moral rights.

Third, unlike political theorists such as Beitz, however, I seek to go beyond merely characterizing the practice within which the international legal human rights system plays such a central role to engage the task of justifying the system of international legal human rights.[19] Further, again unlike Beitz, I explicitly affirm the centrality of international legal human rights to the practice and in so doing acknowledge a much more ambitious and complex agenda for philosophical theorizing.[20] Finally, although I agree with Beitz that a philosophical theory should begin with an inquiry into the functions of the Practice rather than by developing a theory of moral human rights on the assumption that the purpose is to realize them, my conception of the functions is different from Beitz's. His idea that the rights that are central to the Practice—by which he must mean international legal human rights—serve to protect urgent interests is not adequate. For one thing, it does not capture the status egalitarian component. A system of international law, even one that ascribed a set of rights to all individuals, could protect everyone's urgent interests (to some significant extent) without including the status egalitarian features that we find in the existing international legal human rights system. For another, there is a large gap between saying that something is a morally important or urgent interest and showing that there ought to be an international legal human right to protect it. Finally, Beitz's notion that the Practice protects urgent interests is deeply ambiguous, because it could be

---

[19] The closest Beitz comes to engaging the task of justification is when he says that human rights are thought of, in the practice, as protecting "urgent interests" and when he says that the Practice was a response to the perceived threat that states posed to those within their jurisdictions. The former suggestion is not filled out; no theory of urgent interests is provided. In addition, it is not clear that the idea of urgent interests (anymore than the idea of basic interests or that of a minimally good life) can capture the prominent status-egalitarian strain of Practice, as it is shaped by international legal human rights law. Similarly, the notion that the system is designed to protect individuals from harms emanating from their states not only fails to explain why the protection should take the form of international law nor, if it does, why it should be a matter of individual rights.

[20] It is remarkable that Beitz's characterization of the Practice pays so little attention to the role of law in it, as Samantha Besson has noted. Samantha Besson, "Human Rights Qua Normative Practice: *Sui Generis* or Legal?" *Transnational Legal Theory* 1 (2010): 130.

interpreted as the view that international legal human rights have to be grounded solely in the interests of the right-holder or as the view that a proper grounding can appeal to the interests of large numbers of people.

Fourth, unlike political theorists, I have now taken the first steps to articulating this more complex philosophical agenda. As I observed in part I of this chapter, it requires addressing issues that proponents of the political conception of human rights have not yet even formulated. These include whether a system of international legal rights that restricts legal duties primarily to states is optimal or even defensible, whether the legal duties that are correlatives of international legal human rights should be conceived as pertaining only to those over whom the state exercises jurisdiction, whether international legal human rights duties should be incorporated into domestic law automatically upon the ratification of treaties or in some other way and whether the method of incorporation should be uniform among states or not, what sort of supremacy international legal human rights law should enjoy over domestic law, whether states should have default duties, rather than responsibilities, whether the existing division of labor between states, international institutions, and regional institutions regarding the interpretation of international legal human rights is appropriate, whether it would be justifiable to impose international legal human rights obligations on states that do not ratify the relevant treaties, and whether the institutions that play a key role in formulating and implementing international legal human rights are legitimate. Chapter 5 is devoted to the problem of institutional legitimacy, chapter 6 to the supremacy issue.

Finally, I agree with the advocates of the political approach in their criticism of the assumption that international human rights are simply the international legal embodiment of natural rights or of general moral rights of any kind. However, I do not assume that there is no room for appeals to natural rights or general moral rights in the justification of the system of international human rights. I reject moral theories of human rights if they assume that the only adequate justification for international legal human rights will ground them on moral human rights or hold that the task of the philosopher of human rights is largely accomplished by producing a theory of moral human rights.

## Conclusion

Approaching the justification of international legal human rights without the constraining prejudice of the Mirroring View, or more generally, without making unexamined assumptions about the relationship between moral and legal human rights, and without dogmatic assumptions about the proper functions of the system is liberating. It enables one to consider the possibility that the international legal human rights system may serve other functions in addition to that of realizing moral rights. It also permits one to explore the possibility that the functions the system serves are not fixed, but are instead subject to revision and perhaps progressive development, as has been the case with domestic legal systems. Thus, even if it is true that the original function of the system was to achieve something less ambitious—perhaps the international legal embodiment of minimal moral standards for how states ought to treat those under their jurisdiction—it may evolve to perform more ambitious functions, including perhaps a more extensive portion of the work of global justice.

Assuming that the function of international legal human rights is to realize moral rights is no more plausible than assuming that this is all that domestic legal rights do. Abandoning that assumption liberates our understanding of the capabilities of law. The value of law is not restricted to its ability to track the features of a preexisting landscape of moral rights.

# CHAPTER 3

## The Task of Justification

Chapter 2 distinguished between (i) justifying having a system of international legal human rights, (ii) justifying a system that has all or most of the main features of the system that actually exists, and (iii) justifying the inclusion of particular rights within a system of a given type. It also made the case for rejecting the Mirroring View and embracing a justificatory methodology that is pluralistic in two distinct senses: In pursuing any of the three justificatory tasks one should not assume (a) that to justify a legal human right one must show that there is a corresponding, antecedently existing moral right or rely on any premises asserting the existence of moral rights, nor (b) that international human rights law should include only lists of individual legal rights. Instead, one should take seriously the possibility that some, perhaps many justifiable international legal rights of individuals will not have moral human right correlates and that in addition to individual rights-norms the system may also include mere duties (not the correlatives of rights) or prohibitions (on propaganda for war, for example, as does the International Covenant on Civil and Political Rights), as well as group rights (such as the right of political self-determination, which is found in the Universal Declaration of Human Rights, the ICCPR, and the International Covenant on Economic, Social, and Cultural Rights). Taken together, these two methodological directives open up the possibility of a more expansive role for international human rights law than that of realizing moral counterparts of legal rights. We should not assume that the function of the existing system of international legal rights is to realize corresponding moral rights or that this should be its only function. We should not even assume that such a system can only be adequately grounded on moral rights.

Before it is possible to make even a provisional case for having a system of international legal human rights one must first characterize the system type, where this includes a specification of the main functions it is to serve, the chief roles that appeals to its norms are to perform in political discourse and action, the form the norms of the system take, and the sort of authority that the law is supposed to have vis-à-vis domestic law. I began this task in the preceding two chapters; I complete it in this chapter.

## I. *Characterizing the System Type*

There are a number of quite different types of legal systems that might fall under the heading of a system of international legal human rights. Consequently, in order to make headway on the question of justification, it is first necessary to identify the system type. I begin by filling out the previous chapters' shorthand characterization of the main features of the existing international legal human rights system that are relevant to issues of justification. The characterization will be sufficiently abstract so as to apply not only to the existing system but also to a range of possible systems that differ from it in some respects. I will specify the key features with reference to the existing system of international legal human rights, but in a sufficiently abstract way as to make the discussion applicable to a range of systems that share these general features but differ in other respects.

### Functions

Stated abstractly, the most basic function of the international legal human rights system, as I have noted, is *to provide a set of universal standards, in the form of international law, whose primary purpose is to regulate the behavior of states toward individuals under their jurisdiction, considered as social individuals, and for their own sakes.* The phrase 'for their own sakes' is important, because international law prior to the human rights era did regulate the behavior of states toward individuals (e.g., diplomats of other states), not for their own sakes, but in the interest of states. The inclusion of the qualifier 'considered as social beings' is designed to deflect the misguided but common view that the system is grounded in a conception of human beings as so-called atomistic individuals. No one who has read any of the major human rights documents with a modicum of care and who understood how many of the rights they contain protect groups and relationships would make this mistake, but it occurs perennially nonetheless. The authors of the UDHR in particular took considerable pains to make it clear that the individuals to whom that document ascribes rights are social beings, but they underestimated the resilience of false preconceptions.

One advantage of this formulation of the basic idea of the system is that it makes it clear that it is one thing to have a system of law that functions in this way, another to have one that fulfills this function by relying on individual legal rights. That distinction highlights the fact that a justification for a system of the type that actually exists must explain not only why there should be international standards for the behavior of states that are focused on individuals rather than on the interests of states and why these standards should take the form of international law, but also why a prominent role for individual rights norms is appropriate.

Because states can act only through their governments, in practice the standards will apply to governments. On the most plausible interpretation of the character of the norms included in the existing international legal human rights system, the most basic values that the fulfillment of those legal obligations are designed to serve are (1) providing each individual with the opportunity to lead a minimally good or decent life (the well-being function), where this includes both protections from serious and commonly occurring harms and the provision of resources for living reasonably well; and (2) affirming and protecting the basic equal status of each individual, where this includes prohibitions on any form of discrimination, public or private, on grounds of gender or race (the status egalitarian function).

If, as I argued in chapter 1, it is true that from the founding of the international legal human rights system there was a consensus that the duties it was to impose on all states included the central functions of the modern welfare state—roughly, the provision of a set of basic social and economic rights—then the well-being function should not be interpreted too austerely. International legal human rights make a greater contribution to human well-being than merely protecting people from the most serious harms that the state or other agents can inflict.

The difficulty, which I shall explore further in the final chapter, is that there is great controversy—and theoretical uncertainty as well—about how extensive the welfare functions of the state should be and also a reasonable belief that how extensive they should be is, within limits, a matter of democratic choice that can vary across states. The unsatisfyingly vague phrase 'ensuring the opportunity to lead a minimally good or decent life' serves only to signal two things: first, that this function of the system exceeds that of merely protecting people against abuses by the state, and second, that it is a considerably less ambitious goal than enabling people to lead the best possible life. In other words, saying that one function of the system is to ensure that all have the opportunity to lead a minimally good or decent life is simply a way of signaling that the system is founded on the assumption that all states are to perform basic welfare functions, with all the indeterminacy and ambiguity that the latter phrase entails, but with the implicit proviso that what is sought is not maximal well-being (whatever that would mean), but something more like sufficiency.

A question that must be faced sooner or later, however, is this: Given the character of the processes by which international legal human rights law is created, the authority that it claimed on behalf of this law, and the institutional resources for implementing it, is it justifiable for the system to require all states to attempt to discharge the rather robust welfare functions that realization of the full set of existing international legal human rights would require?

To put the point in a somewhat different way: Does the system provide adequate constraints to prevent its demands in terms of positive or welfare rights from becoming too expansive? This is not a question of capacity. The existing system allows for the progressive realization of rights on the part of states that currently lack the resources for their full realization. The issue I am foregrounding here and to which I will return in the final chapter is one of principle.

Taken as a whole, the system also has a second function, as I have already emphasized: to foster the public recognition of equal basic status for all people, in all societies. With few exceptions (such as the restriction of political participation rights to adults), the rights listed in the UDHR and the most general human rights conventions (including the ICCPR, the ICESCR, the Racism Convention, the Slavery Convention, and the Torture Convention) are ascribed to all human beings. Just as important, as I have already emphasized, the scope and weight of the rights are understood to be the same for all to whom they are ascribed, and the conditions of derogation are the same for all. Further, as I have also noted, all individuals are to have recourse, under conditions of equality before the law, to effective remedies to violations of their rights. Finally, some of the major human rights conventions, and in particular the Racism Convention and the Women's Convention, include what I have called strong rights against discrimination on grounds of race or gender. As I argued in chapter 2, these cannot be plausibly understood as serving only to ensure the conditions for being able to lead a minimally good or decent human life, because people can lead a minimally good or decent human life and yet be subject to some forms of discrimination. This would be the case, for example, if well-paid, educated women receive lower salaries than men, simply because they are women or when highly successful people of color suffer similar "soft" discrimination. Nor is it convincing to argue that people cannot lead minimally good or decent lives unless they not only have the same rights as others but also have the same rights with the same scope and weight and subject to the same conditions of derogation and also have strictly equal access to remedies for violations of their rights.

Given the tremendous importance of law in modern society, the equal basic legal status that the system of international legal rights affirms expresses a recognition of equal basic moral status.[1] The most natural explanation of why individuals should be accorded equal basic legal status—and that its protection is a matter of sufficient concern to warrant the use of international law to achieve this—is that all humans *are*, in some fundamental sense, of equal moral status. Later, when I consider whether a right to participate in democratic government should be an international legal human right, I will expand on the idea that under modern conditions not

---

[1] For a lucid elaboration of this point, see Samantha Besson, "The Egalitarian Dimension of Human Rights," *Archiv für Sozial-und Rechtsphilosophie Beiheft* (2012): 19–52.

only equal basic legal status, but also the opportunity to participate as an equal in the most important political processes of one's society is required for the public recognition of equal basic moral status. The idea, in a nutshell, is that under modern conditions, in which the state plays such a pervading and profound role in human life, for a competent individual to be excluded from participation as an equal in the most important political processes of her society would signal a presumption of inferiority that is incompatible with the public recognition of her equal basic moral status.

The existing system of international legal human rights includes not only the right of each individual to participate in the governance of his or her own society, but also the collective right of political self-determination. The inclusion of this latter right reflects the struggle against colonialism that was a powerful formative influence on the system, not just at the system's creation in 1948, but also and even more so during its doctrinal and institutional development in the 1960s and 1970s, when colonized peoples were liberating themselves and achieving representation in the United Nations. Although the right of political self-determination is a collective right, the denial of self-determination can be and was reasonably seen by colonized peoples as an affront to the dignity of each member of a society that is characterized as unfit for self-government. The ideology of colonialism against which the right of political self-determination was asserted viewed a society's supposed lack of capacity for self-government as due in part to the inferiority of the individuals that composed the society. To that extent, the inclusion of the right of political self-determination also contributes to the affirmation of equal basic status for all. Especially in the modern context in which democratic government is widely considered the proper political condition for human beings, a system of international legal human rights that did not include a right of political self-determination would be defective, from the standpoint of affirming equal basic status.

Drawing on historical examples of discrimination, we can formulate a serviceable understanding of what a threat to equal basic moral status is and hence an idea of how various legal rights can guard against such a threat. The public recognition of one's equal basic moral status is threatened when one is treated in ways that, given the historical context, put one at risk of being regarded as naturally inferior in certain respects, where being naturally inferior in those respects is thought to disqualify one from participation as an equal in important social practices or roles, and where natural inferiority is understood as the normal condition of individuals of the sort of human being one is (as opposed to cases of impairment of rationality due to illness or injury, for example). To be regarded as naturally inferior—inferior by virtue of one's nature as a woman, as a person of color, or as a homosexual—is especially threatening because the assumption is that the flaw goes as deep as possible and is irremediable.[2]

The commitment to affirming and protecting equal basic moral status is perhaps most explicit in the inclusion of strong rights against discrimination on grounds of gender or race. Historically, discrimination against women and people of color has usually been justified by appeals to beliefs about supposed natural differences, understood not simply as differences, but as marks of inferiority. In particular, discrimination has been justified on the grounds that women or people of color are naturally less rational than men or whites, against the background assumption that rationality is an especially valuable trait that distinguishes humans from so-called lower animals. In such a context, characterizing certain classes of humans as less rational than others by nature conveys a message of inferiority, even suggesting that they are, in a sense, less than fully human.

In addition, the list of international legal human rights includes so-called positive or welfare rights that, if realized, significantly constrain various social and economic inequalities which, if severe enough, can undermine the public recognition of equal basic status for the worst off in a society. The list includes the right to work. In modern societies, individuals who are deemed able to work but who cannot find work are at risk of being regarded as inferior—relegated to the status of dependent beings who are not contributors to social cooperation. In all of these ways, the system affirms and protects the equal basic status of all people.

Here it is important to distinguish clearly between a description of the existing system and a proposal for how it might best be rationally reconstructed or a hypothesis about what the system is like on

---

[2] The case of discrimination against homosexuals has its own peculiarities. Often those who engage in discriminatory behavior toward homosexuals seem to believe that these persons have a natural or constitutional defect—that they are "not normal" in the sense of being flawed, inferior examples of humanity.

the best interpretation of it, where interpretation can involve selectively emphasizing some features of the actual system and ignoring or downplaying others, for the sake of coherence and moral cogency. At this point, I am simply trying to describe the system. For reasons already noted, I think it is accurate to say that the system includes some rights (and other provisions) that, if realized, help ensure that all have the opportunity to lead a decent or minimally good life, and some rights and requirements regarding equality of rights that go beyond this to affirm and protect basic equal status. Some theorists ignore the status-egalitarian function and others construe the well-being function very narrowly, limiting it to the satisfaction of basic needs.

Theorists in the first group may think that the inclusion of the status egalitarian function is not defensible, perhaps because they think it would make the system vulnerable to the charge that it exhibits a parochial, Western bias. In chapter 7 I explore and allay this worry. Thinkers in the second group may think international legal rights that do more than protect basic needs are indefensible because they think that the only universal moral rights that exist are limited to this role—and because they assume, wrongly, I have argued, that something should be an international legal right only if there is a corresponding universal moral right.

Other theorists may insist that the system of international legal human rights should only serve to secure for all the opportunity to lead a minimally good or decent life (or satisfy basic needs or basic interests) because they want to prevent an overly expansive conception of international legal human rights that would attempt to ensure full flourishing for all. To avoid such overreach, however, it is not necessary to extirpate the system's robust commitment to equal basic status. A system that aims both to ensure that basic interests are protected and promoted (the well-being function) and that equal basic status is affirmed and protected is still much less ambitious than one devoted to ensuring that all lead fully flourishing lives. Such a system's well-being component, including its requirement that the state perform welfare functions, is significantly limited in principle.

All or at least most of the norms included in the UDHR and the various human rights conventions can be understood as furthering one or the other or both of the two basic functions identified above—helping to ensure that all have the opportunity to lead a minimally good or decent life (the well-being function), where this includes both protections from harms inflicted by the state and access to critical goods and services, or affirming and protecting equal basic status for all (the status egalitarian function). However, language in the UN Charter, the UDHR, and the two covenants indicate that the system has a third function as well: to help maintain international peace, on the assumption that states that treat their own peoples badly are likely to be a threat to international peace.[3]

I will focus on the first two basic functions and have little to say about the third function, for two reasons. First, whether or to what extent the system of international legal human rights serves that function is an empirical question that is not easy to answer. There are many factors that are likely to have contributed to the reduction of interstate armed conflict since World War II, and it would be hard-going to try to establish that the modern human rights movement has been a major factor. Second, and more important, the function of promoting international peace and security is not peculiar to the system of international legal human rights in the way the other two functions are; it was the primary purpose of the international legal system prior to the advent of international human rights law. I will focus on what is distinctive of international human rights law.

ROLES IN POLITICAL DISCOURSE AND ACTION

In his path-breaking book *Making Sense of Human Rights*, James Nickel notes that appeals to international legal human rights play a number of distinct roles in political discourse and action. One of the most important is that of supplying standards of conduct for states specified that are conceived as being applicable by third parties, especially other states. In other words, an important function of the system is to enable third parties to hold states accountable for how they treat those under their jurisdiction. The standards of conduct, as they are enshrined in international law, are understood

---

[3] See the Preamble sections of United Nations, *Charter of the United Nations*, October 25, 1945. UN General Assembly, *Universal Declaration of Human Rights*, December 10, 1948, 217 A (III). UN General Assembly, *International Covenant on Civil and Political Rights (ICCPR)*, December 16, 1966, Article 22. UN General Assembly, *International Covenant on Economic, Social and Cultural Rights*, December 16, 1966.

to empower third parties to criticize governments, understood as the agents of states, that failed to satisfy the standards and in such a way as to disable the rejoinder, on the part of the offending government, that "this is none of your business; it is a domestic affair, shielded by the veil of sovereignty."[4]

In this way, international legal human rights function as limitations on sovereignty. They modify the international system's strong affirmation of the sovereignty of the state by introducing a new norm according to which it is appropriate for states and other parties to criticize a state if it violates international legal human rights law. The quite reasonable assumption here is that helping to assure that all have the opportunity to lead a minimally good or decent life and are treated as having equal basic status are sufficiently important to disable assertions of sovereignty.

## THE FORM OF THE LEGAL NORMS

I have already noted, in chapter 1, some key features of the norms that compose the system. They chiefly address duties to states, duties that specify how states are to treat those under their jurisdiction, and largely assign responsibilities, where this means something less than full-fledged duties, to other states when a state fails to fulfill these duties. And in those cases in which the norms take the form of rights, they generally assign rights to all human individuals, not just those who satisfy more specific characterizations than that of being a human individual.

As I also emphasized in chapter 1, it is a striking fact that the UDHR and the various human rights conventions are not restricted to lists of legal rights of individuals. If the chief purpose of international human rights law is to lay down legally binding standards for how states treat those under their jurisdiction, there is no reason why it *should* be restricted to rights-norms. If the more specific purpose of this body of law is to create legal obligations which, if fulfilled, will result in ensuring that all have the opportunity for a minimally good or decent human life and that the equal basic status

---

[4] Joseph Raz, "Human Rights without Foundations," *The Philosophy of International Law*, eds. Samantha Besson and John Tasioulas (New York: Oxford University Press, 2010), pp. 321–37.

of all is affirmed and protected, then there is no need to limit the norms to those that are formulated as individual rights. For example, if propaganda for war is a contributing cause to conflicts that threaten equal basic status and basic interests, then perhaps a prohibition on it should be included in the international legal human rights system, as in fact it is in the International Covenant on Civil and Political Rights.[5] To assume that a prohibition on propaganda for war should be included in a body of international law whose distinctive character is to constrain sovereignty for the sake of individuals only if there is a corresponding moral right to live in a world free of propaganda for war seems not only implausible, but unnecessary. It is implausible because the scope of duties reasonably associated with this right exceeds anything that could be justified by appealing to the interests of the individual right-holder; it is unnecessary, because the moral case for such a prohibition is strong enough without appealing to any such moral right.

Nonetheless, individual rights-norms are prominent in the UDHR and the conventions. So, a sound justification for having a system like the one that exists, must include an account of why there should be a prominent role for individual rights norms, not just duty norms. In chapter 4, I will provide the needed account, arguing that a prominent role for individual rights norms is appropriate, given that one of the major functions of the system is to be the affirmation and protection of basic equal moral status for all.

## The Authority Claimed on Behalf of the Norms

International human rights law, like international law generally, comes in two main varieties: customary and conventional (treaty-based). Basing the Practice exclusively or even primarily on customary law would have serious disadvantages. First, the creation of customary law is a slow process. Second, one of the benefits the founders of the modern human rights practices sought to achieve was the articulation of an authoritative set of standards for the behavior of states toward those under their justification. Treaties are much more apt for this purpose than customary law, whose norms

[5] UN General Assembly, *International Covenant on Civil and Political Rights (ICCPR)*, December 16, 1966, Article 20.

may be inherently abstract and to that extent ambiguous or at least more disputable as to their content than the provisions of treaties. It is likely, however, that the founders of the system hoped for what has actually happened, namely, that the rights norms that were first created by written documents, preeminently the UDHR and the ICCPR, have become a part of customary international law. The advantage of this route to inclusion in customary law is that it allows for the customary norms to partake of the relative determinateness of their conventional predecessors.

If a human rights norm is part of customary international law, then it possesses a more robust legal authority than norms that are exclusively treaty-based inasmuch as customary norms bind every state, even those that have not ratified human rights treaties, so long as a state did not persistently dissent during the process of the formation of the customary norm. Even states that did not exist during the formative period—and which therefore had no opportunity persistently to dissent—are legally bound by customary norms. In this respect, the international legal human rights system is not, and probably was never intended by its founders to be, a strictly voluntary matter.

There is one more respect in which it is inaccurate to say that the authority of international legal human rights is a self-imposed or strictly voluntary under the current system: International law recognizes jus cogens norms, which are binding on all states irrespective of their treaty commitments and regardless of whether they persistently dissent from them or not. Jus cogens norms at present include only the rights against slavery and torture, and, on some accounts, genocide and aggression. Article 2(4) of the UN Charter, which sharply constrains the use of military force, is also widely regarded as jus cogens.

I observed earlier that one impetus for the creation of the international legal human rights system was to try to protect people from serious harms inflicted by their own states. If being bound by human rights law was a purely voluntary affair—and in particular, if the system only applied to states that ratified human rights treaties or did not dissent from customary human rights norms during the process of their formation—the system would appear to be seriously flawed from the standpoint of this objective. The worry is that states that wished to prey on their own people would only have to refrain from ratifying treaties or, in the case of customary norms, persistently dissent. Keeping this in mind, it seems likely that the founders of the system looked forward to a time in which a set of legal standards for the conduct of states that was explicitly embraced by the vast majority of states through treaty ratification would become binding on all states.[6]

It is another question, however, whether it would be justifiable to have a system in which—apart from the norms migrating from treaty to custom—a supermajority of states ratifying a human rights treaty could justifiably impose legal obligations on nonratifying states. Later I will argue that states—all states, whether they ratify human rights treaties or not, and whether they dissent from customary human rights norms or not—have an obligation to support the system of international legal human rights because they are all benefiting from an international legal order that would be morally intolerable in the absence of a system of international legal human rights. If that is so, then it lends credibility to the notion that a supermajority of ratifiers could justifiably impose legal human rights obligations on nonratifiers.

Nevertheless, given the character of the existing international order, there is much to be said for the assumption that human rights law and international law generally should largely be a matter of voluntary self-binding on the part of states, for three reasons. First, there is such a disparity of power among states that the requirement of voluntariness may be necessary simply as a brake on the ability of powerful states to coerce or manipulate weaker states. Second, the international legal order lacks some of the characteristics that make majority rule palatable in the case of domestic societies. To the extent that we find the imposition of the majority's will on minorities acceptable in the domestic context, this is because we are assuming that the majoritarian principle is operating within the context of a constitutional democracy that places limits on what the majority can do and that it is operating within a genuine political community, embedded in civil society institutions that play a role in underwriting a conception of the common good. These assumptions do

---

[6] See Mary Ann Glendon, *A World Made New: Eleanor Roosevelt and the Universal Declaration of Human Rights* (New York: Random House, 2001, p. xvii–ix), pp. 56–83.

not hold at the global level. Third, as I observed in chapter 1, the existence of international human rights law can contribute to compliance with its requirements on the part of states even in cases in which states have no legal obligation under that law. Various actors, from NGOs to states and international organizations, can and do hold states politically accountable for violating international legal human rights even when there is no violation of an international legal duty. Even states that refrain from ratifying human rights treaties, as well as nonstate entities that had no opportunity to ratify them, can be pressured to comply with international legal human rights. *Consequently, the fact that the legal reach of international human rights is constrained by the commitment to voluntariness is not as damaging to the efficacy of the system as it might first appear.*

Notwithstanding these three points, in chapter 8 I will argue that for the most basic legal human rights norms, acknowledgment of their authority should not remain a strictly voluntary matter and that this conclusion is not restricted to the very small set of human rights norms that are now thought to be jus cogens.

### Inherent Dignity?

I now want to note what might at first appear to be an additional feature of the existing system, or at least of what might be called the justificatory rhetoric of the system, as the latter is expressed in the preambles of some of the core documents: the notion that international human rights law is somehow grounded in and intended to affirm the inherent dignity of human beings. I am not sure whether this item should be included among the constraints on a satisfactory justification for the system, for three reasons. First, one can imagine a system with the other five features that did not include it; it refers to the grounding of the system and not to what might be called its functional features. Second, one can state the main functions of the system—understood, say, as constraining sovereignty for the sake of protecting people from the most serious threats to their well-being and affirming their equal basic status—without recourse to the notion of dignity.[7] Third, human rights documents do not develop the

---

[7] Samantha Besson makes this point in "The Egalitarian Dimension of Human Rights."

idea; they do not explain what inherent dignity is or show how it grounds the legal rights they enunciate. Some theorists think this is no accident; they believe that the notion of dignity is so vague that the system would be better off without reference to it or that it adds nothing of value.

Whether or not the notion that the international legal human rights system is grounded in and serves to affirm the inherent dignity of humans is a central feature of the system, it is surely at least a desideratum for a justification for the system that it can make sense of this notion given its prominence. I now want to argue that the conception of the two chief purposes of the system I have articulated makes good sense of the notion of inherent dignity.

I have argued elsewhere that the relevant notion of dignity can be understood to include two aspects.[8] First, there is the idea that certain conditions of living are beneath the dignity of the sort of being that humans are. Thus, for example, we say that when prisoners of war or victims of ethnic cleansing or the elderly or institutionalized persons with mental illness are kept in severely crowded, filthy conditions, this is an affront to their human dignity. Sometimes, when people are in such conditions, we say they are living like animals or being treated like beasts. The implication is that, given the kinds of beings they are, namely, human beings, such a life is unfitting for them, beneath them, incompatible with their dignity as beings of that kind, and that for them to live in those unfitting conditions is an injury or something that is contrary to what they are due. Let us call this first aspect of dignity the *well-being threshold aspect*.

The second aspect of dignity is the interpersonal comparative aspect, the idea that treating people with dignity also requires a public affirmation of the basic equal status of all and, again, that if they are not treated in this way they suffer an injury or a wrong. This second aspect of dignity is difficult to grasp if one approaches it by trying to define the term 'basic equal status' in a positive way. The prospects are brighter if one takes a kind of via negativa, focusing on cases where we have strong and stable intuitions about how unequal treatment constitutes an insult to a person's dignity. When women's testimony in court is systematically discounted

---

[8] Allen Buchanan, "The Egalitarianism of Human Rights," *Ethics* 120:4 (2010): 679–710.

because it is the testimony of women (as occurs in the legal systems of some countries where Islam is the dominant religion), or when a person of color is required to eat in a separate facility or use separate toilets, or when a woman receives less pay than a man doing the same job simply because she is a woman, or when one's child is barred from a public amusement park because she is black, there is an affront to the person's dignity in the interpersonal comparative sense, regardless of whether this kind of behavior tends to undermine their prospects for a minimally good or decent human life. In other words, to characterize what is wrong with such unequal treatment, and to make sense of the idea that it represents a failure to treat the person with dignity, one need not make the case that it is likely to lead to more tangible harms that will prevent a person from having a minimally good or decent life. A person treated in these ways could rightly complain that someone who reduced the wrong she has suffered to a threat to her opportunity to lead a minimally good or decent human life had failed to understand an important aspect of her ill-treatment, namely, the fact that she was being treated as if she were an inferior type of being.

The well-being-threshold aspect of dignity concerns whether one is doing well enough for a being of the sort one is; it makes no reference to how one is treated vis-à-vis others. The interpersonal comparative aspect has to do with whether one is being treated as an inferior relative to other people. The point is that one's dignity can be respected in the well-being threshold aspect and yet may be compromised in the interpersonal comparative aspect. This would be the case in a society in which people of color had quite adequate material wealth and living conditions, but were denied the right to vote or required to eat in separate facilities or use separate toilets. To make the point more vivid, consider how you would feel if you were a member of a group that was always assured nutritious and tasty food, but required to eat it from dishes on the floor, at the foot of a table on which the members of another group dined. Or, to take a real-world example from the colonial era, suppose that, because you were a "native," you were required to step off the sidewalk into the gutter when you approached an Englishman.

Earlier I listed among the features of the existing system that a justification for the system should take into account both the protection of equal basic status and the securing of the conditions for a minimally good or decent life. On the two-aspect understanding of the term 'dignity' this makes sense, given the claim, salient in the justificatory rhetoric of the system, that international legal human rights help affirm the dignity of the individual. If dignity includes both a well-being threshold aspect and an interpersonal comparative aspect, then a system of international legal human rights that affirms and protects the dignity of all people will include rights that function to ensure that all have the opportunity to lead a minimally good or decent life—a life fitting for human beings—and that all are treated in ways that recognize their equal basic status. The qualifier "fitting for human beings" is important; I include it to signal that what I am calling for the sake of brevity the well-being component includes the idea that a good life for human beings typically requires some significant scope for autonomy, or what Nickel refers to as the interest in leading a life.[9]

Some might argue, however, that dignity, properly understood, is an essentially comparative notion and does not include the second component, the well-being threshold idea.[10] On this view, one's dignity is not affronted if one lives in the most squalid conditions, unless this is the result of discriminatory attitudes or practices. I am not sure how to respond to this point, except to say that there does seem to be a coherent and plausible tradition of thinking about human dignity as including the idea that a certain sort of life—one that involves more than merely keeping body and soul together and in which there is scope for a meaningful exercise of the capacity for autonomy—is morally required for beings like us and that if we lack it this is an insult to our dignity. Be that as it may, the main features of my view as presented in this book do not depend on the assumption that dignity has a well-being threshold aspect, not just a comparative aspect. Further, everything I want to say about international legal human rights and their relationship to morality can be said without assuming that all international legal human rights can be seen as affirming human dignity.

James Griffin offers a narrower conception of dignity that appears to be akin to the welfare threshold conception—one according

---

[9] James Nickel, *Making Sense of Human Rights*, revised edition (Malden, MA: Wiley-Blackwell, 2007), pp. 35–37.

[10] Julian Culp, personal communication with the author, September 10, 2012.

to which the proper sort of life for beings like us in a life of normative agency, where this is understood to include access to resources
for achieving some substantial degree of success in pursuing one's
ends. For him dignity, so far as this is relevant to the grounding of
human rights, is a matter of protecting normative agency.[11] On his
view, dignity is a wholly noncomparative notion: One can tell
whether an individual's dignity is being respected simply by determining whether she has ample scope for normative agency, irrespective of whether she is relegated to an inferior position vis-à-vis
others.

However, it is implausible to say that some human rights, including the right to torture, are best understood as protecting normative agency. It is true that being tortured can interfere with one's
ability to operate as a normative agent, but that is not the only or
perhaps even the main reason why there should be an international
legal right to not be subjected to torture. Apart from its impact on
normative agency or on autonomy, torture greatly diminishes a person's welfare, chiefly by being terrifying and painful and because it
tends to damage a person's capacity for trust and intimacy. From the
standpoint of providing a basis for justifying anything like the
system of international legal human rights that now exists, dignity,
understood in Griffin's restrictive way, as respect for normative
agency, or as respect for autonomy, is inadequate. It fails to capture
the best justification for some of the rights in the system that perform the well-being function. And because Griffin's notion of normative agency is wholly noncomparative, it cannot account for the
status egalitarian aspect of the system.

Griffin might say: So much the worse for the system. His main
concern, he would add, is to provide a theory of moral human rights.
This reply is unsatisfying, however, unless Griffin is willing to admit
that his moral theory of human rights sheds little light on the system
of international legal human rights or unless he can tell us why that
system is unjustifiable unless the rights contained in it only have the
function of protecting normative agency. Once we abandon the Mirroring View, nothing in Griffin's work gives us reason to believe that
the system of international legal human rights should have so narrow

[11] James Griffin, *On Human Rights* (New York: Oxford University Press, 2009).

a justificatory base as the protection of normative agency. The same holds for attempts to ground the system of the protection of autonomy (so far as this can be distinguished from what Griffin calls normative agency).

On the face of it, given the threats to which the system was a response, it is implausible to assume that international legal human rights are justifiable only if they serve to protect individual autonomy. Because of the power they wield, states do pose a threat to the autonomy of individuals under their jurisdiction, but they also threaten their well-being in quite direct and unsubtle ways whose moral seriousness is independent of their effects on autonomy. It is more than appropriate that a system of international legal rights should address both sorts of threats.

Note that everything I have said so far is quite compatible with concluding, when all is said and done, that a system like the existing one, which includes provisions for affirming and protecting both aspects of dignity, the noncomparative well-being threshold aspect and the interpersonal comparative aspect, is not justifiable. It might turn out, for example, as James Nickel suggests, that a system that has only the more limited goal of helping to ensure that all have the opportunity to lead a minimally good or decent life is more defensible than one that adds to this the additional goal of publicly affirming and protecting equal status, where this includes providing protections against all forms of discrimination on racial or gender grounds, whether they interfere with the prospects for a minimally good or decent life or not.[12] This might be the case, if, given widespread cultural beliefs, it is simply not feasible to require all societies to strive to eliminate all forms of discrimination on grounds of gender—and *if*, as Nickel supposes, something cannot be a justified international legal right unless it can be realized in the majority of states. Or, one might think that the affirmation and protection of basic equal status, rather than ensuring that all have access to the conditions for a minimally good or decent life is inappropriate, not because it is not feasible, but because basic equal status, understood as barring any form of gender discrimination, is incompatible with the tenets of some reasonable moralities and that imposing such a norm on those who espouse such moralities would be wrong.

---

[12] Nickel, *Making Sense of Human Rights*, pp. 35–37.

In my judgment, Nickel's feasibility requirement is too strong if being realized in the majority of states means being fully realized in them. Torture, usually perpetrated by police personnel, is practiced in the majority of states (in fact, probably in all of them), and eliminating it entirely in any state, much less the majority of them, is probably not feasible. Yet it makes good sense to have laws against torture and to affirm an international legal right not to be tortured. I consider the other objection to including protections of equal basic status that include strong rights against discrimination—that doing so is incompatible with some reasonable moralities—in chapter 7.

For now, I want to home in on an aspect of the system's justificatory rhetoric of dignity that Hans Morsink has especially emphasized.[13] The preambular rhetoric of the major human rights documents, including the UDHR and the two Covenants (ICCPR and ICESCR), refers not just to dignity, but to the *inherent* dignity of the human individual. The most plausible interpretation of this language is that the documents take seriously the idea the each human being is a subject of moral concern *on her own* account or, as one might also put it, that each has moral worth that is not in any way derivative.

It is not surprising that the major human rights documents should emphasize the idea of the inherent dignity of the individual, given that the modern human rights movement was to a significant extent a direct response to the horrors of World War II and the Holocaust, and given the plausible and widespread assumption at the founding of the modern movement that these were due in large part to the effort to implement a fascist ideology that held that some humans have no worth at all and that those who do have worth have it only derivatively, according to their ability to contribute to the life of the nation. In other words, the notion of dignity, understood as having the well-being threshold and interpersonal comparative aspects, is valuable for combating two of the most dangerous tenets of racial fascism: the idea that individuals have no value except so far as they contribute to the good of the nation (radical collectivism) and the idea that there is an order of rank among human beings, the denial of

[13] See Johannes Morsink, *The Universal Declaration of Human Rights: Origins, Drafting and Intent* (University of Pennsylvania Press, 1999) and Johannes Morsink, *Inherent Human Rights: Philosophical Roots of the Universal Declaration* (University of Pennsylvania Press, 2009).

equal basic moral status (radical inegalitarianism). Whether or not it is, strictly speaking, a constraint on the justification for having a system of international legal human rights similar to the existing one, it is at least a desideratum that a justification should be able to make sense of the emphasis on the inherent dignity of all human individuals, if this means that all have equal basic moral worth on their own account. Later I will argue that this desideratum can be satisfied by a justification that does not present international legal rights as mirroring preexisting corresponding moral rights. All that is needed to satisfy the inherent dignity desideratum is that the justification be of the moral-individualist sort—that is, that the chains of argument, for the most part, ultimately appeal to what is conducive to individual well-being or freedom or equal basic status and that the system as a whole affirm the equal moral worth of every human being and help to ensure that each has the opportunity to lead a decent or minimally good human life.

I noted earlier that a justification for having a system of international legal human rights must be two-pronged, addressing both the fact that the rights that compose such a system are *international* legal rights and the fact that they are rights of *individuals*. Most theorists who situate themselves in the broadly liberal tradition find it obvious that, within the state, legal individual rights can provide valuable protections against abuses of state power and would agree that they are especially valuable for shielding individuals from harms inflicted in the name of ideologies, like racial Fascism, that deny the equal basic status of some humans and that deny that individuals have worth or value in their own right, but hold instead that their value derives from their contribution to the nation. Because individual rights, as opposed to mere duties, focus attention on the individual to whom they are ascribed, they are well-suited to express the idea that each individual has moral worth or value, if they are ascribed to all and are understood to be the same for all in terms of their content and weight. If these rights are thought of as sufficiently weighty as to block appeals to what would maximize utility or contribute to the social good, then this helps convey the idea that individuals are morally important in their own right. Further, if these protections for individuals are given the form of legal rights, this conveys a serious social commitment to making them effective, through enforcement if necessary.

In chapter 7, I will probe what I call the Ethical Pluralist Challenge to the project of international legal human rights, the charge that the attempt to create a morally justified system of international legal standards for the conduct of all states is incompatible with a proper recognition of the fact that there is a plurality of valid moralities (or value systems). There I will argue that although valid collectivistic moralities need not recognize individual moral rights, they must concede that individuals are of moral worth on their own account, even though they give greater weight to the moral importance of groups than individualistic moralities do.

## II.  *Why International Legal Rights?*

Yet all of this is not enough; exhibiting the advantages of a system of legal individual rights from the standpoint of securing the well-being and status egalitarian functions is insufficient. We still need to know why there is a need for a system of *international* legal rights. *A substantial part of the answer lies in an appreciation of both the success and the limitations of the domestic constitutionalization of individual legal rights.* At the time of the founding of the Practice, there were a number of examples where domestic constitutional bills of rights appeared to be playing a significant role in protecting individuals. It is unsurprising, then, that in preparing the first draft of the UDHR the original Human Rights Commission surveyed existing constitutional bills of rights and that its members frequently characterized their task as the formulation of an international bill of rights.[14]

If domestic bills of rights were so valuable, why was it thought necessary to formulate an international bill of rights? Instead, why not simply mobilize diplomatic, political, and economic pressure, under the leadership of powerful states that appreciate the importance of constitutional individual rights, to encourage states that lack such protections to remedy this defect? The next chapter answers this question by setting out three arguments for having an international legal human rights system.

[14] See Mary Ann Glendon, *A World Made New* and Hans Morsink, *Inherent Human Rights*, note 13 supra, p. 149.

# CHAPTER 4

## The Case for a System of International Legal Human Rights

The preceding chapter set out the most important requirements for a sound justification for having a system of international legal human rights like the existing one. This chapter offers three distinct justificatory arguments that satisfy those requirements and then sketches arguments to justify the inclusion of particular rights from each of the major categories of international legal human rights in the system. It also considers several potential countervailing considerations—reasons against having a system of this type. The chief remaining piece of the justification puzzle, an assessment of the legitimacy of the institutions through which international legal human rights are created and realized, is taken up in the next chapter.

The first two arguments present powerful reasons for having a system of international legal human rights, reasons that apply to a broad range of actors, individual and collective, private and public. The third shows why states and their governments have a special moral obligation either to support the existing international legal human rights system or to undertake alternative major reforms to remedy the defects of the international order that such a system serves to counter.

### I. *Argument 1: The Argument from Benefits*

There are seven reasons for having a system of international legal individual rights like the existing one, corresponding to seven valuable benefits that such a system can provide. These benefits fall under the following headings:

i. Encouraging the creation or improvement of domestic bills of rights through the establishment of international legal obligations.

ii. Providing legal backup for failures in the implementation of domestic bills of rights.

iii. Enhancing the legitimacy of the state, by providing independent adjudication of claims that citizens make against it, including claims made on the basis of domestic constitutional rights.

iv. Contributing to better understandings of domestic constitutional rights by providing a focus for supranational legal processes that can help develop better informed, less-biased approaches.

v. Supplying institutional and doctrinal resources for morally progressive developments of international humanitarian law (the international law of the conduct of armed conflict).

vi. Constituting a unified legal framework for coping with genuinely global problems — serious threats to human well-being for which individual states cannot be reasonably held culpable (such as grave cumulative effects of negative environmental externalities) or which are not cases of states failing to protect the rights of their citizens (such as the plight of stateless persons).

vii. Helping to correct for an inherent flaw of democratic states, namely, the fact that democratic accountability chiefly makes government responsive to the preferences of citizens, often at the expense of a due consideration of the rights of foreigners.

Each of these seven beneficial functions of international legal human rights will be explained in turn.

A cautionary word about my method of proceeding is in order. For each of the benefits, I will provide evidence that the existing international legal human rights system actually provides the benefit. But I will not try to show that the existing system does this well enough to justify *it*, all things considered. My primary aim is to begin the task of answering the more general justificatory question distinguished in chapter 1, namely, whether there is a justification for creating or, if it already exists, supporting a system similar in important respects to the existing one. Appealing to the performance of the existing system, rather than being an effort to show decisively that *it* is justified, has two other purposes: First, it will clarify the various benefits that a system of international legal human rights can provide by giving concrete, actual examples; and second, it will show that the benefits I describe are more than theoretical possibilities for a system of international legal human rights—that they can be achieved under conditions that are not unrealistic. This leaves open the possibility that even if the existing system does not presently deliver the benefits well enough to justify its existence, given that the system has significant moral costs, it nevertheless may be possible to improve the existing system in ways that would make it justifiable.

A further qualification: I do not claim that the founders of the international legal human rights system had all of these benefits in mind. I use the term 'benefits' rather than 'purposes' to avoid controversies about what the actual purposes of the founders were, recognizing that a system can have functions that were not intended or clearly envisioned by those who created it. My aim in this section is to construct the best justification for a system similar to the one we have, not to provide a causal account of why the actual system was created.

### (i) Encouraging and Improving Domestic Constitutional Bills of Rights

Promulgating a list of international legal rights, with corresponding legal obligations on the part of states, especially if it is supported by the authority of the UN—arguably the only international institution with credible pretensions to genuine inclusiveness and global moral standing—could both encourage those societies lacking domestic bills of rights to create them and provide a model for them to emulate. There is evidence that this has indeed occurred, especially in the cases of peoples emerging from colonial domination and former socialist states undergoing liberal democratization.[1] In addition, in the case of societies that have incomplete domestic constitutional rights regimes, a well-crafted international list of rights can encourage

---

[1] *Human Rights Here and Now: Celebrating the Universal Declaration of Human Rights*, Nancy Flowers, ed., www.1.umn.edu/humanrits/edumat/hreduse-ries/.../short-history.htum (University of Minnesota Human Rights Center).

improvements. To the extent that the domestic constitutionalization of individual rights—*rights-constitutionalism*—is a morally progressive development, the fact that a system of international legal human rights can assist it counts in favor of having such a system.

There are other ways in which states might be encouraged to adopt or improve constitutional rights systems, for example, through international declarations or goal-setting exercises that lack the force of international law. The mechanism of international law has two advantages, however. First, and most obviously, it makes it clear that states have legal obligations to promote certain rights within their jurisdictions, not just that it would be a good thing if they did, while at the same time providing an authoritative initial formulation of what these rights are and, perhaps more importantly, processes for interpreting these obligations that conform to principles of legal reasoning. So far as states give more weight to international legal obligations than to less formal undertakings, the system of international legal human rights is likely to be more effective than nonlegal alternatives. Second, when states incur international legal obligations, this creates the possibility of eventually developing legal institutions that will hold states accountable for fulfilling them. Legal obligations have the advantage of a presumption that enforcement (eventually if not presently) is appropriate.

There is yet another reason in favor of devising a new type of international law as the mechanism for furthering the project of domestic rights-constitutionalism. If the need for domestic constitutions that include individual rights is due in part to the fact that international law empowers states to treat those under their jurisdiction badly by creating a "veil of sovereignty," then it is especially appropriate that international law should be modified so as to help remedy this defect. I elaborate this idea in Argument 2 below.

### (ii) Providing Backup for Failures of Domestic Protection of Rights

Even in societies that have comprehensive constitutional individual rights, there can be failures of implementation, and the existence of a system of international legal rights can help prevent or ameliorate such failures. Societies that generally do a good job of protecting the rights of their citizens often fall short in the case of particular groups—women, racial or ethnic minorities, migrants, indigenous people, or gays, lesbians, or transgender people. And in cases of perceived national emergency, as in war or in the wake of dramatic terrorist acts, the rights of all citizens may be imperiled by state action taken in the name of national security. In some cases, domestic courts appeal to international legal human rights to justify decisions to prevent or remedy both kinds of failures.[2] The fact that international legal human rights are law, not simply a statement of supposed moral rights, empowers domestic courts to invoke it to correct for lapses in the state's protection of rights. The ability to perform this backup function is a second important consideration in favor of having a system of international legal human rights.

Even though there may be some differences in domestic and international lists of rights, there is sufficient overlap to make the backup function significant. That there should be considerable overlap is not surprising, given the fact, noted earlier, that the drafters of the Universal Declaration of Human Rights (UDHR) looked to influential domestic bills of rights for guidance and given that the UDHR and the ICCPR have subsequently influenced the content of many domestic bills of rights.

It is important to understand that a system of international legal rights can perform the backup function even if (a) there are no *international* institutions for enforcement of international legal human rights, and (b) even in cases where no significant *external* pressures can be brought to bear on states when they fall short in implementing their own domestic constitutional rights. With respect to (a), it must be emphasized that most legal enforcement of international legal human rights is not achieved through the actions of international institutions but through the operations of domestic

---

[2] See, for examples, Dudgeon v. United Kingdom, 4 Eur. Ct. H.R. 149 (1981), which held that Irish law criminalizing "buggery" between consenting adults violated the right to privacy under Article 8 of the European Convention on Human Rights, and UN Human Rights Committee judgment against similar laws in Tasmania (Toonen v. Australia, Case No. 488/1992, U.N. Hum. Rts. Comm., 15th Sess., U.N. Doc CCPR/C/50/D/488/1992 [1994]). For other examples, see Robert O. Keohane, Stephen Macedo, and Andrew Moravcsik, "Democracy-Enhancing Multilateralism," Institute for International Law and Justice Working Paper No. 2007/4 (New York University Law School, 2007).

institutions. In states where the judiciary is relatively independent and there is a culture of compliance with its decisions, a court's ruling that the state violates a citizen's international legal human rights can result in the state taking corrective action, even in the absence of any possibility of enforcement by agents outside the state. With respect to (b), there is impressive evidence that some states respond to pressures from *domestic* groups mobilized under the banner of international legal human rights.[3]

So, neither international institutions capable of enforcement nor effective external pressure appear to be necessary for a system of international legal human rights to perform the function of providing backup for failures in the implementation of domestic constitutional rights. Of course, when there are international enforcement mechanisms and powerful external pressures (as when economic sanctions are threatened or membership in beneficial organizations such as the EU or NATO are made conditional on improved human rights performance), a system of international legal human rights will perform the backup function more effectively and the case for having such a system will be correspondingly stronger.

### (iii) Enhancing the Legitimacy of States

There are two senses of 'legitimacy': one normative and one sociological. An institution is legitimate in the normative sense if it actually has authority or, as I shall explain in chapter 4, if it warrants a certain public standing that involves various aspects of respect. An institution is legitimate in the sociological sense if it is widely *believed* to have authority or to be worthy of respect. Sociological legitimacy is normatively important, to the extent that an institution's ability to perform its functions depends on whether it is perceived to have authority or warrant respect.

When a system of international legal human rights performs the backup function just described, it can contribute to the state's legitimacy in the normative sense, given the plausible assumption

that the legitimacy of the state depends in part on its at least providing minimally adequate protection of its citizens' human rights.
But a system of international legal individual rights can also contribute to legitimacy in the sociological sense. If citizens know that
when it comes to legal claims they make against their state the state
is not the final arbiter in its own case, this can bolster the belief that
the state is legitimate.[4] Thus the public's knowledge that the system
of international legal human rights is performing the backup function can enhance sociological legitimacy. So, to the extent that it is
important not only whether the state is legitimate, but also whether
it is believed to be legitimate, there is value in having a system of
international legal human rights.

On some accounts, the public knowledge that the state is not the
final arbiter in its own case would increase legitimacy in the normative sense as well. This would be the case for views on normative
legitimacy according to which the state must not only protect human
rights or satisfy other requirements of justice, but must also be seen
to be doing so. In other words, if one's view of normative legitimacy
includes a publicity requirement of this sort, then a state's acknowledgment of the supremacy of international human rights law, by
providing a publicly ascertainable indication that it takes the human
rights of its citizens seriously and recognizes its own limitations, can
increase its legitimacy. In the next chapter, I explore in much more
detail how participation in a system of international legal human
rights can enhance a state's legitimacy.

### (iv) Contributing to Better Understandings of Domestic Constitutional Rights

It is a perennial complaint in some quarters that international legal
human rights betray a parochial scheme of values and, more specifically, that they are infected by the particular cultural biases of

---

[4] Stephen Gardbaum, "Human Rights as International Constitutional Rights,"
*The European Journal of International Law*, 19:4 (2008): 762–65. See Samantha Besson, "The Human Right to Democracy—A Moral Defence, with a Legal Nuance,"
in *Souveraineté populaire et droits de l'homme*, Collection Science et Technique de
la Société, Strasbourg: Editions du Conseil de l'Europe 2012, pp. 47–75, available at
http://www.venice.coe.int/docs/2010/CDLUD%282010%29003-e.pdf.

"Western" societies, whose members are said to have played a disproportionate role in formulating them. Interestingly, those who voice this complaint seem to be unconcerned about the risk of cultural biases in domestic bills of rights. The most influential domestic bills of rights—those that have been most widely imitated in constitutions across a diversity of societies—may be the French Declaration of the Rights of Man and the Citizen and the US Bill of Rights. Both of these documents and many of their numerous offspring present the rights they enumerate as *universal rights*, not rights peculiar to people in a particular society. Even when, as in the title of the French Declaration, a distinction is made between the rights of man and those of the citizen, there is the strong suggestion that a citizen of any state ought to enjoy these rights. (The title of the document refers to the rights of *"the* citizen," not the rights of French citizens.) Given that this is so, the question arises as to whether in some cases domestic bills of rights fail to deliver on the promise of universality, and instead exhibit a parochial bias due to the particular historical-cultural context in which they originated. The worry is not only that some constitutional rights might be parochial while being presented as universal, but also that their parochialism might be an expression of the biases of a particular ethnic group or class within a given society.

The existence of a system of international legal human rights can help ensure that domestic bills of rights are not distorted by parochialism if two conditions are satisfied: First, the system exerts significant influence on the original formulation or subsequent interpretation of the items included in domestic bills of rights; and second, the system includes effective measures to reduce the risk of parochialism in its own formulation of rights.

I have already indicated that the first condition is satisfied with respect to the existing system of international legal human rights: The UDHR and the International Covenant on Civil and Political Rights (ICCPR) in particular have influenced the creation of domestic bills of rights in a number of states and, at least in states whose courts recognize the supremacy of international human rights law or look to it as a legitimate interpretative source, international legal human rights influence the interpretation of domestic constitutional rights.

Chapter 7 addresses the question of whether the second condition is met. But for now I will only note that there is abundant evidence that both in its origins and its subsequent development the existing international legal human rights system includes impressive provisions for reducing the risk of parochialism in how human rights are conceived. The strenuous efforts of the drafters of the UDHR to include a wide range of cultural perspectives have been well-documented.[5] Moreover, the initiative to draft an international bill of rights came chiefly from weaker states in Latin America and Asia and in the face of reluctance if not outright opposition on the part of the most powerful Western states and the Soviet Union.[6] Further, there is clear evidence that anticolonialist (and hence "non-Western") views were not only voiced in the deliberations that led to the drafting but also found their way into the final document, in particular with respect to the unambiguous assertion that the rights therein contained apply to all persons, including those currently under colonial domination[7] and the enunciation of a right of self-determination of *all* peoples.

It would be a mistake, however, to assume that whether the existing system of international legal human rights includes protections against parochialism depends solely or even chiefly on whether such measures informed the drafting of the founding documents. What matters is whether the system subsequently developed institutions and principles that provide protections against parochialism in the ongoing interpretation and reinterpretation of international legal human rights and in particular in the processes by which new human rights conventions are created.

Elsewhere I have argued in detail that this is precisely what has occurred.[8] Here I only wish to suggest that a system of legal rights that is created and developed through the participation of people from many cultures should be less prone to parochialism in

---

[5] Mary Ann Glendon, *A World Made New* (New York: Random House, 2001), pp. 56–83.

[6] Ibid., pp. 5–12.

[7] Article 2 of the UDHR states that "Everyone is entitled to all the rights and freedoms set forth in this Declaration [and that] . . . no distinction shall be made on the basis of the political, jurisdictional or international status of the country or territory to which a person belongs, whether it be independent, trust, or nonself-governing or under any other limitation of sovereignty."

[8] Allen Buchanan, "Human Rights and the Legitimacy of the International Order," *Legal Theory* 14:1 (2008): 39–70.

its understanding of those rights, other things being equal, than one that operates solely within a domestic cultural context. For brevity, let us refer to this as the epistemic advantage of international human rights law.

Earlier I observed that international human rights law can be seen as supporting the project of domestic rights-constitutionalism. If the object of that project is for all states to have constitutions that ascribe rights to their citizens that have a credible claim to universality, then using international law to further that project makes sense, given its epistemic advantage.

### (v) Supplying Resources for Developments in International Humanitarian Law

International humanitarian law is that part of international law that regulates the conduct of armed conflict. International human rights law and international humanitarian law have distinct origins and, until very recently, have developed independently from one another. International humanitarian law originated in an international order that did not yet view individuals as subjects of international law — that was not yet transformed by the momentous advent of the post-World War II human rights regime. Hence it is not surprising that international humanitarian law is not framed in the language of individual human rights. International humanitarian law originated as part of an international legal system that was designed to regulate the behavior of states toward one another, and to do so chiefly in the interest of states.

To the extent that the statist origins of international humanitarian law still influence its content and institutional development, reconceptualizing it as a branch of international human rights law would not only help to correct for any statist biases, but also could strengthen its implementation by harnessing it to the resources of the larger human rights movement. The point is not that traditional international humanitarian law does not take the well-being of individuals into account, but rather that subsuming international humanitarian law under the system of international legal human rights would unambiguously convey the message that the most important aim of constraining the conduct of war is to protect individuals, not to benefit states. It would also make absolutely clear that the constraints on war are not conditional on reciprocity in their observance, but are instead grounded in proper regard for all human individuals. For it is a distinctive feature of the notion of human rights (moral and legal) that individuals do not have to earn them by respecting the rights of others.

For the system of international legal human rights to exert a morally progressive influence on international humanitarian law, nothing as radical as subsuming the latter under the former may be required, however. In fact, there is evidence that the influence of the existing international legal human rights system has already begun to stimulate progressive developments in international humanitarian law, without anything as momentous as a merger of the two types of law. For example, the concept of war crimes has recently been expanded to include mass rapes. Rape was recognized as a violation of international legal human rights before it was seen to fall within the scope of war crimes. Moreover, the effective use international legal human rights discourse by NGOs appears to have played a major role in this change. It can also be argued that the 1977 Additional Protocols to the Geneva Conventions strengthen the conventions by including human rights provisions not previously found in them.[9] Finally, James Nickel has suggested that international legal human rights law has had another, arguably progressive influence on international humanitarian law: Conceptualizing the traditional protections provided by international humanitarian law as human rights increases their weight in international legal reasoning, making them more resistant to certain trade-offs.[10] These developments have been succinctly[11] summarized by Robert Sloane as follows: "[Modern international humanitarian law] signifies a major postwar shift . . . away from an interstate model grounded solely in simple reciprocity and interstate dynamics and toward a model justified more explicitly by international human rights law's solicitude for the individual and normative commitment to a universal conception of human dignity."

[9] Frits Kalshoven and Lisabeth Zegveld, *Constraints on Waging War: An Introduction to International Humanitarian Law*, Third Edition (Geneva: ICRC, (International Committee of the Red Cross) 2001), p. 34.

[10] James Nickel, personal communication, June 16, 2011.

[11] Robert Sloane, "Prologue to a Voluntarist War Convention," *Michigan Law Review*, 106:443 (2007–2008): p. 483.

*(vi) Constituting a Unified Legal Framework for Coping with Genuinely Global Problems*

As we have seen, the value of having a system of international legal human rights depends in large part on whether there are deficiencies in domestic law that such a system can ameliorate. There are two kinds of threats to human well-being and equal basic status that present serious problems for even the more enlightened domestic legal systems. The first is the vulnerability of stateless persons. Domestic constitutions ascribe rights chiefly to citizens. When rights are ascribed to noncitizens, they typically apply only to those noncitizens within the state's territory. Not surprisingly, domestic constitutions do not affirm rights for stateless persons elsewhere.[12] International legal human rights are ascribed to all individuals, including those who are stateless, irrespective of where they are.

The second problem that domestic rights regimes have difficulty addressing is harms that states individually cannot effectively cope with and for which it would be inappropriate to hold them responsible, in the absence of any voluntarily assumed special international legal obligation. These include harms to health and well-being caused by environmental degradation, but also damage caused by international terrorists or pirates on the high seas. To cope with this second category of threats, states not only need to cooperate, but also to coordinate their cooperation on a single set of standards. Framing the standards in terms of international legal human rights not only gives them greater legal weight, but also enlists the impressive political and legal resources of the international human rights movement. Thus, for example, if the more severe harms that may occur as a result of global climate change are conceived of as violations of international legal human rights to an adequate standard of living or to health or even to physical security in extreme cases, the efficacy of mobilization to prevent them may be increased.

Both in the case of stateless persons and that of global environmental threats, voluntary solutions may be blocked by the free-rider problem, because averting the threat has the characteristics of a public

---

[12]   Gardbaum, "Human Rights as International Constitutional Rights," pp. 764–65.

good. To the extent that obligations under international human rights law are treated as among the most weighty international legal obligations rather than just matters of morally admirable policy or bureaucratic requirements, conceiving of these threats as violations of international legal human rights can do something to counteract the incentives for free-riding.

In the final chapter, I will qualify this benefit significantly. There I will argue that even if international legal human rights law can help us conceptualize the damage caused by jointly produced pollution or the plight of stateless persons, it is at present not well-equipped to provide guidance for remedies. The problem is that existing international human rights law is primarily designed to hold each state accountable for how it treats those under their jurisdiction, on the assumption that the state is itself in control of these matters. The predominate conception of duties in international human rights law therefore does not capture the need for collective action by the community of states to remedy problems that are not caused by any particular state's actions or omissions—or at least it does not provide an assignment of duties whose fulfillment would solve the collective action problem. For now, however, I only wish to emphasize that international human rights law does something valuable when it provides a way of conceptualizing the harms caused by cumulative damage to the environment and at least creates a presumption that helping to remedying them is an appropriate task for international law—even if the current form of the law suffers serious limitations so far as this task is concerned.

## (vii) Helping to Correct an Inherent Flaw of Democracy

It is a virtue of democracy—on some accounts its premier virtue—that government officials are accountable to their fellow citizens. That is the good news. The bad news is that the democratic commitment to the accountability of government to citizens tends to produce not just accountability, but near exclusive accountability. Democratic electoral processes and constitutional checks and balances create formidable obstacles to government taking into due account the legitimate interests of anyone who is not a citizen. In other words, democracy has an inherent structural bias toward excessive

partiality or, if you will, against cosmopolitanism.[13] This bias is most
evident in the case of accountability through periodic elections: Foreigners have no votes.

A system of international legal human rights can provide resources for domestic and transnational groups to exert pressure on
domestic government officials to take the rights of foreigners into
account and to that extent can ameliorate the structural bias of democracy. From the standpoint of institutional design, a commitment
to international legal human rights can be seen as a self-binding
mechanism for democratic peoples to help counteract this structural
bias of their own constitutions. Even those democratic states (if
there are any) whose implementation of individual rights for their
own citizens is so perfect as to render the backup function of international legal human rights otiose would still have this reason for
supporting a system of international legal human rights.

This benefit could become much greater if international legal
human rights law were modified in two respects: first, if it came
to include more robust responsibilities on the part of other states,
either individually or collectively, to take action when a state fails to
fulfill its human rights-correlative duties toward those under its own
jurisdiction; and second, if the extraterritorial human rights obligations of states become more substantial. By extraterritorial human
rights obligations here I mean primarily obligations of states under
international human rights law not to violate or to help realize the
human rights of foreigners within the territories of other states. At
present international human rights law is more successful in ascribing duties to states regarding those under their jurisdiction than
in ascribing either default duties or extraterritorial duties. Nonetheless, even in the absence of clear legal duties of these two latter sorts,
there is value in the fact that citizens can invoke the authoritative
lingua franca of international legal human rights in their efforts to
make their governments take more seriously the interests of foreigners. For as I have already emphasized, states—and nonstate actors such as corporations—can sometimes be held accountable for

---

[13] Note that this point does not assume an extreme cosmopolitan point of view.
It only assumes that states should systematically give some independent weight
to the well-being and freedom of foreigners, not that they should be given equal
consideration.

violations of international legal human rights norms even when the corresponding legal duties are not ascribable to them.

In the past decade or so, there has been a new development in the direction of the first change: the enunciation and elaboration of the Responsibility to Protect (R2P) doctrine. R2P contains three "pillars": first, the responsibility of states to protect the human rights of those under their jurisdiction, along with the idea that sovereignty is grounded in the discharging of this responsibility; second, the responsibility of the society of states to help states build the capacity to discharge the first responsibility; and third, the responsibility of the society of states to act when a state fails egregiously to protect basic human rights within its territory.[14]

It is not an accident that the term 'responsibility' rather than 'duty' is employed here. The development of R2P is both a recognition of the deficiency of a system of international law that does not assign clear default duties to states—duties to act when a state fails to protect the human rights of those under its jurisdiction—and an expression of the unwillingness to go the whole distance toward remedying that defect. At this point it is impossible to know whether R2P will eventually evolve into an unambiguous affirmation of genuine default duties—and whether, if it does, it will be appropriately embodied in international law and made effective.

## II. *Argument 2: International Legal Human Rights as a Necessary Condition for the Justifiability of the International Order*

The traditional international legal order conferred impressive—and extremely dangerous—rights, powers, and privileges on states while at the same time imposing scandalously minimal requirements for statehood or, rather, for what qualifies a group to count as the government representing a state. The international order is often described as "the state system," and until the advent of the modern human rights movement, its norms governed the relationships among states, and international law did not even recognize individuals as

---

[14] The UN General Assembly first adopted the "Responsibility to Protect" doctrine in UN General Assembly, *2005 World Summit Outcome*, paragraphs 138–45.

having rights on their own account. Generally speaking, the international order, at least in its legal structure, largely treated individuals as if they were of consequence only so far as their interests affected the interests of states.[15]

## The "Veil of Sovereignty"

The rights of sovereign states conferred by the traditional international order—or perhaps more accurately, the rights that constituted that order—included first and foremost an extremely robust right against interference in the "domestic affairs" of states. Operating behind the veil of sovereignty, states had great latitude as to how they treated those under their jurisdiction. It may be true, as Gary Bass has argued, that at least since the mid-nineteenth century, the international order tacitly recognized something like a right to intervene on humanitarian grounds when states severely abused certain minorities (e.g., Christians in Syria), but this right, if one can call it that, was neither clearly formulated nor institutionally embodied.[16] Nor is it clear that it was accorded to any other than a handful of states.

## The Resource Control Norm

The extremely robust right against interference in a state's domestic affairs, taken by itself, contributed significantly to the vulnerability of individuals to abusive behavior by their own states. It erected a formidable obstacle to efforts by oppressed people to enlist the help of external agents in combating tyranny. But there were several other norms of the international order that exacerbated the problem of vulnerability. Among the most important are the resource control norm, the borrowing privilege, and the right to limit or completely prohibit immigration.

According to the resource control norm, any government that the rules of the international order recognizes as legitimate has a right to

---

[15] The humanitarian law of war, which began to develop prior to the modern human rights movement, is a partial exception to this generalization.

[16] J. Bass, *Freedom's Battle: The Origins of Humanitarian Intervention* (New York: Knopf, 2008).

dispose of the natural resources within the state's territory. As Thomas Pogge has pointed out, this norm gives governments virtually blank checks to sell or lease the country's natural resources to the highest bidder, without regard for the well-being of the general population.[17] In brief, the resource control norm confers awesome power over resources without any checks to ensure responsible stewardship.

## The Borrowing Privilege

A second norm, whose destructive effects are also emphasized by Pogge, empowers states (or, in practice, the governments of states) to borrow, again without any restrictions. The effect of this norm is not only to lessen the incentives for governments to make the country self-reliant in financial matters, but, much worse, to enable irresponsible, inept, or corrupt governments to burden their populations with debts that can extend over generations and pose a formidable obstacle to economic development and to the efforts of individuals to improve their lot in life. As with the resource control norm, a power is conferred without provisions to prevent it from being exercised in deleterious ways—and in conditions under which it is virtually guaranteed that abuses will occur.

## Control of Immigration

Under the traditional international legal order, states also have an almost unlimited right to prevent foreigners from settling in or even entering their territories, as well as the right to withhold from them the rights usually accorded to citizens if they are allowed to enter. This norm greatly compounds the damaging effects of the preceding three norms, because it makes the option of exit impractical for those whom other states are unwilling to accept. When governments persecute some people within their jurisdiction or abuse all of them, or when they squander resources, or pile up mountains of debilitating debts, those who suffer from these actions may find no other country willing to accept them. By weakening the credibility of the

---

[17] Thomas Pogge, *World Poverty and Human Rights* (Cambridge: Polity Press, 2008).

threat of mass exit, the norm that confers the power to prohibit immigration deprives the oppressed of what might otherwise be an effective means of resisting tyranny or at least escaping it.

I have characterized these four norms of the traditional international order as conferring rights, powers, and privileges on states, but in describing their effects the focus has been on the behavior of governments. This is not a mistake or an equivocation. Although the most basic norms of the international order are formulated in terms of states, they are applied to the behavior of governments, on the assumption that they are the agents through which the state acts.

## The Principle of Effectivity

The destructive potential of the four norms of sovereignty noted above is exacerbated by a fifth norm, the Principle of Effectivity, which determines who counts as the government of a state. According to this principle, all that is required for a group of people to qualify as the government of state is that it exercise effective control over a territory with a relatively stable population and be capable of entering into relationships with other states.[18]

The Principle of Effectivity imposes no normative criteria whatsoever on what counts as a legitimate government. It is simply an instance of the more general principle that might makes right. In a world in which coming to be recognized as the legitimate government of a state means gaining all the powers, rights, and privileges that accrue to states, especially the right to control resources and the borrowing privilege, the Principle of Effectivity creates strong incentives for groups to gain control over a territory, by any means available to them, including the killing of rivals and the overthrow of existing governments.

## Extreme Inequality of Power to Shape the International Order

There is one final feature of the international order that contributes to the vulnerability of many people: the fact that it is, to a significant degree, crafted—and often selectively implemented—to further the

[18] General Act of the 1885 Conference of Berlin, Article 35 available at http://courses.wcupa.edu/jones/his312/misc/berlin.htm. Isla de Palmas (United States v. Netherlands), 1928.

interests of the most powerful states. The most powerful states play a disproportionate role in determining what is customary international law, because their behavior counts more heavily in evaluating whether the requirement of "state practice" is met in the identification of an emerging customary norm. Likewise, the most powerful states are better able to shape treaty law, either by exerting pressure on weaker states to ratify treaties they favor or by refraining from ratifying treaties they dislike and thereby limiting their effect. In our world, where the interests of states and global corporations are often aligned—and sometimes at odds with the interests of ordinary people and especially the world's worst off—the disproportionate ability of powerful states to shape the international order, especially in its economic and financial institutions, can be highly destructive.

A disinterested visitor from another planet who became acquainted with the four norms of sovereignty and the Principle of Effectivity, who was aware of the fact of radical power asymmetries among states, and who was not lulled into uncritical complacency by familiarity with the traditional system or by an inability to imagine alternatives, could only conclude that it was not designed for the benefit of all. Instead, he would conclude that, to a considerable extent, it was artfully designed to serve the interests of a tiny minority of the world's population.

Taken together, these six flaws are so severe as to make the system morally unjustifiable, unless they can be significantly mitigated. The system of international legal human rights has the potential to ameliorate the damage caused by all of these flaws of the international legal order, with the exception of the last one, or so I shall argue.

At least in the case of the first flaw, the virtually unlimited license for states to abuse those under their jurisdiction, the potential has been actualized to some extent. International human rights law has served as the authoritative lingua franca for imposing standards on states as to how they must treat those under their jurisdiction, and the institutions of the international legal human rights system have provided an important resource for various parties who strive to hold states to those standards.

Here it is important avoid a common mistake, and one that I have already flagged: gauging the power of international human rights law by the strength of international institutions. As Beth Simmons,

Kathryn Sikkink, and others have documented, most of the enforcement of international human rights occurs through domestic institutions (chiefly courts and legislatures) and the key agents in the process of "mobilizing for human rights" are often domestic groups, operating through domestic civil society institutions and practices.[19]

Although international institutions for implementing it are generally weak, the existence of international human rights law plays a significant role in empowering more capable agents and institutions. One way in which this empowerment occurs is that international human rights law provides a focal point for domestic reform efforts, especially in the case of states that have ratified human rights treaties. Domestic activists can appeal to the international legal obligations their states have undertaken and legitimately appeal to international organizations in their struggle for better compliance.

So far, the Practice has been less successful with respect to modifying the other norms or mitigating their damaging effects. Apart from including in its major documents the right of individuals to exit their state—the importance of which should not be underestimated—international human rights law has done little to moderate the norm regarding control of immigration, except by encouraging the recognition of a very limited right of sanctuary for victims of political persecution.

With respect to the resource control norm, international human rights law has had some impact so far as it has supported the notion that all people have a right to democratic government and includes a number of rights which, if realized, tend to create the conditions for democratization. To the extent that states become democratic, the accountability of the government to the people lessens the risk that the resource control privilege will be abused. When governments are accountable through democratic processes, they are less able to pillage the country's resources to line their own pockets.

In the case of the borrowing privilege, the prospects are less encouraging. Even where governments are responsive to the public, irresponsible borrowing can and does occur, because the public may

---

[19] See Beth A. Simmons, *Mobilizing for Human Rights: International Law in Domestic Politics* (Cambridge: Cambridge University Press, 2009) and Kathryn Sikkink, *The Justice Cascade: How Human Rights are Changing World Politics* (New York: Norton, 2011).

be all too willing to impose burdens on future generations. The most promising role for international human rights law and the activism for which it provides a focal point in mitigating the damage of the borrowing privilege norm lies in supporting domestic rights regimes that limit the discrepancy between the interests of government officials and the interests of the present public. For the present, at least, the resources of international human rights law and of international law generally for protecting the interests of future generations appear to be much more meager.

If states conscientiously implemented the various social and economic rights that further the well-being function of the international legal human rights system—thus securing for all the conditions for a minimally good or decent life—this would preclude the worst abuses of the resource privilege. Unfortunately, the various domestic, regional, and international agents and institutions of the Practice have been much less successful in holding states accountable for realizing these rights than has been the case with the civil and political rights. Whether this discrepancy can be reduced or eliminated is one of the greatest challenges for the Practice.

It is important to understand that from the standpoint of international human rights law the social and economic rights are not of lesser priority. They are on an equal footing, so far as the law is concerned, with the civil and political rights. Nevertheless, there are two special difficulties in holding states accountable for their realization, and this fact lessens the ability of this sort of right to constrain abuses of the resource control right and the borrowing privilege. First, some states lack the capacity to realize some of the social and economic rights. The doctrine of "progressive realization" is intended to cope with this problem, but makes it more difficult to hold states accountable. Second, as a broad generalization, it may be more difficult for outsiders to determine the extent to which the failure to realize social and economic rights is the result of deficiencies in state policy as opposed to being the consequence of structural features of the international order and in particular of its economic and financial institutions and practices.

In chapter 8, I will explore the implications of the fact that whether the well-being function of international legal rights can be realized in a particular state can depend not only upon its own actions, but also upon how that state fares in a global basic structure that arbitrarily favors the more powerful states. I will argue that existing international legal human rights law, designed as it is primarily to impose duties on states regarding their treatment of those under their jurisdiction, is not well-suited to cope with detriments to welfare due to the global basic structure.

An additional consideration is often invoked in this context: It is said that the social and economic rights, being "positive" rights, are necessarily more indeterminate or more open-ended than the "negative" civil and political rights and that this fact also makes it harder to hold states accountable for their realization. This last consideration is often overstated and depends on an exaggerated contrast between civil and political rights and social and economic rights. The realization of civil and political rights involves the fulfillment of extremely demanding positive duties and these, too, are necessarily indeterminate. For example, as I noted in the preceding chapter, to realize various rights to physical security, including the rights against torture and against arbitrary deprivation of life, as well as the rights to due process and equal treatment under the law, a state must undertake large-scale, costly social policies, including the training, monitoring, and disciplining of the police and the personnel of penal institutions, supervision of the training of judge and lawyers, and much more. Despite the special problems involved in holding states accountable for the realization of social and economic rights, existing international human rights law has the potential to limit the opportunities for states abusing the borrowing privilege and the right to control resources indirectly, by holding them accountable for realizing social and economic rights, simply because fulfilling these obligations is incompatible with the worst abuses of these incidents of sovereignty.

One way in which progress could be made in this regard would be for international financial institutions such as the International Monetary Fund and the World Bank to alter their lending policies to make them more effective in reducing the risk of damaging borrowing and for the more economically developed states to restrict the ability of corporations based in them to make resource extraction deals with states that are damaging to their populations. Considerable human rights activism is already focused on both of these reforms. How successful they will ultimately be remains to be seen.

Sporadically, there have been some potentially valuable efforts to replace the Principle of Effectivity with a standard of recognition that is normatively demanding. The idea, mentioned earlier with respect to R2P, that sovereignty is conditional upon the discharge of responsibilities toward those over whom it is exercised, seems to be gaining traction. In the case of new states emerging from the dissolution of Yugoslavia and the Soviet Union, there have been political efforts, with varying degrees of success, to make recognition conditional on the provision of credible guarantees of protections for the human rights of national minorities. There have also been failures, as with the case of the recommendations of the Badinter Commission.[20] This European commission recommended that no member state of the Council of Europe grant recognition to new states emerging from the dissolution of Yugoslavia unless the new states gave assurances that they would respect the rights of minorities within their borders. Unfortunately, Germany, and then other countries, granted recognition in the absence of guarantees.

The prospects that international human rights law will mitigate the effects of the profound inequality of power among states are, if anything, less encouraging. The resources of an international law-based human rights practice for constraining the ability of the most powerful states to shape the rules of the international order and their implementation in ways that are damaging to others are quite limited. This is not surprising, given that the most basic idea of the human rights enterprise, so far, has been to develop international legal standards for how states treat those under their jurisdiction—not to regulate power relations among states. In the final chapter I will elaborate this point, arguing that it indicates a major limitation on the power of human rights law, at least as it has been understood up until now.

It remains to be seen how successful practice that is grounded in appeals to human rights law will ultimately be in mitigating the deleterious effects of the four norms of sovereignty. Be that as it may, the existence of an international legal human rights system is an important resource for making headway on them. If this is the case, then, given the moral necessity of mitigating the negative effects of

[20] The Arbitration Committee of the European Community's Conference for Peace in Yugoslavia, 1991–1993.

these norms, one important reason for having such a system is that it is necessary for making the international order justifiable.

The four norms of sovereignty, and above all the right against intervention in domestic affairs that international order conferred on states, in combination with the morally undemanding Principle of Effectivity, not only empowered states to abuse their peoples; it also enabled them to ignore or actively suppress efforts on the part of the population to insist that the state perform basic welfare functions, not just provide security and refrain from abuses that detract from their welfare. Given the tremendous power the modern state wields over human lives, the robust authority it claims, and the resources at its disposal, it is reasonable for people to expect the state to provide basic welfare services, not just to provide security, and do so in ways that do not inflict abuse on them.

In other words, in the modern context at least, the state's performance of welfare functions is arguably a necessary condition for its justification.[21] If this is so, and if the international order equips states with powers that they can and sometimes do use to evade their responsibility to perform welfare functions—or to provide basic social and economic benefits only to some but not all of those under their jurisdiction—then the international order is unjustifiable, unless it is modified so as to reduce this risk. A system of international legal human rights that includes rights with correlative duties on the part of states to provide basic social and economic benefits to all those under their jurisdiction is justified, therefore, as a necessary condition for the justifiability of the international order.

## III. *Argument 3: The Special Obligation of States and Governments*

The third justificatory argument focuses on the obligation of states and their governments to cooperate to remedy the flaws that make the international order morally unjustifiable. The obligation falls on states and their governments for two reasons: They are the chief

[21] This is not to say, as some have tried to argue, that the satisfaction of *egalitarian* principles of distributive justice is a necessary condition for the justification of the modern state. In my judgment, efforts to establish the stronger claim have clearly failed.

beneficiaries of the international order in general and in particular of the dangerous norms of sovereignty discussed above, and they are in the best position to correct its flaws because the international order is created and sustained by them. If the international order is morally unjustifiable without a system of international legal human rights and if states and their governments have an obligation to render it justifiable, then they have a special obligation to support the system of international legal human rights.

The moral weight of this obligation and the costs which an agent may rightly be expected to bear in discharging it will vary across states, depending on how much power they have to influence the character of the international order and upon the resources at their disposal. The most powerful states (and their governments) have an especially stringent obligation and should be expected to bear greater costs in discharging it, not just because they have greater resources, but also because they derive proportionately greater benefits from the international order.

## The Natural Duty of Justice

In an earlier book on the philosophy of international law, I argued that the natural duty of justice requires support for the international human rights system.[22] The natural duty of justice, as I understood it there, is the moral duty to support institutions that help achieve justice if they exist and to help create them if they do not. The duty is called natural because it exists independently of obligations that institutions impose on us. The three justificatory arguments I have just sketched are compatible with what I said in that earlier work. With respect to the first argument, most if not all of the benefits the system provides are important from the standpoint of justice. With respect to the second argument, the flaws of the international order that the system of international legal human rights system ameliorates cause injustices. With respect to the third argument, the duty to create and sustain just institutions—in this case to ameliorate the injustices of the international order detailed in the second argument—falls most heavily on states and their governments, for the reasons already noted.

[22] Allen Buchanan, *Justice, Legitimacy, and Self-Determination: Moral Foundations for International Law* (New York: Oxford University Press, 2004).

## IV. *Why Individual Legal Rights?*

In chapter 3, in laying out the requirements for justification of the system, I noted that the basic idea of the system might have been implemented without introducing any individual rights into international law; instead, a system of duties might have been utilized, so long as it focused on the importance of individuals, rather than the interests of states. I also noted that an adequate justification for a system like the existing one should explain why it is important, nonetheless, to include a prominent role for individual rights norms. Now I want to provide the explanation. I need to do this to counter a potential objection, namely, that while the combined weight of the three justificatory arguments makes a strong case for having a system of international law that performs the same functions the existing legal human rights system does, those functions could be performed adequately by a system that does not feature individual rights, but relies only on (mere) duty norms.

### *Individual Rights as Nonpaternalistic Protectors of Interests*

In other words, I need to show that the prominent role accorded to individual legal rights in the existing system is justified. There are several reasons for preferring a system that has this feature. First, at least in the case of rights that can be wielded (invoked or waived) by the right-holder, rights-norms express a kind of respect for the individual as an autonomous agent, and the idea of human dignity, as James Griffin has emphasized, is historically associated with the capacity for autonomous agency.[23] In other words, rights that can be wielded by the individual provide protections, but in a nonpaternalistic way, because it is up to the individual to actuate the protections or not. This is an important advantage, if, as I have argued, one of the main functions of the system is to help ensure that all have the opportunity to *lead* a minimally good or decent life, what I have called the well-being function of the system. A system of legal norms could perhaps express a commitment to the idea that individuals are beings who are capable of autonomy without the norms being

---

[23] James Griffin, *On Human Rights* (New York: Oxford University Press, 2008) pp. 9–27.

formulated in terms of rights, but rights language is especially well-suited for this purpose.

## Individual Rights as Facilitating Efficient Fulfillment of Duties

Second, as I noted in chapter 2, considerations of efficiency also make individual legal rights attractive. If individuals have legal standing to press for the fulfillment of the correlative duties, then all that is required to prompt enforcement of the duties is a complaint by one individual.

## Individual Rights and Status Egalitarianism

There is a third and more important reason for assigning a prominent role to individual rights in the system: Doing so best serves the status egalitarian function. The public—indeed international—recognition of each individual's basic moral status is unambiguously affirmed by ascribing international legal rights to all. And given that the ascription of these rights to all occurs in a system that has the other status egalitarian features, any attempt by states to discriminate among different individuals as to the content or weight of the rights or as to the conditions of abrogation or any failure to make effective remedies for rights-violations available to all is prohibited. That is a very strong affirmation of equal basic status. A robustly egalitarian system of international legal rights of all individuals helps to affirm the equal basic moral status of all by creating a universal legal status that applies to all people everywhere.

It is perhaps true that in principle a system of international law could affirm everyone's equal basic status without including any individual rights norms, relying instead only on duty norms, so long as the duties were crafted in such a way as to require states to affirm and protect the equal basic moral status of all. But by assigning a prominent role to individual rights, the existing system affirms and protects equal basic status for all in the most transparent and direct way. By according a prominent role to individual legal rights, the existing international legal human rights system not only encourages states to act in ways that affirm and protect equal basic moral status, it also does so using norms that are themselves partly constitutive of that status in its most visible, public aspect.

## V. *Justifying the Status Egalitarian Element*

Justificatory arguments 1 and 2, when taken together with the three advantages of individual rights described at the end of the previous section, constitute a strong case for having a system of international individual legal rights that includes both rights designed to prevent the state from abusing its power and rights that require it to perform basic welfare state functions. It is perhaps not so obvious that they provide strong support for the status egalitarian function. In other words, it is not clear how the first two justifying arguments can support all of the status egalitarian elements I identified in chapter 2: the strong rights against discrimination on grounds of gender or race, the ascription of rights to all, with equal content and weight, nondiscrimination as to conditions of abrogation, and the requirement of equal access to remedies for rights-violations.

Similarly for the third argument. It is relatively uncontroversial to say that an international order that equips states with powers that allow them to harm those under their jurisdiction or to evade their responsibilities for performing basic welfare state functions is seriously flawed and that governments have an obligation to ensure that this order is modified to include a system of international legal human rights that reduces those risks. It is more problematic to claim that governments are obligated to support international legal human rights that require them also to eradicate all forms of private discrimination on grounds of gender or race. For one thing, it would be difficult to show that such discrimination is largely a result of features of the international order. Unless we are willing to undertake a significant revision of the existing system, then, it is necessary to justify the inclusion of the robust status egalitarian elements in the system, including the prohibitions on all forms of gender and racial discrimination, both private and public.

### *The Importance of Affirming and Protecting Equal Basic Status*

In brief, we need to determine whether achieving the social recognition of every person's basic equal status is of such importance that international law should be harnessed to help achieve it. There are two aspects to the question or rather two assertions to be evaluated. The first is an assertion about morality and may be called the Principle of Equal Status, which holds that all human individuals have the same—and important—basic moral status. The second is an assertion about the proper business of international law, namely, that it may be appropriately employed to help ensure that the equal basic moral status of all individuals is publicly affirmed and protected.

I believe that the Principle of Equal Status is correct, but I am not sure how to provide an argument to support it. A commitment to acknowledging equal basic status for all is so fundamental to my moral outlook that I worry that any other moral principle I might invoke to try to support it would be no more intuitively plausible and possibly less so. Further, because I believe that the Principle of Equal Status is a genuine moral principle and an extremely basic one, not merely a parochial preference, I see no reason why it should not be affirmed by every legal system, whether domestic, regional, or international. I suspect that most philosophers working on human rights do not deny that all individuals have equal basic moral status, but that some have serious reservations about the assertion that it is the proper business of international law to affirm and protect equal basic moral status. Nonetheless, let us consider both the Principle of Equal Status and the assertion that it is the proper business of international law to affirm it.

## The Principle of Equal Status

Consider first the Principle of Equal Status. Suppose, as seems to me to be reasonable, that the weight of historical experience concerning what often happens when people *are not* treated as having equal basic status is sufficient to create a presumption in favor of affirming and protecting equal basic status for all. Or, suppose that, independently of any such historical considerations, one simply finds it intuitively plausible that the default position should be a presumption of equality of basic status.

In either case, given the presumption of status egalitarianism, the burden of argument can be shifted: One can call attention to the fact that the supposed justifications for not treating everyone as having equal basic status seem to be uniformly defective. When justifications are given for discrimination against women or people of color, they always seem to rest either on factually false assumptions about the natural characteristics of the group in question (women by nature are less rational or intelligent than men, blacks by nature are not fully rational and less morally developed than whites, are better suited to menial jobs, etc.), or on implausible assumptions about which characteristics are determinative of basic status (e.g., that if A is somewhat less intelligent than B, then A is of an inferior basic status). If justifications for unequal basic status are defective in either or both of these ways, and if a presumption of equal status is reasonable, then an insistence that everyone be treated as if they had equal basic status is reasonable.

### Arguing for the Principle, Rather than Presuming It

No doubt some will regard the move of starting with a defeasible presumption of equal basic status as question-begging. They will hanker after an argument to show why everyone's equal basic status should be protected and affirmed that does not begin with a presumption of equality. They will demand support for the Principle of Equal Status itself. I am not certain that such an argument can be provided, though in a recent article I have tentatively attempted to provide it.[24] Without repeating the intricacies of that discussion, I will note that the success of an argument for the Principle of Equal Status depends not only on being able to show that all people possess some characteristic or capacity that confers a high moral standing. It is also necessary to explain why those who have that characteristic to a higher degree do not have a higher moral status. In other words, it is necessary to make a convincing case that basic status is a threshold (not a scalar) concept *and* to give a cogent account of location of the threshold that yields the intuitively rights result, that is, the conclusion that all humans, or at least all humans who are not seriously deficient in the characteristic or capacity in question, lie at or above the threshold.

---

[24] Allen Buchanan, "Moral Status and Human Enhancement," *Philosophy & Public Affairs* 37:4 (2009): 346–81.

In my judgment, the most likely candidate for a feature that exhibits the required threshold effect and makes sense of the idea that those at or above the threshold all deserve a special sort of moral standing is *the capacity for responsiveness to reasons*—the ability to give and take reasons for or against various actions and practical stances, reasons that are interpersonally accessible. To put the same point in somewhat different terms: what matters for basic status is whether one has the capacity for participating in practices involving rational accountability. The idea, roughly, is that if one has the capacity to engage with others as members of a community of beings who are responsive to reasons, then one has an especially important moral status, the same moral status as all others who have this capacity, regardless of whether some may be more adept at exercising this capacity. In Kantian terms, if one has this capacity at all, one is a moral subject, a being with moral duties, and it is the fact that one is a being with moral duties that makes one an object of morality in a very special sense: It confers the especially high moral standing that we assume human beings have vis-à-vis other beings in our world. In the same paper, I argue that attempts to understand basic moral status in terms of interests, as opposed to the capacity for responsiveness to reasons, cannot achieve a cogent explanation of a threshold; instead, they can only underwrite the idea of a gradient of moral standings.

Without in any way minimizing the difficulty of fleshing out such a broadly Kantian attempt to argue for The Principle of Equal Status that I tentatively endorsed in that work, I would like to point out that the problem of justifying a commitment to equal basic status for all is not in any way unique to the international legal human rights system. It is a problem for morality, as increasingly large numbers of human beings are coming to conceive morality. In other words, the commitment to equal basic moral status that I have argued is present in the international legal human rights system is not an anomaly. It is simply an expression of the increasing salience of an idea that is arguably one of the most momentous improvements in human morality, the abandonment of various forms of tribalism in favor of a genuinely cosmopolitan outlook.[25]

---

[25] Allen Buchanan, "Human Rights and Moral Progress," *Human Rights: The Hard Questions*, eds. Cindy Holder and David Reidy (Oxford: Oxford University Press, 2013).

It is all too obvious, of course that this Kantian understanding of the basis of equal basic moral status does not apply to all human individuals, but rather only to those who have some minimal cognitive skills. Yet some international legal human rights are ascribed to all human individuals. This fact is not damaging for the normative framework I am proposing. If one of the two main functions of the international legal human rights system is to require states to secure the basic well-being of all those human individuals under their jurisdiction, then this can be understood to apply to cognitively compromised individuals as well as the cognitively normal. Thus, in my view, the fact of severe cognitive impairment does not exclude an individual from protection by the system. In contrast, for theories like James Griffin's, which attempt to ground human rights solely on normative agency or autonomy, the implications are quite different. That sort of view excludes from the human rights domain all individuals that lack the capacity for normative agency or autonomy—at least if one assumes, as Griffin and other proponents of the Mirroring View do, that what is true about moral human rights constrains what sorts of international legal human rights there ought to be.

But what are we to make of the fact that the international legal human rights system ascribes robustly egalitarian status to all individuals? It seems to me that there are only two alternatives for those who subscribe to a Kantian understanding of equal basic moral status of the sort I favor. Either one must admit that the robust status egalitarian features of the system are a case of overreach—that the full panoply of status egalitarian features found in international human rights law should not in fact be extended to all human individuals, but only to those who have the capacities needed for equal basic moral status. Or, one must argue that those individuals who are so impaired as to lack equal basic moral status are so vulnerable, as regards the threats to their basic well-being, that the best course is for international human rights law to treat them as if they had equal basic moral status. In other words, even if, as I have argued, it is implausible to argue that the robust status egalitarian features of the system are needed to perform the basic well-being function in the case of cognitively normal individuals, one can make the case that they are needed in the case of severely impaired individuals. Given the neglect and abuse that severely cognitively impaired people have suffered and their limited ability to protect themselves, the latter alternative seems to me to be the more plausible. The central point here is that there can be a sound moral justification for according individuals equal status *in international law* even if some of them do not have full equal basic *moral* status, due to severe cognitive impairments. Just as we should not assume that legal rights must mirror moral rights, similarly, we should not assume that legal status must mirror moral status.

There is, of course, a more nuanced alternative—and in fact it has been advocated in the bioethics literature and put into effect in some countries. We can presumptively accord severely cognitively impaired individuals the same basic legal status as the rest of us but permit exceptional treatment of them, either as a matter of law or of less formal social practice, under certain extreme circumstances. For example, in the case of an individual who is wholly and permanently unconscious, we can allow termination of life support. The point is that a permanently unconscious individual is not capable of well-being, at least well-being of the sort that we aim to protect through the implementation of legal human rights. For such individuals, the argument that according full equal legal status to severely impaired individuals is needed to ensure their well-being is adequately protected no longer applies.

## Equal Basic Status and the Proper Functions of International Law

As I already indicated, my surmise is that philosophers who advocate expunging or toning down the robust status egalitarianism of the international legal human rights system do not reject *moral* status egalitarianism—they endorse the principle that all human beings (or, on some variants, all persons) have an equal basic moral status. Instead, they take exception to the idea that it is the proper business of international human rights law, and the practice built upon it, to affirm equal basic status as robustly as it does. In particular, they may be doubtful, as Beitz is, that the system should include strong rights against discrimination on grounds of gender. So now, while fully acknowledging the inconclusive character of my discussion of the Principle of Equal Status, let us ask whether it is the proper business of international law, and in particular international human rights law, to affirm equal basic moral status for all. Notice that this way of formulating the matter leaves it open as to whether the principle of equal basic status is correct or whether, even if it is not, there are good reasons to treat everyone *as if* they had the same basic moral status.

### Worries About the Feasibility of Affirming Equal Basic Status in International Law

We can begin with what some, including Beitz, apparently find to be the most problematic robust egalitarian element of the system, strong rights against discrimination on grounds of gender. Beitz thinks that these rights are a "hard case"—that is, he doubts that they are genuine human rights, by which I take him to mean that he has serious reservations as to whether they should be included in the system of international legal human rights. Before examining this worry, I simply wish to note that international human rights law is equally as prohibitive of all forms of racial discrimination. It is difficult to imagine why one would think that it is appropriate for international law to include prohibitions of one sort of discrimination but not the other. Yet those, like Beitz, who have questioned whether international legal human rights should prohibit all forms of gender discrimination have not voiced a similar concern about rights against racial discrimination.

Beitz thinks that something should be an international legal human right only if the violation of it is properly a matter of international concern. He apparently thinks that a necessary condition for something being a matter of international concern is that there must be some effective way for states or international organizations or some other sort of external agent to exert pressure on a state that violates the right. He doubts that this is possible in the case of strong rights against discrimination on grounds of gender, for two reasons: First, he thinks that there is insufficient knowledge as to how to alter the deeply-engrained patterns of discrimination that exist in some societies, and second, he also seems to doubt the effectiveness of external efforts to change these patterns (perhaps because of the lack of knowledge of how to do so, but also perhaps simply due to how well-established they are).[26]

---

[26] See Charles Beitz, *The Idea of Human Rights* (New York: Oxford University Press, 2011) pp. 187–96 for his views on women's human rights.

Kristen Hessler has shown that Beitz underestimates both the extent of our knowledge about how to achieve a reduction in gender discrimination and the effectiveness of external pressure on states where such discrimination exists, when this pressure is properly integrated with indigenous activism.[27] She also points out that Beitz's argument yields unacceptable results: The same deeply-engrained social practices and attitudes that make it difficult to end discrimination against women in employment (something ruled out by the strong antidiscrimination rights in existing international human rights law) also contribute to violations of their most basic legal human rights, including the right against arbitrary deprivation of life. (That is, in some societies, honor killings or lethal abuse of women by their spouses may be just as entrenched in sexist social practices and value systems as unequal pay for equal work.) So, if strong rights against discrimination on grounds of gender are not suitably included among the international legal human rights because certain attitudes toward women are deeply engrained and recalcitrant to effect pressures from external agents, then neither is the right against arbitrary deprivation of life. Like Hessler, I take this to be a reductio of Beitz's view. His reflections on the difficulty of ending gender discrimination, then, do not give us reason to conclude that even though equal basic moral status is a valid moral principle, it should not be taken seriously in international legal human rights law.

## Is the Affirmation of Equal Basic Status in International Law Intolerant?

Some who may believe that equal basic status is a sound moral principle reject the status egalitarianism of international human rights law for a different reason. On their view, it is justifiable and commendable to have an international legal human rights system, to require all states to recognize for all a set of rights that provide important protections of basic interests all humans tend to have. But, they say, international legal norms requiring strong rights against gender discrimination, and perhaps the other status egalitarian features of

[27] Kristen Hessler, "Hard Cases: Public Health and Women's Human Rights," talk delivered at Duke University Trent Center for Bioethics, April 14, 2011.

existing human rights law as well, exhibit the vice of intolerance, at least from a liberal point of view.[28] In other words, they believe that the well-being function is within the bounds of tolerance but that the status egalitarian function is not. They think that liberal toleration requires refraining from imposing principles on people that are contrary to their moral views, so long as the latter are "reasonable" or at least "not unreasonable." And they apparently think that moral views that condone gender discrimination and other forms of inequality that are incompatible with the robust status egalitarianism of international legal human rights are reasonable or at least not unreasonable.

I doubt that this is a stable position. What is the principled reason for maintaining that it is *not* intolerant to require all states to accord all those under their jurisdiction the same set of rights—where this means recognizing that everyone's basic interests are worthy of serious protection—but that it *is* intolerant to require all states to provide equal protection of those same basic interests by including provisions to ensure that the rights in question have the same scope and weight and that effective remedies are available for all? Where is a principled line to be drawn between those inequalities that must be tolerated and those that must not? And if tolerance does not bar the international legal human rights system from requiring the other status egalitarian features—equal content and weight, equal conditions of derogation, and effective remedies for all—why does it preclude strong rights against gender discrimination?

It seems to me, then, that the intolerance objector faces a painful dilemma: He must either reject as intolerant all the status egalitarian elements of the international legal human rights system, not just the strong rights against gender discrimination, and assert that it is intolerant for international law to prohibit states from using domestic law to assign systematic inequalities in status that are far more serious than violations of strong rights against gender discrimination; or he must abandon his allegation that it is intolerant to include strong rights against gender discrimination in international human rights law. I do not see how he can draw a principled line that rejects

---

[28] John Rawls, *The Law of Peoples* (Cambridge, MA: Harvard University Press, 2001). Joshua Cohen, "Minimalism About Human Rights: The Most We Can Hope For?" *Journal of Political Philosophy*, 12:2 (2004): 190–213.

strong rights against gender discrimination as intolerant and at the same time hold that it is not intolerant for international law to require that all states affirm the other elements of equal status—to require that they respect the same set of rights for all, with the same scope and weight, not discriminate as to the conditions of abrogation, and provide effective remedies for all.

If the intolerance objector bites the bullet and says that tolerance forbids including any of the status egalitarian features, then he is advocating a truly radical revision of international human rights law that amounts to eviscerating it. He is also committing himself to the repugnant view that tolerance requires not using international law to prevent domestic law from supporting caste systems or their moral equivalents—forms of society in which all have the same basic rights formally speaking, but in which the scope and weight of rights, the conditions of abrogation, and the availability of remedies for violations of them vary systematically among individuals, depending on which groups they belong to.

There is another, even more serious objection to the intolerance view. Elsewhere I have argued in detail that the understanding of tolerance that leads to such a radical conclusion is highly implausible, in part because it treats as reasonable, or at least as not unreasonable, moral views that assign inferior statuses to women or people of color on the basis of patently false factual beliefs—beliefs about supposed natural differences among different groups of human beings that do not stand up to empirical scrutiny.[29] Tolerance is an important virtue, perhaps especially so from the standpoint of a broadly liberal perspective. But from a liberal perspective, tolerance is at bottom a matter of showing respect for individual human beings, considered as moral equals—as beings who are capable of being responsive to reasons but also prone to differences in what they value. It is not tolerance, but rather exaggerated humility,

---

[29] Rawls tries to use the notion of a cooperative scheme, as opposed to a form of society based on force, to draw a principled line as to what ought to be tolerated. I argue that this strategy fails—that the idea of a cooperative scheme cannot show why human rights, as they operate in the Practice, should be restricted to the very lean list of rights Rawls endorses. Allen Buchanan, "Taking the Human Out of Human Rights," pp. 37–48 and "Justice, Legitimacy, and Human Rights," pp. 22–26, both in *Human Rights, Legitimacy, and the Use of Force* (New York: Oxford University Press, 2010).

to refuse to employ as potentially powerful an instrument as international law to support the public acknowledgment of equal basic status and to help dismantle legal orders and social practices that relegate some human beings lesser status on the spurious grounds that they are naturally inferior.[30] The problem with a conception of tolerance that rules out affirmation of equal basic status as a function for international human rights law is that, by ignoring the most basic epistemic standards for what counts as a not unreasonable moral view, it confuses exaggerated humility with tolerance. Respecting persons does not require caving in to discrimination based on gross factual errors about natural differences among human beings. At this point in human history, given the damage that has been done by such views, and given the increasing availability of knowledge to debunk them, tolerance does not require caving in to them.

### Intrasocietal or Global Equal Basic Status?

There is a profound ambiguity in the assertion that the international legal human rights system is designed in part to affirm and protect equal basic status for all. This assertion admits of an intrasocietal or a global interpretation. On the former, the commitment is to affirming and protecting each person's equal status *within his or her own society*, that is, vis-à-vis other members of that society; on the latter, the commitment is more ambitious: to affirm and protect the equal status of each human being vis-à-vis all other human beings.[31] My surmise is that the current international legal system, with its primary emphasis on setting standards for how

[30] Thus far, I have only argued that there is a strong case for international human rights law affirming and protecting equal basic status for all who have the characteristics that confer equal status. Some human beings, however, permanently lack the capacity for responsiveness to reasons; yet they are accorded rights under international human rights law. This latter fact is not as embarrassing to my view as it is for those who think that international legal human rights should mirror moral human rights. On my view, international human rights law is an instrument that can rightly serve a number of moral purposes. This leaves room for the possibility that extending some international legal human rights (e.g., the right against torture and against arbitrary deprivation of life) to human beings who lack the capacity necessary for equal basic moral status is morally justifiable.

[31] I thank Julian Culp for pressing me to explore this ambiguity.

each state should treat those under its jurisdiction, focuses on intrasocietal equal basic status so far as its ascription of determinate duties to states is concerned.

Of course, there is one sense in which the system does address basic equal status on a global basis: It ascribes international legal rights to all human beings and, so far as they all have these legal rights, they have an equal legal status under international law. But there is one important respect in which the system does not affirm equal basic status in a global sense: There are no analogs, at the level of global governance institutions, of the rights of citizenship that the system confers at the domestic level. If, under modern conditions, exclusion from meaningful participation in domestic governance institutions is incompatible with equal basic moral status, then it is hard to see how similar exclusion from global governance institutions is morally acceptable. As global governance institutions become more powerful, the fact that most of the world's population has little opportunity for occupying important roles within them or exerting significant control over those who occupy these roles will increasingly expose the limitations of existing international human rights law as a means of affirming equal basic moral status at the global level.

Even if the existing international legal system is designed only to affirm and protect intrasocietal, rather than global equal basic status, the best understanding of the moral basis for the system points in the direction of a commitment to securing global equal basic status. In the final chapter, I will begin to explore the meaning of global equal basic status and try to determine whether existing international law has the resources to extend the affirmation of equal basic status to the global level.

## VI. *Countervailing Considerations*

So far, I have set out three distinct justifications for an international legal human rights system: One that appeals to the benefits of such a system, one that shows that the existing international order is unjustifiable in the absence of such a system, and one that shows that states and their governments have a special obligation to create and sustain such a system. I have also explained why it is appropriate that the system accord such a prominent role to individual legal rights. I have thus taken the first step toward answering what may be the most neglected question in current philosophical theorizing about human rights, the most general justification question: Why have a system of international legal human rights? I have also provided the initial materials for the first step in answering the question of whether the *existing* international legal human rights system is justified by showing that, to some extent at least, it performs these valuable functions and provides significant resources for remedying some of the most serious flaws of the international order.

The combined weight of these arguments only makes a prima facie case for the international legal human rights system, however.[32] One must consider the other side of the ledger: the considerations against having such a system. Even those who are impressed by the three justificatory arguments set out above might conclude that, *in the case of the existing system of international legal human rights—* whatever may be the case for a more ideal system—the negatives outweigh the positives.

There are four main objections to having an international legal system of human rights similar to the one that now exists: (i) given the great disparity of power among states, such a system is too prone to abuse by the most powerful states, who will use feigned concern for human rights to pursue their geo-political and economic ends (the Inevitable Abuse Objection); (ii) the institutions through which the system is implemented are illegitimate (The Legitimacy Objection); (iii) such a system unjustifiably intrudes on collective political self-determination, either at the level of states or for groups within states (the Self-determination Objection); (iv) a system of individual rights is incompatible with a proper appreciation of the fact that there is a plurality of reasonable or valid moralities, some of which are "collectivistic" in nature and which cannot accommodate the individualism which a system of individual rights presupposes (the Reasonable Ethical Pluralism Objection). Chapters 5 and 6 address objections (ii) and (iiii) respectively; chapter 7 takes up objection (iv).

---

[32] Nor does it show that having a system of international legal rights is the *only* way to achieve all of these benefits. That would be an excessively strong requirement for the system being justified.

*Human Rights Law as a Weapon of the Powerful*

Here I will only respond in a preliminary way to (i), the Inevitable Abuse Objection. It claims that the value of a system of international legal human rights is undercut, in our world, by the great disparity of power among states and the fact that states tend to pursue their own perceived interest. In such a world, international legal human rights become weapons for the powerful to prey on weak states or levers to manipulate them. There are several replies to this objection, the most important of which I will only outline here. In the concluding chapter, after my view of the system of international legal rights and its limitations is on the table, I will return to this issue.

First, one can reject the increasingly discredited extreme Realist view of world politics that the Inevitable Abuse Objection assumes. Liberal theorists of international relations have marshaled impressive evidence that liberal democratic states do not behave in the ways extreme Realists assume all states do. In particular, they show that in liberal democratic states domestic groups do care about human rights, not just their states' interests narrowly defined, and that these groups exert influence on state policy accordingly.[33] Since some of the most powerful states are liberal, this significantly limits the risk of abuse.

Second, one can argue that even though powerful states sometimes use international legal human rights as weapons or levers in the pursuit of their own interests, their capacity for predation would be even greater if there were no international legal human rights system. In other words, the very power asymmetry that creates opportunities for abuses of the system would be even more dangerous if the system did not exist. As a generalization, it seems fair to say that power unrestrained by law is more dangerous than power restrained by law, at least if the content of the law is not too morally flawed. Even though powerful states can sometimes evade the constraints of international human rights law and sometimes appeal to it to further their own ends at the expense of human rights, the system does place some constraints on their propensity to behave badly.

---

[33] For a concise discussion of liberal theories and their criticisms of Realism, see Buchanan, *Justice, Legitimacy, and Self-Determination*, pp. 31–45.

It is true that some states have used their own legal system to perpetrate great wrongs. But usually their abuses of the law have consisted of the systematic revocation of the legal rights of certain classes of individuals. In contrast, no individual state, no matter how powerful, is able unilaterally to revoke the international legal human rights of its citizens.[34] Indeed that is one important respect in which international human rights law is an improvement on domestic systems of rights.

Even when a government's abuse of the legal system is severe, the law still provides some constraints on the exercise of power. For example, Hitler and his henchman were masters at perverting the German legal system, but they nonetheless felt obliged to convey the appearance of legality and in doing so subjected their exercise of power to some constraints.[35] Similarly, even though the apartheid system was created by South African law, the legal system imposed some limitations on how the architects of apartheid could pursue their goals. In particular, the integrity of some judges, who refused to treat the law as a mere instrument of political power, was a thorn in the side of the apartheid regime.

I surmise that in the domestic case most people would prefer to have a legal system that included individual rights, even though they recognize that power asymmetries among members of society create the potential for abuses of it. That is, most of us think that the risk that the powerful will prey on the weak is less in the case of even a defective legal system than where there is no law. If that preference is reasonable, then it would be hard to make the case that the risk that powerful states will misuse the system of international legal rights is so great that the world is better off without the system, because the power asymmetries among states, and hence the potential for predation by the stronger in a lawless condition, are arguably as great if not greater than in the domestic case. I think it is much more likely that an extremely powerful state would perpetrate great wrongs simply by ignoring international human rights law than by manipulating it to its own advantage. To manipulate the system

---

[34] Human rights conventions, unlike some other types of treaties, typically cannot be repudiated at will.

[35] Richard J. Evans, *The Coming of the Third Reich* (London: Allen Lane, 2003).

effectively, one must act as if one takes it seriously and doing that inevitably means being constrained by it.

Even if the risk that powerful states will use human rights to dominate or manipulate other states is significant, the risk that states will abuse their own citizens is arguably greater, in particular because aggressive behavior toward foreigners is more likely to result in the formation of military alliances against it than domestic abuses are. As long as there are effective ways of limiting the potential for abuse of the system of international legal rights by powerful states, the risk that they will abuse it in their relations with other states may be a good bargain, if what we get in return is a system in which states publicly acknowledge that there are limitations on what a state may do to its own citizens, specified by global standards in the creation of which weak and powerful states participate.

Apparently, the representatives of weaker states who spear-headed the movement to create the founding document of the modern human rights era, the UDHR, thought that the risks that powerful states would manipulate international legal human rights for their own purposes were less serious than the risks of living in a world without international legal human rights. There is something to be said for the assumption that they were in a better position than any-body else to evaluate the relative risks that powerful states posed to weaker ones with or without a system of international legal human rights. The fact that powerful states were less than enthusiastic about the project of creating the UDHR suggests the same conclusion: If they thought that human rights law would be merely another tool with which they could pursue their own interests, they would have embraced it with relish.

Third, one can note that the seriousness of the threat that the system will be manipulated by powerful states depends upon how appeals to international legal human rights function in the larger in-ternational system. The greatest threat, presumably, is that powerful states will cite human rights violations in another country as a rea-son for military action against it for the purpose of advancing their own geo-political aims. How serious this risk is will depend upon the combined weight of the various constraints on military interven-tion that the larger system includes. An international system in which there are robust norms constraining military intervention will make it harder for powerful states to use the violation of international legal human rights as a pretext for aggression than one that lacks them. In the existing system, highly restrictive norms regarding the use of force, anchored in the UN Charter and the authority of the Security Council, place significant limits on the ability of powerful states to use human rights in predatory ways.

I do not pretend to have laid the Inevitable Abuse Objection fully to rest at this point. Remember, my ultimate goal in this book is not to provide a full justification for having a system of international legal rights similar to the existing one, but rather to make clear what all is involved in such a justification, to take the most important steps toward a full justification, and to show that there is good reason to think that a full justification is possible.

## *The Path-Dependent Character of Justification*

At this point, I want to emphasize a simple but powerful methodological point that strengthens the three prima facie justifications that I have advanced: Any attempt to justify the existing international legal human rights system (or a system similar to it) should take the historical context into account. In particular, justification should not proceed in a vacuum, ignoring the path the world has taken. In our world, the case for having an international legal human rights system like the one we have—a system that gives a prominent role to individual rights that serve to constrain sovereignty for the sake of individual welfare and equal basic status, and for which supremacy over domestic law is claimed—is greatly strengthened by four facts about the historical context. First, the notion of universal individual rights was already widely understood and had already proved politically effective in the democratic revolutions of the late eighteenth century and in the abolitionist and feminist movements of the nineteenth and early twentieth centuries; second, in a number of domestic constitutions, individual legal rights, typically justified on universalistic grounds, had already shown some efficacy in constraining state power and improving human lives; third, the interwar experiment of international recognition of group rights, conducted under the League of Nations, was judged to be a failure; and fourth, the notion of individual rights understandably seemed to be a powerful tool for repudiating the racial fascist ideology that had, in the eyes of many people, been responsible for the horrific destruction of World War II and the Holocaust, because it aptly expressed a rejection of two core elements of that ideology, the belief that the individual had value only so far as he contributed to the nation and the rejection of equal basic status for all human beings. In a different historical context, the case for creating a system of international law prominently featuring individual legal rights for all people might have been much weaker; but that does nothing to detract from the justification of the existing system, given its context.

The lesson here is that it is a mistake to be overly abstract in considering whether having a system of international legal human rights similar to the one we have is justified. When we situate the task of justification in its historical context, the system looks much more attractive than if we pose the question of justification abstractly. It might be the case that most or all of the seven benefits that the system of international legal human rights performs could *in principle* be achieved by a radically different system of law—for example, one that only imposed duties without recognizing rights, or which accorded more prominence to group rights than individual rights, or which relied on protecting individuals by recourse to domestic constitutional reforms without recourse to international law, or which utilized some other, nonlegal institutional means. Given the actual historical context, however, those possibilities do not undermine the case for the existing system.

Further, to justify this system, it is not even necessary to show that it is the *best* feasible system for performing these beneficial functions. A system of law may be worthy of our strong support, and the actions undertaken by its agents or others who seek to promote compliance with its norms may be justifiable, even if it is not optimal. This is especially true if the system in question demonstrates the capacity for significant improvement.

I believe this latter condition is satisfied in the case of the system of international legal human rights. To take only some of the most obvious improvements: It has become more politically effective over time (partly due to the emergence of powerful human rights NGOs), it has developed more adequate institutionalization, it has extended the commitment to equal basic status to include unambiguous and strong protections against both public and private discrimination on grounds of gender and race, and, through the addition of specialized treaties (such as the conventions of the rights of children, of migrants and their families, and of the disabled) it has done much to answer the perennial criticism that universal individual rights are too abstract to do the moral work they need to do.

One final methodological point: Showing that it is reasonable to support the system that already exists is an easier task than justifying the creation of such a system. If the system is functioning fairly well and the functions it is performing are laudable, if it is capable of improvement, and if the transition to an alternative system would be either risky or costly, then it may be rational and even morally obligatory to support it, even if it exhibits flaws that would be intolerable if one were creating a system from scratch.

## VII. *Must All States Participate?*

In this chapter so far, I have produced three arguments to justify having a system of international legal human rights similar to the existing one, identified possible countervailing considerations and begun to assess them. What I now want to emphasize is that the *weight* of these justificatory arguments can vary depending upon the nature of the state in question. If this is the case, then a general justificatory approach, which glosses over differences among types of states, will only take us so far.

Clearly the magnitude of the seven benefits listed under justificatory argument 1 will vary across states. For example, some states may be quite legitimate without participation in the system of international legal human rights (consider, for example, Sweden). For states where the risk that the domestic constitutional arrangements will fail to protect human rights are lower, the value of the backup function served by the international legal human rights system will be correspondingly less.

It might be thought that the situation is different with respect to argument 2 (according to which an international legal human rights system is needed to make the international order justifiable by mitigating the risks to people that its norms create) and argument 3 (according to which states and governments have a special obligation to institute such a system of international legal human rights or support it where it exists, because they are the chief beneficiaries of an international order that is morally unjustifiable without it). These two justificatory arguments seem to apply equally to all states. As I have already noted, however, they too may carry more weight with respect to some states than others.

## Support Versus Participation

Notice, however, that the second and third arguments only establish the conclusion that states are obligated to *support* a system of international legal human rights, that is, to contribute to the establishment and maintenance of such a system. They do not show that every state has an obligation to *participate* in such a system, where this means ratifying its treaties and acknowledging the supremacy of international human rights law over their domestic law. To see why this is so, it is necessary to distinguish several types of states.

Let us use the label "Type A states" for states that have two characteristics: (1) they are *internally and externally rights-respecting*—they do an excellent job of realizing the rights of those under their jurisdiction and do not violate the rights of foreigners—and (2) they achieve this without participating in an international legal human rights system. Presumably, Type A states have an obligation to participate in the international legal human rights system only if their nonparticipation would be damaging to the efficacy of the system. According to the three justifying arguments above, Type A states, like other states, have an obligation to support a system of international legal human rights, but there are various ways they can fullfil this obligation without themselves participating, so long as their lack of participation does not undermine the system. For example, they can contribute funds and expertise to international human rights institutions.

Now consider two sub-types both of which have both of the features of Type A states, but which differ in this respect: for Type A1 states, whether they participate in the international legal human rights system makes a difference as to the success of the system; in contrast, Type A2 states are not very influential, so whether they participate or not makes no significant difference to the success of the system. It would seem that while Type A1 states have an obligation not just to support the international legal human rights system, but also to participate in it, Type A2 states only have an obligation to support, but not to participate.

The United States does a comparatively good job though very far from a perfect job of realizing human rights internally, but it has a much less admirable record in its treatment of foreigners, especially in its almost ceaseless military interventions and its covert activities in support of or against various governments.[36] Moreover, it is so influential that were it to abstain completely from participating in the international legal human rights system, this might well have serious effects. So, it appears that it has an obligation not just to support the system, but also to participate in it.

It is worth pointing out that the clearest examples of states that respect the rights of foreigners as well as those of their own citizens and that are not very influential when it comes to the success of the international human rights endeavor, tend not to be *self-sufficient* with respect to human rights protection. They are participants in the supranational European legal human rights system.

Consider a hypothetical case of a human rights-self-sufficient Type A2 state that is a modification of an actual one: Think of Denmark as it is, except assume that it does not participate in the international legal human rights system or the European human rights system. Suppose that is, that this country is doing very well in respecting human rights, internally and externally, by relying only on its own legal system, without incorporating in it any supranational human rights law, and that it is not so influential that its nonparticipation impairs either system. Call this country Denmark 2. Why should it participate in either the international legal human rights system or the European system (as opposed to merely supporting it)?

## Why Support Is Insufficient

There are at least two reasons why a country like Denmark 2 should participate in some supranational legal human rights system. First, doing so "locks in" the admirable human rights protections it already has; in other words, participation is a kind of self-binding mechanism. The fact that it is widely held that human rights treaties cannot be exited unilaterally facilitates their self-binding function. The

[36] There are at least two areas in which the domestic human rights record of the United States is, in my judgement, disgraceful. The first is in the mass incarceration of people of color in the war on drugs; the second is the treatment of migrants illegally crossing the southern border.

locking-in function of participation is important, because one should not assume that the social, cultural, and economic conditions that currently result in strong support for the domestic system of rights will persist indefinitely. Second, participation exhibits an admirable commitment to the principle that a party to a dispute should not be the final judge in its own case. This principle of impartiality, which is arguably an important constituent of the ideal of the rule of law, is especially compelling in the case of disputes over very important matters, including human rights.

Abiding by this principle of impartiality is of great important in situations where there are allegations that a state's behavior has negatively impacted the human rights of foreigners. As I have already noted, the case of the United States clearly illustrates the sad truth that a state that generally does a creditable job of respecting human rights at home can go seriously astray in its actions beyond its own borders (or in its treatment of noncitizens within its borders). This risk is exacerbated if the state can rest assured that it is accountable to no one for its judgment that it is not violating human rights. Instead of exacerbating the risk, the state can reduce it by refusing to insist that it is the final judge of whether it is violating human rights and instead acknowledging the supremacy of international human rights law, where this means subjecting itself to the judgment of bodies that are not subordinate to it.

Extremely powerful states are more likely to be able to engage in actions that can seriously impact the human rights of foreigners; and because they are powerful they are less vulnerable to retaliation and sanctions, and are better able to weather adverse reputational effects, at least in matters in which they see themselves having an important interest. Consequently, such states are especially in need of a form of self-binding that make them accountable to someone other than themselves. So powerful states have especially weighty reasons to participate in the international legal human rights system, and this is true even if, as in the case of the United States, they have highly developed legal systems and generally do a good job of protecting human rights internally.

## The Implausibility of Exceptionalism

At this point, some American politicians and constitutional lawyers would protest that my argument overlooks an important fact: The legal institutions of the United States are much more highly-developed and trustworthy from the standpoint of protecting individual rights than international legal human rights institutions, and American Constitutional law is a far superior resource for properly determining the scope of individual rights than the vagaries of international law. Why, they ask, should a country like the United States embrace an inferior system for the protection of human rights? The principle that one should not be the final judge in one's own case is not absolute. In this case it is outweighed by the fact that the alternative is reliance on inferior institutions, institutions that are themselves defective from the standpoint of the ideal of the rule of law.

The obvious difficulty with this reply is that it ignores what I have emphasized, namely, the fact that despite its virtues, the American legal system has often not done a good job of protecting the rights of foreigners. Further, its record in protecting the rights of those under its jurisdiction is far from perfect. As noted earlier, like other countries, it continues to fail to provide equal protection to certain minorities and in times of perceived national security crises has a tendency to give short shrift to the rights of citizens generally. So, it, too, needs the backup supplied by international legal human rights. Further, because the United States is so influential, its participation is important for the success of the system as a whole.

Given the strength of the case for its participation, the appropriate response to the undeniable flaws of the international legal human rights system is for the United States to direct its efforts toward helping remedy them, not to refrain from participating. Alternatively, it could invest more heavily in improving the institutional resources of the regional human rights system in which it now participates (though rather less than whole-heartedly) with other Western Hemisphere states. The only alternatives are not being the ultimate judge in one's own case, on the one hand, or relying on inferior supranational institutions, on the other. Instead of using the weakness of regional or international human rights institutions as a reason for not fully participating in them, the United States should invest more heavily in their improvement.

There is one final reason why it would be especially problematic for a very powerful country merely to support the international legal human rights system without being a participant in it, where this means acknowledging the supremacy of international human rights law. As I have already emphasized, there are extreme disparities of power among states and quite predictably this produces serious injustices. The most powerful states are able to shape the rules of the international order to their advantage, at the expense of less powerful states and their populations. The result is unfair trade, financial, and intellectual property rights regimes. In such a situation, for the most powerful states to support a system of international human rights law that they expect others to participate fully in, while not recognizing its authority over themselves, would give a very strong signal that they do not take seriously the unjust inequalities of the international order and that they reject the idea that international law should apply equally to all states.

In the final chapter I will make a stronger point: To the extent that it is feasible, the international legal human rights system can be and should be harnessed to a goal that goes beyond merely regulating the behavior of states toward those under their jurisdiction; it should also become an instrument for mitigating the structural injustices of the international order. To make headway on this additional goal, the full participation of the most powerful states will obviously be necessary.

The reflections of this last section are not intended to establish conclusively that every state has an obligation to participate in an international or regional legal human rights regime. The primary goal was to provide justifications for having an international (or at least supranational) legal human rights regime. Yet these arguments also make a strong case for the conclusion that at least the vast majority of states, and especially the more powerful ones, have an obligation to participate in such a system.

## International or Regional?

Before proceeding to the task of showing how to justify the inclusion of various particular rights in a system of international legal human rights that has the main features of the existing system, I want to suggest why it is important to have an international legal human rights system, rather than relying solely on regional systems. The point is not that there should be one type of system or the other, but not both. Instead, it is that there are strong reasons to have an international system, even if it is true that the best arrangement is to also have regional systems.

There are two chief advantages of having an international system. First, an international system manifestly and publicly embodies the idea that how a state treats those under its jurisdiction is the legitimate concern of all states and indeed of all people, not just those that happened to be in some particular region. Second, an international system not only enables its human rights law to serve as a focus for mobilizing the widest possible range of actors for the sake of realizing human rights.

In chapter 7 I will take up the Ethical Pluralist Challenge, which denies that the international legal human rights system does or could be an instrument for pursuing universal values. If that objection were sound—and I shall argue that it is not—then, at most the justifications I have articulated so far would only extend, at most, to more limited supranational human rights system, not to an international one. Different regional systems might aptly embody values that are predominant in their regions, but there could be no international system embodying universal values.

## VIII. *Justifying Particular Rights for Inclusion in the System*

Having presented arguments in support of having a system of international legal human rights like the existing one, I turn now to the application of the pluralistic methodology I have been advocating to the task of justifying the inclusion of particular rights in such a system. My aim is not to provide a full justification for the rights included in the existing international legal human rights system. I doubt that this can be done, because I suspect that there are some cases of rights inflation. Indeed, given the messy and relatively undisciplined nature of the process by which human rights treaties are created, it would be surprising if that were not the case. Furthermore, if, as I have argued, one of the chief functions of the system is to ensure that states perform basic welfare functions, but the system lacks the doctrinal or institutional resources to do much to specify what this encompasses, then there will be opportunities for rights inflation. Those devising human rights treaties may be tempted to include rights that would make more sense if the goal were to ensure maximal human flourishing rather than to ensure that all have the opportunity to lead a minimally good or decent life.

Nor will I attempt to provide a conclusive, fully fleshed-out justification for any of the particular international legal rights I consider. My goal is much more modest: to reinforce my case for a pluralistic justificatory strategy by showing that adequate justifications can be given for rights from each of the major categories of international legal human rights without appealing to a list of antecedently-existing moral human rights. This more modest goal is appropriate, given that my chief aim in this book is not to produce a moral theory of international legal human rights, but to make some progress on laying out the options for how to engage in theorizing them. In the end, it may turn out that even if an *adequate* justification for many of the items included in the existing system of international legal human rights can be given without relying on premises about moral human rights, the *best* justification will ground at least some international legal human rights on corresponding moral human rights or on some moral rights or other.

The categories of international legal human rights I consider are (1) civil rights (in particular, rights of due process and equality before the law); (2) social and economic rights (in particular, the rights to health and to a basic education); (3) political rights (in particular, the right to democratic governance); and (4) economic liberties (rights to engage in economic activities without undue interference by private or public actors). In doing so I will cover more thoroughly some of the ground traversed in chapter 2, when I made the case that appealing to corresponding moral rights is neither necessary nor sufficient for justifying legal rights.

## Rights to Due Process and Equality Before the Law

This category encompasses a number of rights that both protect individuals from abuses of the legal system (the protective function) and make the legal system an effective resource for them to deploy in pursuing their legitimate interests (the facilitative function). It includes, but is not limited to the right to be apprised of the charges against one in criminal proceedings, the right to a fair trial, the right to legal counsel and representation, and the right to equal access to legal remedies for violations of rights. In light of the justificatory arguments for having a system of international legal rights set out in part III, there is a strong case for including these rights in such a system. Given the importance that these rights generally have for individuals, it is beneficial to enact them in a system of law that is independent of the domestic system and can provide backup for it. Affirming these rights in international law makes sense, in other words, because of the obvious drawbacks of relying exclusively on one's own legal system to ensure that it is not abused and that its resources can be effectively utilized by all.

Including rights of this sort in the system of international legal human rights serves both of the chief functions noted above: It helps to ensure that all individuals have the opportunity to lead a minimally good or decent life (the well-being function) by protecting them against abuses of the legal order and helping to ensure that all are able to utilize the law as a resource for the pursuit of their legitimate interests; and, because these rights are ascribed equally to all, with equal weight and content for all, are subject to the same conditions of derogation for all, and are accompanied by equal rights to remedies for their violation, it affirms and protects equal basic status (the status egalitarian function). This same form of justification, which, I would emphasize, is a type of moral-individualistic justification, can be used to justify the inclusion of many rights, from a number of different categories, in the system of international legal human rights, as the following further illustrative cases show.

Before proceeding to examples from other classes of rights, I should emphasize that nothing I have said implies that there is no moral right to due process. There may well be; but if there is, it has a much more limited content than that ascribed to the legal right that goes under that label. The moral right has a much less demanding set of corresponding duties, because the demanding set of duties we ordinarily associate with the legal right to due process are simply not justifiable from a standpoint that grounds duties solely in morally important aspects of the individual right-holder.

## The Right to Education

In domestic legal systems and in the international system of legal human rights, the right to education is usually understood to be a legal entitlement to basic education. Basic education, in the modern context, is understood to include a package of services and opportunities designed to produce the most important bodies of knowledge and skills for acquiring knowledge, given the demands of modern society. The institutional investment required for realizing the right to education thus understood is enormous. Educational institutions must be developed, monitored, sustained, and modified over time so as to ensure that the basic education provided is suitable, given the changing demands of an evolving economy. This would be true even if (as is now virtually nowhere the case) most basic education were exclusively private. To ensure that private education is adequate, a good deal of social investment and government oversight and regulation is necessary. In addition, there would still be a significant role for government investment in the educational research needed to ensure that the requirements that private providers of education must meet are up-to-date. Here, as with the other rights already considered, there is no prospect of justifying the inclusion of this right in a system of legal rights if we are limited to strictly subject-grounded modes of justification. But because the duties that correspond to moral rights are directed, morally owed to the right-holder, the justification of the duties must be solely subject-grounded. The legal right to basic education does not suffer this limitation. In addition to the benefits to the individual right-holder, it is legitimate to appeal to broader social benefits in making the case for this right. Among other things, having an educated citizenry contributes to economic productivity, which in turn can raise the standard of living, and it is also valuable from the standpoint of deliberative democracy. The importance of any particular citizen being educated does not lie solely or even mainly in how being educated benefits him. This is not to deny that a legal entitlement to basic education is extremely important from the standpoint of the individual right-holder; it is only to emphasize that to justify a legal right to basic education one can and should appeal to much more than that.

From the perspective of helping to ensure that all have the opportunity to lead a minimally good or decent life alone, the case for a legal right to basic education is strong, and the arguments offered in part III show why there are important advantages in including such a right in a system of international law, rather than relying only on domestic legalization. The point is that we can justify a legal right with much more extensive correlative duties if we can appeal to the importance of helping to ensure the opportunity for a minimally good or decent life for large numbers of individuals.

One might also argue, however, that under the condition of a modern economy, individuals who do not have a basic education are at risk for being relegated to a position of inferiority and that therefore this right is also justifiable from the standpoint of the status egalitarian component. However, the importance of basic education for being able to lead a minimally good or decent life (under modern conditions) is sufficient in itself to justify the inclusion of this right in a list of international legal human rights.

## *The Right to Health*

In a much earlier paper, I argued in detail that it is a mistake to think that the case for a legal entitlement to healthcare depends upon the existence of a moral right to healthcare.[37] In chapter 2 I began to extend that point to a right to health, understood as including access to healthcare but also the provision of other conditions that are important for health, such as public health measures. Here I want to elaborate that argument.

Suppose, as some have argued, that there is no moral right to health (or healthcare) but instead there is a moral duty of beneficence that encompasses providing assistance to those in ill health and doing something to prevent ill health. In traditional terms, we can say that there is no perfect duty to contribute to the health of others (no duty that is the correlative of a claim-right), only an imperfect duty.

A person who seeks to act conscientiously to fulfill her imperfect duties of beneficence will care about the effectiveness of her efforts. And even if she is not obligated to help all in need, she will be concerned about all who are in need and will prefer ways of discharging her duties of beneficence that contribute to ensuring that all who are in need are helped. She will also recognize that in many cases the effectiveness of giving is subject to threshold effects or to economies of scale. When the well-being of individuals depends upon a massive collective enterprise (such as medical research or public

---

[37] Allen Buchanan, "The Right to a 'Decent Minimum' of Health Care," *Philosophy & Public Affairs* 13:1 (1983): 55–78.

health measures), success will not be achieved unless a certain threshold of contributions is met. Hence the conscientious person of beneficence will wish to avoid contributing to projects that may fail to reach the threshold of resources needed for success. In other cases, even if smaller scale endeavors will have some effect, a more ambitious effort will be much more effective, due to economies of scale. Hence the conscientious person of beneficence will be sensitive to the fact that the greatest benefits may not be achievable by individual or small scale group giving. In both cases, such a person will care about how she discharges her duties of beneficence. She will also understand that if beneficence is not coordinated, there will likely be both gaps and redundancies: Lack of coordination will result in less than optimal beneficence. If she is both conscientious and rational, she will come to the conclusion that an institutional approach to beneficence, rather than purely individual efforts, will be morally better.

Thus, even if there is no individual moral right to health (or, more generally, to beneficence), there is a strong case for having institutions that can achieve coordinated, efficient efforts to ensure that all have access to the most important conditions that affect health, so far as these are properly subject to social control. Under modern conditions, the state is the only institution capable of playing this role in a comprehensive way while at the same time ensuring that the question of priorities in beneficence can be made subject to the most inclusive, democratic, public deliberation.

Having a legal entitlement to health has an additional advantage: If it is funded by a reasonable system of taxation, it can provide assurance to each citizen that all are bearing their fair share in achieving coordinated, effective beneficence. To summarize: Even from the standpoint of an imperfect duty of beneficence—and without the assumption that there is a corresponding moral right—the desirability of effective, coordinated beneficence and of a fair distribution of the burdens of providing it provide a strong argument for a legal entitlement to health.

The same sorts of considerations are also sufficient to ground many other social and economic rights. The modern welfare state can be seen as a device for achieving efficient, coordinated beneficence, for achieving a fair distribution of the costs of doing so, and, to the extent that it is democratic, for providing a public forum in which informed, rational deliberation about the priorities among human needs and the best means of responding to them can occur. International human rights law that includes social and economic rights can then serve the purpose of providing international support for state-centered, collective beneficence projects.

## The Right to Democratic Government

There are two quite different ways to argue for the legal right to democratic government, whether at the domestic or international level. One can argue, as I have already suggested, that, at least under modern conditions in which the state looms so large in human life, a proper public recognition of the equal basic moral status of all individuals requires that competent individuals are to have a legal entitlement to participate, as equals, in the most important processes by which the laws governing their life together are created.[38] Alternatively, one can argue that the secure realization of some other particular legal or moral right or rights requires a legal entitlement to equal participation. Although I think that the first argument is powerful if fleshed out properly, I will concentrate on a particular version of the second, because I think it relies on less controversial premises.

Thomas Christiano has advanced a forceful, empirically informed version of the second argument. He appeals to the best available comparative data to support the contention that a human right to equal political participation in democratic government—for brevity, a right to democracy—is justifiable because it is the most reliable way of securing the right to physical security. Christiano, like most other philosophers, does not distinguish clearly between legal and moral human rights, but what he says about his conception of a right indicates that he is talking about a moral human right to democracy.

For reasons already noted, I do not think his argument works for a moral right to democracy, if the right is construed as including not only the negative right not to be prevented from·voting or running for office, but also the battery of rights usually associated with democracy, including the rights to freedom of expression, association,

---

[38] Thomas Christiano, *The Rule of the Many* (Boulder, Colorado: Westview Press, 1996) and *The Constitution of Equality: Democratic Authority and Its Limits* (New York: Oxford University Press, 2008).

and assembly. Realizing these latter rights typically requires positive and quite extensive (and expensive) actions, not just refraining, on the part of the state. (For example, it may need to take actions on a wide front to ensure that unpopular minorities can effectively exercise their rights to freedom of expression, assembly, and association, and to prevent their being intimidated so that they refrain from voting.)

Quite apart from that, the right to democratic government presumably includes the right to free, fair, and reasonably efficient elections. To do this may be quite expensive. The difficulty is that the full range of duties whose realization is required cannot be grounded solely in any aspect of the individual right-holder, whether it be his will or interests or something else of moral significance.

I think the inadequacy of Christiano's argument is even clearer if we also include rights to access to media for getting one's political message across or rights to campaign funding. The point, which should be familiar by now, is that the right to democracy, understood in a suitably expansive way, entails very demanding duties that involve massive social investment in institutions, extensive limitations on the liberties of many individuals, and large-scale social practices which cannot be justified from the standpoint of a conception of rights that is solely subject-grounded. Christiano's argument cannot establish the existence of a moral right to democracy that has the content we would reasonably expect of a legal right to democracy, because such a legal right has corresponding duties that are more extensive (and expensive) than the duties that can be grounded exclusively in any morally important aspects of the particular right-holder.

Recall the difference between moral and legal rights I emphasized earlier: Legal rights can have much greater scope, that is, more extensive corresponding duties, because to justify having legal duties owed to individuals one may appeal to interests other than those of the right-holder. Keeping this difference between moral and legal rights clearly in view, one can modify Christiano's argument linking democracy and physical security rights as follows: Drawing on the empirical evidence he cites, one can argue that a domestic legal entitlement to democracy (understood to include at least the rights to vote and run for office, and the rights to freedom of association, assembly, and expression, along with provisions for free and fair elections, if not also the right to campaign funds and access to media) *for most citizens* is needed to secure domestic legal rights to physical security for all, but that a proper regard for equal basic status requires that this complex legal right be extended to all citizens. Next, one can argue, for reasons adduced in the preceding Section, that the best way to make a legal right to physical security secure and effective is to back it up with an international legal right to democracy.

At no point does one need to show that there is an antecedently existing moral right to democracy, in order to provide a "linkage" argument connecting legal rights to physical security to the legal right to democracy. That is a good thing if, as I have argued, there is no moral right to democracy of the scope that we reasonably expect of a legal right to democracy.

Notice that the style of argument I am advocating avoids another problem to which Christiano's argument is liable. His argument that the right to democratic government is necessary for securing rights to physical security depends on the empirical claim that everyone's physical security is better protected in societies with democratic governments. But that being the case is compatible with an adequate level of physical security for all being attained by a legal order in which *most*, but not all people have the right to equal participation in the basic political processes.

In other words, Christiano's argument trades on an equivocation: The 'right to democracy' can mean either a right to democratic political institutions or a right of all to participate as an equal in them. The instrumental argument from what tends to be required for physical security only establishes a right to democracy in the first sense. It only shows that everyone is entitled to live in a democratic state, not that everyone is entitled to participate as an equal in democratic processes.

What Christiano's version of the argument overlooks—and what renders it invalid—is the fact that the benefits of democracy for rights to physical security can be secured by arrangements that fall short of an equal right to political participation *for all*. This would be the case if the physical security interests of the majority who had the right to political participation were sufficiently congruent with those of the minority who did not have this right.

The fact that rights to physical security for all can be effectively realized without extending the right to democracy to all is no embarrassment for the style of argument I am advocating. On my view, all that is necessary to establish that there should be a legal entitlement to democracy for all is, first, a strong correlation between *widespread* equal participation and physical security and second, an additional premise to the effect that a proper regard for basic equal moral status makes it unacceptable to extend the right to equal participation to most while denying it to some. The reason that it would be unacceptable to restrict the right to political participation is that any basis that could be adduced for excluding some people while granting the right to others would be incompatible with a proper regard for the basic equal status of all. If, for example, women or people of color were excluded, this would, for obvious historical reasons, be unacceptable, independently of whether this restriction would make the right to physical security less effective for women and people of color. If, alternatively, only people whose IQs were in the top quintile were accorded a legal right to democratic participation, then those who were not granted the right could rightly complain that they were not being treated as having equal basic moral status, on the grounds that this sort of difference in intelligence is not an appropriate basis for such a momentous distinction in legal status as this.[39]

### Economic Liberties

James Nickel has rightly emphasized the importance of economic liberties for individual well-being and autonomy (and, one might add, for the flourishing and in some cases even the surivival of groups and communities as well).[40] International human rights law requires states to secure an impressive set of economic liberties for all individuals under their jurisdiction. It also includes economic rights (to primary education, to "social security" broadly construed, and to health) that serve to make the economic liberties effective—and to prevent the use of economic liberties by those who have access to resources from disadvantaging those who do not. Economic liberties in international human rights law include

---

[39] This argument is developed in more detail in Buchanan, "Moral Status and Human Enhancement."

[40] James Nickel, "Economic Liberties as Fundamental Freedoms," *Making Sense of Human Rights* (Malden, MA: Blackwell Publishing, 2007), pp. 123–36.

the right to own property (both individually and with others, where this is not restricted to personal (that is, nonproductive) property), equality before the law regarding the making and enforcement of contracts, the right to work, the right to choose an occupation, freedom from slavery and involuntary servitude, the right to form and join labor unions, and rights against gender and racial discrimination in all spheres of society, including commerce, where this encompasses the requirement of equal pay for equal work and nondiscrimination in access to loans.[41] Economic rights are valuable, but economic rights combined with economic liberties are better still. Similarly, economic liberties are important, but are likely to be effective for all only if they are accompanied by economic rights that equip individuals with the resources to use them effectively.

John Tomasi has rightly criticized theories of justice in the broadly Rawlsian tradition for giving short shrift to economic liberties,

---

[41] The UDHR, Article 13, affirms the "right to freedom movement and residence within the borders of each state" and "the right to leave any country, including [one's] . . . own." These rights prohibit one important restriction on effective economic activity, namely, barriers to freedom of movement to seek economic opportunities. In Article 16, the UDHR affirms "the right to own property alone as well as in association with others" and specifies that "no one shall be arbitrarily deprived of his property." These two rights are also obviously important for the ability to engage in economic activities. Article 22 of the UDHR forbids discrimination in payment, affirming "the right to equal pay for equal work." In Article 23 the UDHR affirms "the right to form and to join trade unions." The ICCPR, Article 8, forbids slavery and involuntary servitude, like the UDHR affirms freedom of movement (Article 12), and (Article 26) emphasizes equality before the law, not just in criminal proceedings, but across the board, where this extends to commercial contracts. The ICESCR (Article 6) affirms the right to work and to freedom of choice of occupation, the right to equal pay for equal work (Article 7), the right to nondiscrimination in advancement in employment (Article 7), and the right to form and join trade unions (Article 8). The Racism Convention and the Women's Convention emphasize that all international legal human rights are to be enjoyed equally by all persons, regardless of race or gender, and prohibit discrimination in any area of life, including private commercial activities. The Women's Convention (CEDAW), Article 11, after affirming the right to freedom of occupation, affirms "the right to promotion" and "the right to equal remuneration, including benefits, and to equal treatment in respect of work of equal value, as well as equality of treatment in the evaluation of the quality of work." Article 13 of CEDAW affirms the equal right of women "to bank loans, mortgages and other forms of financial credit." If there is a deficiency in international human rights law's protection of individuals' efforts to improve their lot by economic activity, it is the lack of explicit prohibitions on

noting that the only economic liberties recognized in Rawls's theory are the right to own personal property (not productive property), the right to choose an occupation, and the right against slavery and involuntary servitude.[42] Tomasi's criticism is not applicable to the international legal human rights system. This, I suspect, is only one case among several in which contemporary moral and political theory has failed to take an advantage of an opportunity to learn from contemporary human rights practice and the law that undergirds it.

The failure of many states to realize a robust set of economic liberties for all is a significant cause of economic underdevelopment—and of poverty for millions of people. It is also a serious obstacle to people improving their condition through activities over which they exercise a significant degree of control and in which their own choices matter. When a person's economic liberties are secure—and when her economic rights position her to use these liberties effectively—she be will better able to pursue her own conception of the good in significant degree through her own efforts, in cooperation with others she chooses to work with, exercising her own judgment as to which of the available options she is likely to be able to pursue most successfully, and avoiding excessive dependence on the state. It is therefore not hard to justify the inclusion of the above set of economic liberties in both domestic and international legal systems of rights, especially from the standpoint of their contribution to enabling a person to *lead* a minimally good or decent life.

One should not underestimate the importance of economic liberties from the perspective of the status egalitarian function of the system of international legal human rights, however. Being able to engage effectively in productive activities, without being liable to discrimination, and being able to avoid being relegated to the status

---

corrupt government practices that hinder economic activities, such as the necessity of giving bribes in order to obtain licenses, and on government toleration of private individuals' coercive interference with the economic activities of others, in cases where no racial or gender discrimination is involved.

[42] John Tomasi, *Free Market Fairness* (Princeton, NJ: Princeton University Press, 2012).

170 of a dependent recipient of public support can also contribute to the

of a dependent recipient of public support can also contribute to the affirmation of one's equal basic status.

The right to economic liberties, as I have described it so far, only entails negative duties—duties to refrain from interfering with legitimate economic activities on the part of individuals. As such, these duties apply to everyone, including the state. If they only require various agents to refrain from engaging in morally unjustifiable interferences with others, it is much more reasonable to say that there are moral rights of this sort and that the legal rights of the same name can be viewed as attempts to realize in law antecedently existing moral rights.

In other words, most of the duties entailed by the right to economic liberties might seem to be sufficiently undemanding that the right appears to be justifiable as a moral right from a solely subject-grounded standpoint. As distinct from the other rights considered in this section, this seems to be a case where the Mirroring View makes good sense. We can begin the process of justifying an international legal right to the economic liberties by first showing that there is a corresponding moral right, a right with the same content, that is, that entails the same duties as the legal right. (The word 'begin' here is important, because one cannot simply conclude that there ought to be a legal right to R simply because there is a moral right to R.)

Matters are not quite so simple, however. Even if many of the duties associated with the legal right to economic liberties are, as negative duties, relatively undemanding, some are not, at least on some reasonable understandings of the content of the legal right. In many economically less developed countries and some economically developed ones, private agents interfere systematically with the economic liberties of certain classes of individuals—for example, members of ethnic minorities or low-caste individuals, people of color, or women—by practicing discrimination toward them in economic matters. To prevent this from happening, the state may have to undertake massive and expensive social policies. It is not obvious that this highly demanding duty can be justified from a strictly subject-grounded standpoint. If it cannot, then even if most of the content of the international legal human right to economic liberties can be seen as a legal realization of a corresponding moral right, not all of it can be.

In this section I have deepened my argument that to justify international legal human rights it is neither necessary nor sufficient to
first show that there are antecedently existing, corresponding moral
rights. Instead, one can argue for enacting international legal human
rights, as I have demonstrated, by appealing to the fact that the legal
entitlements in question would serve the interests or autonomy of
many people, or help protect their equal basic status, while justifying the ascription of the rights to all rather than merely to most on
the grounds that to do otherwise would not show proper regard for
equal basic status.

## Conclusion

Building on the account of the requirements for justification laid
out in the preceding chapter, this chapter has achieved two goals.
First, I have advanced three arguments for a system of international
legal human rights like the existing one. Second, I have given, in
broad outline, sample justifications for including in that system
representative rights from each of the most basic types of international legal human rights, justifications that vindicate the pluralistic
methodological approach I have been advocating. In addition, I
have made substantial headway on the task of and addressing identifying possible countervailing considerations that would defeat the
three justificatory arguments. In the next chapter I turn to a remaining key element of justification: determining whether the chief institutions of the existing international legal human rights system are
legitimate.

A final word of caution is in order. As I noted in chapter 2, in recognizing the legitimacy of justifications for particular international
legal human rights that do not appeal to the existence of corresponding moral rights, but instead allow appeals to the interests of many
people, I am not endorsing consequentialism. On my view, the justification for any particular international legal human right is subject
to an important anticonsequentialist constraint: the commitment to
equal basic moral status for all. The kind of justifications I have
sketched above are not consequentialist. To say that it is legitimate to
appeal to interests in addition to those of the right-holder in order to
justify having a legal right does not commit one to the thesis that
maximizing aggregate interests is what matters. The justifications

I have sketched are faithful to the core idea that each individual matters, morally speaking, on her own account—in that sense, they are moral-individualistic justifications. They merely also acknowledge that appeals to the interests of large numbers of such individually important individuals can justify a wider range of duties than any appeal to the interests of the right-holder herself can.

# CHAPTER 5

# An Ecological View of the Legitimacy of International Legal Human Rights Institutions

It bears repeating that my aim in this book is not to provide a conclusive justification for having *a* system of international legal human rights, much less a full vindication of *the existing system* and of all the particular norms that constitute it. Instead, it is (i) to show that justifying the system of international legal human rights should be a central aim of any philosophical theory of human rights that purports to shed light on the moral status of contemporary human rights practice; (ii) to explain how complex the task of justification is and how insufficient for executing it having a satisfactory moral theory of human rights would be; and (iii) to make a strong prima facie case that the existing system as a whole has what it takes to warrant our support of it on moral grounds, even if some aspects of it are defective and should be the object of serious efforts at improvement. In chapter 3, I argued that a justification of the international legal human rights system should consist of three stages: first, justificatory arguments calibrated to the type of system in question where the specification of the system type includes the functions of the system, the sorts of norms it includes (rights-norms, duty-norms, etc.), the roles of appeals to its norms in political discourse and mobilization for action, and the authority that is claimed on behalf of the norms; second, arguments to show which particular rights ought to be, or may rightly be, included in the system, given that it is a system of that type; and third, arguments to show that the key institutions through which the system operates are legitimate. Stages one and two were traversed in chapter 4. This chapter begins stage three, by offering a general account of institutional legitimacy and then applying it to some of the key institutions of the international legal human rights system.

## I. *A General Account of Institutional Legitimacy*

### *The Character of the Philosophical Debate*

The philosophical literature on institutional legitimacy has been preoccupied chiefly with the legitimacy of only one kind of institution—and a quite peculiar kind at that—the state. Consent, Natural Duty, Fairplay, Razian Service, and Associativist theorists have tried to articulate the conditions under which individuals have an exclusionary, content-independent moral duty to comply with the state's directives.[1] In some cases, what are labeled as accounts of legitimacy have been restricted to attempts to supply a necessary condition for the justification of imposing rules by coercion, in spite of the fact that it makes sense to speak of the legitimacy of institutions that do not wield coercion.[2] This restriction is perhaps understandable, given that philosophers have mainly been concerned with the legitimacy of the state, the paradigmatically coercive institution.

Recently, there has been some attention to the legitimacy of international institutions. But theorists have not squarely addressed the task of developing a *general* account of institutional legitimacy that would apply both to the state and to other institutions, including international ones.[3] In fact, they have not even acknowledged the

[1] For detailed characterizations of the various accounts, see Thomas Christiano, "On Authority," *Stanford Encyclopedia of Philosophy*, http://plato.stanford.edu/entries/authority; and Massimo Renzo, "Associative Responsibilities and Political Obligation," *Philosophical Quarterly*, 62:126 (2012): 106–27. I do not include Rawls's theory as developed in *Political Liberalism* because it is intended to be a theory of legitimacy only for liberal societies and focuses only on liberal state institutions.
[2] This is true, for example, of Rawls's liberal principle of legitimacy, which is designed to supply only a necessary condition for a liberal political order to be fully legitimacy, not a full account of legitimacy.
[3] John Tasioulas is an exception. John Tasioulas, "The Legitimacy of International Institutions," *The Philosophy of International Law*, eds. Samantha Besson and John Tasioulas (Oxford: Oxford University Press, 2010), pp. 97–118. In my judgment, the Razian Service conception of legitimacy that Tasioulas endorses has

need for a general account and have actually defined legitimacy in a way that applies only to certain sorts of institutions, namely, those that claim the right to rule, as when they begin their analyses simply by asserting that legitimacy *is* the right to rule.[4] Instead, for the most part, they have presented accounts of when there is a moral duty to obey the law (as such, independent of the particular content of the laws) as if they were accounts of institutional legitimacy. In doing so, they have encouraged the assumption either that legitimacy is simply a matter of having the power to create moral duties by issuing laws or that this power is a necessary condition of legitimacy. I will argue that both assumptions are mistaken.

The term 'legitimate' is coherently applied to a wide range of institutions, including some that neither claim the right to rule nor attempt to rule in any significant sense. This category includes quite different institutions, from NGOs to international organizations and agencies that merely serve to provide authoritative information that states utilize to coordinate their behavior. In particular, it is problematic to say that some of the key institutions of the international legal human rights system, such as the treaty bodies that monitor compliance, *rule*, given that they possess no enforcement powers and merely issue admonitions to noncomplying states. Similarly, it would be odd to say that the UN-based committees through which human rights declarations are first formulated and then passed by the General Assembly and later (in some cases), revised, and reformulated

---

problems. First, without a comprehensive theory of "best reasons," it provides little guidance for how to determine the criteria for legitimacy for any particular type of institution. Second, it sets too high a standard for legitimacy: Given an adequate understanding of the practical function of legitimacy assessments, it appears that an institution could be legitimate even if following its directives did not allow one to do *better*, according to one's best reasons for acting, than one otherwise would if one pursued any alternative; in other words, the Razian conception mistakes legitimacy for optimality or confuses being the *best* practical authority with being legitimate. Third, given that the "best reasons" for one individual may be different from those for other individuals, it is not clear that the Razian conception can do much service in solving the practical problem of achieving convergence on criteria for determining when *we* should regard an institution as having the status associated with legitimacy.

[4] See, for example, Thomas Christiano, "On Authority," and Samantha Besson, "Sovereignty, International Law and Democracy," *The European Journal of International Law*, 22:2 (2011): 176.

as human rights treaties, rule in any significant sense. They merely produce documents that states are free to ratify or reject. They do not create laws.

Other international institutions may be said to rule, but only in a much weaker sense than states do. For example, the World Trade Organization (WTO) has rules that are legally binding on its member states by virtue of their having ratified a treaty, but the judgments of its dispute resolution body are not coercively enforced commands. Instead, they are permissions that simply release the state in whose favor the judgment is made from some of the rules that ordinarily bind member states, in effect restoring them to the condition of having liberty rights they had, as sovereign states, prior to ratifying the WTO treaty. If this body judges that a country has been wrongly treated by another country, the aggrieved country is permitted to engage in retaliatory trade restrictions on goods from the country judged to have been at fault, even though such actions are forbidden by the terms of the WTO treaty.

Even if we accept the standard philosopher's assumption that legitimacy is the right to rule (ignoring institutions that do not purport to rule in any significant sense and the distinction between stronger and weaker senses of ruling), there is still an ambiguity. It is one thing to rule in the sense of creating duties by issuing directives, quite another to do this and also back the duties with coercion. It would be surprising if an account of legitimacy that sufficed for the former also sufficed for the latter, given how morally problematic coercion is. Presumably, the criteria for legitimacy in the case of an institution that wields coercion will be more demanding.

On the face of it, it is unlikely that a single substantive account of legitimacy could both cover the whole range of institutions to which the term is sensibly applied and at the same time be very informative as to what the criteria for legitimacy are, in the absence of information about the specific functions of the institution in question and the context in which it operates. It is doubtful that the criteria for legitimacy are the same for institutions that rule in the robust way that states do, for institutions that rule only in a weaker sense (as with the WTO), and institutions that don't rule at all. Nonetheless, it might still be the case that there is a general concept of institutional legitimacy that applies across a wide range of cases and provides significant guidance for developing more specific conceptions of legitimacy that apply to different types of institutions, when it is deployed in conjunction with information about the natures and functions of particular institutions. I shall argue that this is the case.

There are two quite different possible responses to the lack of a general account of institutional legitimacy. The first is to say that different concepts of legitimacy apply to state-like versus nonstate-like institutions and to acknowledge that philosophical theories of legitimacy only aim to explicate the former. Thus, those philosophical theories that begin with the assumption that legitimacy is the right to rule would acknowledge that they are not explicating *the* concept of legitimacy but rather *a* concept of legitimacy that applies to institutions that claim the right to rule (or, alternatively, that claim the right to rule in something like the robust sense in which states do). Alternatively, those who take up this first task might describe it as seeking a theory of institutions that claim the right to rule, while remaining agnostic on whether there is a single concept of legitimacy that applies to institutions that do not claim the right to rule.

These responses are unsatisfying, however, not only because unified theories are preferable, other things being equal, but also they leave unexplained the fact that the same term, 'legitimacy,' is applied both to state-like and nonstate-like institutions. The second, more cogent response is to explore the possibility that there is one concept of legitimacy that applies to both state-like and nonstate-like institutions — a general concept of institutional legitimacy — to try to explicate it, and then to explore how the various philosophical accounts relate to it. That is the approach taken in this chapter.

*Strategy*

In the remainder of the first part of this chapter, I argue that there is a general concept of legitimacy that applies across a wide range of institutions and that a proper understanding of it leads to the conclusion that while different criteria of legitimacy may apply to different types of institutions, there are several basic considerations — in fact, those that tend to be invoked frequently in real-world controversies about institutional legitimacy — that are usually relevant to legitimacy assessments across a fairly wide range of cases. In part II, I apply this understanding of legitimacy to several key institutions in the system of international legal human rights, taking into account their distinctive characteristics and functions.

## The Metacoordination View

I call this general concept of institutional legitimacy the Metacoordination View. It includes two key ideas. First, the distinctive practical role of legitimacy judgments is that they serve to solve a metacoordination problem: How to converge on public standards that institutions are to meet if we are to accord them the peculiar standing that they generally must have if they are to supply the coordination needed to achieve important benefits or avoid serious costs, and accomplish this without excessive costs. Second, this problem is to be solved in circumstances in which we should expect more of institutions than that they provide some benefits relative to the noninstitutional alternative but in which it would be unreasonable to expect them to be either fully just or optimally efficacious.[5] Although they require more of institutions than that they must be better than the noninstitutional alternative, reasonable assessments of legitimacy do not require them to be fully just or to be the perfectly efficacious in producing the benefits they are designed to deliver.[6] Nor do they require that the institution do a better job than all other feasible alternative institutions.

Recognizing that we should require more of institutions than that they make us somewhat better off than we would be without

---

[5] This idea was first introduced but only lightly sketched in Buchanan and Keohane, "The Legitimacy of Global Governance Institutions," *Ethics & International Affairs*, 20:4 (2006): 405–36.

[6] In some cases, legitimacy is not an issue. Consider the rule of the road, assuming that the rule of the road has not been coercively imposed by someone lacking the proper authority to do so, but instead has simply evolved as a social practice, the mere salience of the convention is sufficient reason to keep following it, because there is nothing else at stake—no controversial distributive implications of accepting one convention rather than the other, and so on. The concept of legitimacy typically comes into play when there is something at stake other than mere coordination—where it is reasonable to expect more of an institution than merely achieving coordination or merely serving as an effective instrument for some other purpose. In particular, the coordinating functions of many institutions are unlike the rule of the road in that they have distributive effects that are subject to moral evaluation.

them, but that we should not require them to be fully just or optimally efficacious, limits the problem of coordinating on support for institutions but does not solve it. The difficulty is that there is a range of alternative sets of normative criteria that could be applied to institutions that occupy the space of possibilities between being merely somewhat better than the noninstitutional alternative and being fully just or perfectly efficacious. The metacoordination problem is this: How can we succeed in converging on a set of normative criteria somewhere within this space in a reasonable, nonarbitrary manner? The goal is not simply agreement that we should support the institution, but rather agreement that is morally appropriate.

The object of achieving such convergence is to give an institution that satisfies the criteria upon which we have converged the sort of *standing* that is necessary for it to have if it to do its job effectively. Both the reasonableness of the normative criteria and whether they are satisfied by particular institutions must be sufficiently apparent to enough people for the institution to enjoy the standing that is necessary for its well-functioning.[7] In other words, institutions cannot generally function so as to coordinate our behavior in beneficial ways—or at least cannot do so without excessive costs in terms of coercive enforcement—unless enough people can converge in their individual judgments as to whether the institution is worthy of support. Criteria of legitimacy serve as coordination points to solve this metacoordination problem.

The term 'metacoordination' signals that there is a more basic coordination problem that must first be solved if institutions are to be able to function to coordinate our behavior in various beneficial ways. We must first coordinate on normative criteria that an institution

---

[7] It might be thought that where one solution to a coordination problem is salient, there is no metacoordination problem to be solved. This is true for some very simple coordination problems with very simple solutions, but in the case of the more important institutions, the fact that an institution exists, while making it salient, does not suffice, both because the institution's operations may have side effects that are unacceptable or controversial and because it will be reasonable to demand that its operations by which it achieves coordination are morally appropriate. In either case, the point is that mere success in achieving coordination is not sufficient for the institution to be worthy of support.

must satisfy if we are to give it the support it needs to coordinate our behavior for the achievement of various ends.

The notion that the term 'legitimacy,' when applied to institutions, indicates a certain standing is crucial. Having standing is a matter of the institution being recognized, in a social practice, as commanding certain forms of respect. Thus, when it comes to legitimacy assessments, the proper perspective is social, not individual: The primary question when legitimacy judgments are at stake is not whether I (or you) should take a certain stance toward an institution; it is whether *we* ought to regard the institution as having a certain standing. On this view, whether or not I or you, as individuals, ought to act respectfully toward the institution depends ultimately on whether it is worthy of having this social standing.

To reiterate: The basic idea is that the distinctive function of legitimacy assessments is to determine when institutions are worthy of having the special standing that is usually required for their performing the tasks for which they are designed and doing so without unacceptable costs. The object of the social practice is to develop shared *criteria* that institutions must satisfy to warrant that standing *and* shared *standards* for determining whether those criteria are satisfied, standards that can widely be seen to be met or not met. On this understanding of what legitimacy is about, the goal for the philosopher, after an initial clarification of the social role of legitimacy assessments, is to contribute to the development or maintenance of morally defensible social practices of assessing legitimacy for various types of important institutions. It is not to *discover*, through a priori reasoning, a timeless set of necessary and sufficient criteria of legitimacy for all institutions.

### Justice, Advantage, and Legitimacy

The point of the social practice of making legitimacy judgments is to achieve a compromise between institutional optimality, on the one hand, and the need to secure the social support that an institution must have if it is to provide its distinctive benefits without excessive costs, on the other. 'Optimality' here covers the maximal achievement of a range of goals, including, but not restricted to justice. For institutions that do not purport to play a significant role in promoting justice or in specifying what justice requires, legitimacy assessments mainly serve to signal a preferred trade-off between optimal efficacy in achieving the specific benefits the institution is designed to provide, on the one hand, and the need to achieve sufficient support of the institution to achieve those goals to some significant extent on the other, even if not optimally. In the case of this sort of institution, failing to regard it as legitimate unless it was optimally efficient would usually be self-defeating—it would deprive us of important benefits in pursuit of instrumental perfection. Examples of this sort of institution include international institutions that enable states to coordinate on global regulatory regimes, international postal systems, and those that assign segments of electromagnetic wave spectra for communication technologies.

Other institutions, including preeminently the state, serve to specify and to promote justice. Here too, legitimacy assessments are attempts to strike a compromise between optimality and the need to support some institution in order to reap benefits that only institutions can provide.

Generally speaking, institutions can provide their distinctive benefits without undue costs only if they enjoy widespread support. But in most cases it would be unreasonable to make our support conditional on their performing *optimally*: The best would be the enemy of the good. This is true whether the good the institution is designed to produce is justice or something more mundane, such as a global postal system.

The idea that it would be unreasonable to use an instrument unless it is optimally efficacious is clear enough when applied to institutions whose functions are less important than that of promoting and specifying justice. The case of the latter sort of institutions deserves further discussion.

There are several reasons why we should not expect institutions to be fully just or to promote justice optimally, as a condition of our granting them the special standing they need to deliver the benefits we require of them (and to do so without unacceptable costs). First, there is disagreement about what justice requires and this disagreement is likely to persist; yet we need institutions and we need them now.

To the extent that there is agreement or at least a broad consensus about what constitutes the worst injustices, reasonable criteria for legitimacy will take this into account: Serious injustices will count against legitimacy and may render an institution illegitimate if there is no reasonable prospect that they will be ameliorated. But that is quite different from requiring that institutions are to be just if they are to be accorded the special standing that legitimacy connotes.

Second, there is uncertainty about what justice requires, especially perhaps as regards distributive justice at the global level. But again, we cannot wait till this uncertainty dissipates before attempting to determine which institutions we ought to support.

Third, justice, in the absence of institutions, is often indeterminate. The standard example is property rights, but the point applies to other regions in the domain of justice as well. Noninstitutional moral reasoning may yield the conclusion that there ought to be a legal system of property rights and may tell us something about its broad contours, but institutionalized reasoning, in the context of a legal system that recognizes property rights and methods and principles for resolving conflicts among them and for determining their scope, is necessary if we are to know what our property rights are.

Finally, attaining justice under present conditions may not be possible, and progress toward closer approximations of justice will often require well-functioning institutions, both because institutions may be needed to affect changes in the direction of justice and because they can make more determinate what the goal of progress is. The most we can reasonably hope for may be an approximation of justice. To refuse to recognize institutions as legitimate on the grounds that they are less than fully just would therefore be self-defeating *from the standpoint of justice*. It is thus incorrect to describe the aim of legitimacy assessments as the striking of a compromise between justice and expediency. The effort to determine how well an institution must promote justice if we are to give it our support is motivated by the commitment to justice.

Although it will generally be unreasonable to insist on optimality, there are usually strong reasons to insist that institutions do more for us than provide some significant advantages relative to the noninstitutional alternative, at least in all but the least favorable circumstances. An institution may make us better off relative to that and yet be extremely unjust, inefficient, unaccountable, seriously lacking in integrity, unfair in the distribution of the benefits it provides, and it may also be a usurper. Even in the case of institutions that are not designed to promote justice but to provide more mundane goods, the question of whether we should support them cannot be reduced to the question of whether they are efficacious; moral considerations are relevant. In particular, we can reasonably demand that the institution provide its benefits without perpetrating or supporting major injustices.

As I shall argue more fully in the next part, the Metacoordination View makes sense of the concerns voiced in real-world discussions of legitimacy. It has no difficulty explaining the attention paid in actual controversies about legitimacy to institutional origins, procedures, and outcomes, to the fit between institutional behavior and the goals and principles invoked to justify institutions, to fairness, and to accountability and transparency, because all of these considerations can be relevant to the question of whether we ought to accord an institution the sort of standing that it needs to provide the benefits that are invoked to justify it and do so without excessive costs. Which particular considerations are relevant and what weights they should have in an assessment of legitimacy will vary, depending upon the kind of institution in question and upon how critical it is to have a functioning institution of that sort, in the particular circumstances. The remainder of this section outlines the main features of the Metacoordination View and makes a case for it.

## The Centrality of Coordination

Whatever else they do, institutions enable large numbers of individuals to coordinate their behavior. Sometimes, coordination is itself the only goal: The problem to which the institution is a response is a pure coordination problem. In other cases, the collective action problem the institution is designed to solve is not a coordination problem or at least not a pure coordination problem. This is so when the goal is to secure public goods whose achievement is potentially blocked by free-rider or assurance problems. But regardless of what sort of problem it is designed to solve, the solution will depend upon the institution's success in coordinating the actions of many individuals.[8] Institutions typically do this by assigning different tasks to different individuals within some overall plan of action. In other words, they define and assign roles that function together in a coordinated way. In addition, other parties, even if they are not called on to coordinate their behavior for the achievement of the institution's goals, must not interfere with the institution's operations or the efforts of other individuals to support them.

## Aspects of Standing

I have said that for institutions to achieve the coordination needed to provide their benefits, or at least to do so without unacceptable costs, they must have a certain standing, at least in the eyes of sufficiently large numbers of people—people who are in a position either to withhold cooperation or to interfere with it. I have also said that endowing an institution with the relevant sort of standing requires solving a metacoordination problem, namely, converging on the same set of normative criteria that the institution is expected to satisfy if it is to have this standing—settling on some set of requirements the institution will be expected to meet, in the space between mere advantage relative to the noninstitutional alternative and optimality. For now, as a first approximation, let us say that this special standing is a type of respect, but that the particular form it takes will vary among individuals and groups, depending on the nature of the particular institution and their relationship to it. In the case of those who are addressees of the institution's directives, showing respect need not mean uniformly complying with those directives or regarding oneself as duty-bound to comply with them, but it will usually at least require regarding the fact that the directive issues from this institution, independently of the particular content of the directive, as a reason to take them seriously. For others to whom the institution's directives are not addressed, but who are in a position to affect its ability to achieve coordination, respect will generally mean, at the very least, not interfering with its efforts to promulgate and promote compliance with its directives or to carry out other functions.

---

[8] For a valuable discussion of the centrality of coordination in legitimacy, see Samantha Besson, "The Authority of International Law—Lifting the State Veil," *Sydney Law Review* 31 (2009): 343.

In addition, for addressees and nonaddressees alike, recognizing an institution as legitimate also usually requires showing a kind of impersonal respect for the institution's agents. For example, even when one disagrees with them and even when one refuses to comply with their orders or attempts to thwart their application to others, one treats them in ways that acknowledge that they are the agents of an institution that is worthy of respect. (One would treat such individuals quite differently if one thought they were simply private agents, acting for their own purposes, or if one thought they were the agents of an institution one regards as illegitimate.) The respect accorded to individuals who are agents of legitimate institutions is not the same as the respect owed to all persons as such; nor is it the appraisal-respect or esteem that is accorded to individuals on the basis of judgments about their personal characteristics. It is respect accorded to an individual by virtue of the fact that she occupies a role in or speaks as a representative of an institution that is thought to be worthy of respect. It is a kind of status respect, as opposed to individually merited respect, that is derivative on the standing the institution enjoys.

Finally, regarding an institution as legitimate has implications for how we ought to respond to its failings. Generally speaking, the proper response to deficiencies in legitimate institutions is reform, not revolution, to attempt to modify it so as to remedy its flaws rather than to scrap it. Thus, the means that one may rightly take to resist the workings of a legitimate institution are generally more morally constrained than those one may deploy against an illegitimate one.

## Standing and the Right to Rule

The notion of standing is broader than the idea, almost uniformly taken for granted in the philosophical literature, that a legitimate institution is one that has the right to rule. It may be true that for some institutions, including preeminently states, legitimacy connotes the right to rule. But as I have already noted, apart from the fact that there are stronger and weaker senses of ruling, the idea of a right to rule is completely out of place when it comes to many institutions to which the terms 'legitimate' and 'illegitimate' are commonly applied. By concentrating on the state, the coercive institution par excellence, philosophers have overlooked the fact that there is a quite general concept of legitimacy that applies not only to the state but also to a wide range of institutions that do not use coercion to back commands. The common initial assumption of the philosophical literature should, therefore, be revised to read as follows: *For those sorts of institutions that attempt to rule*, legitimacy is the right to rule. The idea that legitimacy connotes a kind of standing—that is, being the proper object of forms of respect that may vary among different parties—is broad enough to capture both the cases where the notion of the right to rule is applicable and those in which it is not; and it is also broad enough to cover cases where ruling involves coercion and when it does not.

## The Inadequacy of Coercion and Self-Interest

If the point is to ensure that an institution achieves the coordination that makes it valuable, why not simply employ sufficient coercion to ensure that enough people follow its directives and enough others do not interfere with it? The first thing to note here is that, as I have already observed, not all institutions wield coercion. In addition, for some institutions, using coercion would be unacceptable, given the values and goals the institution is supposed to serve. But suppose we restrict our vision to those institutions where coercion is both feasible and not ruled out in principle. There are three main practical reasons for not relying exclusively on coercion. First, to endow an institution with a capacity for coercion sufficiently robust to achieve compliance with its directives and noninterference with its operations through exclusive reliance on fear of penalty may be dangerous. Such power is likely to be abused, and if it is, there will be little prospect for holding those who wield it accountable. Second, even if we set the problem of dangerous concentrations of power aside, exclusive reliance on coercion may be very costly. If people only comply or refrain from interfering out of fear of a coercive response, it will be necessary to invest heavily in the machinery of enforcement. Third, since enforcement will inevitably be imperfect, compliance and noninterference may be inadequate if a sufficient number of relevant individuals and group do not have other motives for compliance, motives that do not depend on the fear of a coercive response. In brief, the police will not always be around when opportunities for noncompliance present themselves. If an institution is generally regarded as having the standing described above, then the costs of enforcement and the risks of extremely robust coercive capacity will be reduced, and imperfect enforcement need not seriously impair the institution's functioning. This is why, considered simply from a practical standpoint, it is valuable to be able to converge in our legitimacy assessments.

Where enough people can converge in their legitimacy assessments, metacoordination can be achieved even when an exclusive appeal to self-interest (whether it takes the form of the threat of coercion of or more positive rewards) would not suffice. This is advantageous, because even in case of well-designed institutions, the congruence between what the institution requires of us if it is to function well and the dictates of individual self-interest will not be perfect. If enough people internalize common standards for legitimacy, then the institution will receive sufficient support, even in cases where neither the fear of coercion nor more positive self-interested motivation suffice. For this reason we may call the kind of metacoordination that is the object of a social practice of legitimacy assessments *principled* metacoordination.

There is also a moral advantage to being able to converge on normative criteria for assessing the legitimacy of institutions. Achieving support for institutions by appealing to normative criteria, rather than merely to the fear of coercion, shows respect for individual autonomy by acknowledging the importance of our being able to act on what we consider to be good reasons. It also enables a kind of moral community, for two distinct reasons. First, so far as participation in the practice is open to all, all regarded as beings who are entitled to have reasons for supporting institutions apart from those that are created by the threat of coercion.[9] Second, the effort to converge on criteria for legitimacy helps to create a community bound together by principles, not just force.[10]

I can now offer a more complete account of the distinctive function of a practice aimed at achieving convergent legitimacy assessments: It supplements or substitutes for coercion and positive appeals

---

[9] I am indebted to Thomas Christiano for making the importance of this point clear to me.
[10] I thank Julian Culp for clarifying this point.

to self-interest in achieving support for valuable institutions by supplying normative criteria that institutions must satisfy to be worthy of support, in conditions in which it is reasonable to require more than benefit relative to the noninstitutional alternative but in which it would be unreasonable to require full justice or optimal efficacy.

So far I have emphasized the positive aspect of a social practice aimed at achieving convergent legitimacy assessments, its role in solving the metacoordination problem described earlier. It also plays a role in coordinating noncooperation with an institution, if the institution fails to satisfy the standards for legitimacy. In both cases, the point of the practice is to coordinate our responses to the institution, without relying exclusively on coercion or a complete congruence of individual interests and institutional demands.

*Variable Criteria*

Real-world assessments of institutional legitimacy seem to take for granted the commonsensical notion that the criteria for legitimacy may vary according to what sort of institution is being assessed. The criteria assumed or asserted to be relevant to assessing the legitimacy of NGOs differ from those applied to the UN Security Council or the WTO. The Metacoordination View can shed light on why different criteria are appropriate in different contexts, despite the common applicability of the notion of legitimacy. In particular, it can explain why more demanding criteria for legitimacy are appropriate for some institutions.

First, other things being equal, it is reasonable to expect institutions that rule in the most robust sense—those that issue orders that they coercively enforce—should meet higher standards than those that do not. This makes sense, both because coercion in itself is exceptionally morally problematic and because coercive power is likely to be abused. Other things being equal, the bar ought to be set higher for coercive institutions, because the risks of according them standing are likely to be greater. Second, other things being equal, an institution that claims *exclusive* legitimacy in its domain of operation should meet higher standards than one that does not. For if an institution is regarded as exclusively legitimate in this sense, alternative institutions may not be allowed to compete with it, including institutions that might do a better job or be morally superior.

There is a third variable that should also influence criteria for legitimacy: the importance of the job the institution is needed to do. If the failure to gain sufficient support for an institution to function effectively would be disastrous, then it may be reasonable to settle for less. For example, if the only institution able to deal effectively with the problem of climate change is not democratic, then it may be unreasonable to judge the institution to be illegitimate in spite of this deficiency. For other institutions, where the need for them is not so dire, or where there is reason to believe that they will not reliably perform their functions unless they are democratic, or where their being democratic is both feasible and compatible with their performing their functions, it will be reasonable to require them to be democratic.

According to the Metacoordination View, positive legitimacy assessments are judgments that an institution is worthy of our support. Whether it is worthy of our support depends, in part, on what risks we incur by supporting it. Those risks vary, depending on whether the institution wields coercion, whether it attempts to exclude others from operating in its domain, and on how vital the benefits it provides are. In the case of international institutions, including those that figure importantly in the system of international legal human rights, not being democratic need not be an obstacle to legitimacy, if democracy is not feasible in their case, so long as they supply morally important benefits and do so in ways that are not morally objectionable.

Even though, for reasons just noted, we should not expect one set of criteria for legitimacy for all institutions, there are several rather commonsensical criteria that are presumptively appropriate for a wide range of institutions, and they are reflected, as I have already suggested, in actual attempts to assess the legitimacy of particular institutions. These include (1) good or at least not seriously tainted origins; (2) the reliable provision of the goods the institution is designed to deliver (at least under reasonably favorable circumstances); (3) institutional integrity, that is, a reasonable match between the institution's most important justifying goals and principles and its actual performance (absent some appropriate explanation for a mismatch along with evidence that the problem will be ameliorated); (4) the avoidance of serious unfairness; and (5) accountability of the most important institutional agents.

These criteria are not necessary and sufficient conditions; instead they are best regarded as what Rawls in a different context called "counting principles": The more of them are satisfied and the greater degree to which they are satisfied, the more confident we should be in judging the institution to be legitimate. Generally speaking, institutions that exhibit these characteristics to a high degree are more likely to be effective in achieving the ends we want them to achieve and less likely to produce unwanted results or produce good results in morally objectionable ways. If this is the case, then giving them our support will be a good bargain for us.

### Legitimacy Assessments and Risk Management

The basic point can be put in terms of risks and benefits, if we take care to construe these terms broadly enough, so as to include moral considerations. Whenever we bestow the standing on an institution that the term 'legitimacy' connotes, we empower it. But empowerment always involves risks: The agents of the institution may misuse the power bestowed on it. There are two ways to reduce the risk that this will happen. First, we can be selective as to which institutions we empower; this is the function of legitimacy assessments. Second, we can create mechanisms to constrain the institutional agents' ability to act badly. Principal-Agent theory systematically explores the options with respect to this second strategy.

The two strategies converge in this sense: Our criteria for determining which institutions to empower should reflect our knowledge of the design features needed to achieve appropriate constraint of institutional agents. Since neither strategy by itself is likely to be fully effective, the best alternative will be a combination of both. The trick is to pursue the mixed strategy in a way that reduces the risk of bad institutional behavior without depriving ourselves of the benefits that only institutions can provide. This means not being overly demanding with regard to the standards we expect institutions to satisfy if we are to support them and not imposing constraints and incentives on institutional agents that undercut their ability to function effectively.

The first strategy is our concern here. In pursuing it—in determining whether we ought to accord an institution the sort of respect that is necessary for it to have the power needed to do the job we want it to do—we need to weigh the risk that institutional power will be abused (or simply wasted) against the benefits we expect to gain by empowering the institution. Criteria for legitimacy should help us determine whether the benefits of institutional empowerment outweigh the risks. These criteria should reflect knowledge of the risks that an empowered institution poses and the institutional characteristics that reduce the risks.

## Standards

In many cases it will be difficult for outsiders and even for some agents within an institution to make reliable judgments about whether appropriate criteria for legitimacy are being satisfied. In these circumstances, standards that can serve as reliable proxies for criteria are extremely valuable. I use the term 'standards' to distinguish these proxies from the criteria of legitimacy. For example, in the case of a complex institution that operates on the basis of special expertise, ordinary people and even the smartest and most educated outsiders may not be in a position to judge reliably how well the institution is accomplishing its justifying goals or how closely it is adhering to its own procedures. But outsiders will be able to judge that the institution is extremely secretive and that it systematically attempts to block efforts by outside experts to evaluate its performance. Consider an analogy familiar to economists: I may not be able to determine for myself whether the used car I am thinking of buying is mechanically reliable, but if the car dealer refuses my request to have it examined by an independent mechanic, this gives me good reason to doubt that it is. The general point is that in addition to providing criteria, an account of legitimacy should recognize the value of standards that can serve as reliable proxies for criteria and clearly distinguish between the two.

If, as I have argued, the distinctive function of the concept of legitimacy, across all or at least most of the various contexts in which it is applied, is to enable a social practice whereby shared legitimacy assessments promote principled metacoordination, either in support or in criticism of institutions, then it is not enough to have shared criteria for legitimacy. In addition, there must be a widespread consensus on the standards that are to serve as proxies for criteria, in cases in which it is difficult for outsiders to ascertain directly whether appropriate criteria are satisfied.

## Theoretical Desiderata

There are three main reasons to adopt the Metacoordination View: (1) It makes better sense of actual controversies about the legitimacy of a wide range of institutions than the standard philosophical accounts, including institutions that do not purport to rule in any significant sense; (2) it explains the distinctive function of legitimacy assessments, both making clear why legitimacy is not to be confused with justice or instrumental optimality and at the same time showing why considerations of justice and efficacy are relevant to legitimacy; and (3) by offering an understanding of legitimacy that applies to noncoercive as well as coercive institutions, and to institutions that rule as well as those that do not, it avoids conflating whether an institution is legitimate with whether it is justified in using coercion and conflating legitimacy and the right to rule. The Metacoordination View thus avoids the parochialism of philosophical accounts which target a very peculiar institution, the state.

The Metacoordination View, as I have developed it so far, is an illumination of a *concept* of legitimacy that has application across a wide range of coercive and noncoercive institutions. It is not a full-blown *theory* of legitimacy. Indeed, it casts doubt on the possibility of developing a substantive, action-guiding theory of legitimacy that would cover all the different sorts of institutions to which this very general concept can be applied.

The core idea of the Metacoordination View of the concept of legitimacy is that legitimacy assessments are best understood as contributions to a social practice aimed at achieving principled metacoordination in support of or in criticism of institutions, a social practice that implicitly proceeds on the assumption that present circumstances are such that it is reasonable to expect more of an institution than that it make us marginally better off than the noninstitutional alternative but unreasonable to expect it to be fully just or optimally efficacious. This understanding of the role of the general concept of legitimacy leads quite naturally to a distinction between *criteria* and *standards* (understood as proxies for the satisfaction of criteria), because the point of the practice cannot be achieved unless an institution's satisfaction of the relevant criteria can be perceived by various relevant agents, most of whom will not have insiders' knowledge about the workings of the institution.

This account of the general concept does not itself specify criteria of legitimacy, much less standards of legitimacy. Indeed, it explains why we should reject the assumption that we should expect an analysis of the concept of legitimacy to yield any determinate criterion of legitimacy, much less a single criterion that is applicable to all institutions. But it does provide guidance for developing criteria of legitimacy in the light of the facts about particular institutions and their functions, and it explains why criteria without epistemically accessible standards are insufficient. Although the Metacoordination View tells us we should not expect a universal set of criteria for legitimacy, it does tell us that criteria should lie within a range, between the excessively demanding requirements of full justice or optimal efficacy and the excessively forgiving requirement of bare advantage relative to the noninstitutional alternative. The Metacoordination View also tells us that how demanding the criteria should be within those limits should vary according to how important achieving metacoordination of support for an institution is in a particular case and whether the institution claims exclusive authority over a given domain. Further, if we add plausible assumptions about the morally problematic character of coercion and about the risk of abuse that coercive power entails, it implies that how demanding our criteria should be will vary depending upon whether an institution wields coercive power.

## Democracy Is Not Necessary for Institutional Legitimacy

Given its account of the nature of legitimacy assessments, the Metacoordination View guards us against the assumption that democracy is a necessary condition for institutional legitimacy, even for institutions that rule in some significant sense. It opens us to the possibility that, depending on its functions, an institution that is not democratic may nonetheless be worthy of the kind of standing that is necessary for it to perform those functions with acceptable costs. More specifically, it forewarns us against the mistaken assumption that if democracy is a necessary condition for the legitimacy of the state, it is also a necessary condition for quite different institutions. The Metacoordination View enables us to understand what is common to legitimacy assessments—namely, a judgment as to whether the risks and costs of according an institution a particular kind of standing are worth the benefits that its having that standing will make possible—while at the same time making it clear that the criteria for conferring standing may differ greatly across different types of institutions.

Another virtue of the Metacoordination View is that it encourages us to take seriously what goes on when legitimacy assessments are made and contested, and this in turn leads to the identification of certain recurrent considerations that are voiced across a wide range of institutions. These fall under the headings of acceptable origination, procedural virtues, fairness (or avoidance of serious unfairness), congruence between justifying goals and principles and actual performance (that is, institutional integrity), effectiveness in producing specific outcomes, accountability, and transparency. If the task is to converge on criteria that fall between the extremes of bare advantage and full justice or optimal efficacy, these criteria make sense. They are often relevant to determining whether conferring standing on an institution is a reasonable, chiefly because, when they are satisfied, the result tends to be a reduction of the risks that we incur by giving the institution the standing connoted by the term 'legitimate.'

Given the attractions of the Metacoordination View of the *concept* of legitimacy, it is plausible to use it to develop a set of desiderata for a philosophical *theory* of institutional legitimacy. In the space remaining I can only sketch some of the more obvious desiderata.

The first desideratum is generality. A philosophical theory of legitimacy should operate with a *concept* of legitimacy that applies to a wide range of institutions, while recognizing that different criteria of legitimacy may be appropriate for different types of institutions. Second, a theory should recognize that the stringency of the criteria for legitimacy should vary depending upon how crucial the achievement of metacoordination is, on whether the institution is coercive, and on whether it claims exclusive authority in a given domain. Third, a theory should accommodate the notion that as conditions improve we should expect more of institutions if we are to regard them as legitimate. Fourth, a philosophical theory of legitimacy should recognize the fact that participants in the social practice in which legitimacy assessments occur include not just those to whom the directives of institutions are addressed, but others as well. The standard philosophical accounts speak only to the responses of addressees.[11] Of course, their proponents could argue that how a nonaddressee should respond—in particular, whether he should interfere with the institution's operations or not and whether he should treat the institution's agents with respect— is wholly derivative on whether the addressees ought to take the directives as authoritative. The Metacoordination View, in contrast, makes room for the plausible possibility that nonaddressees' responses should be determined in part by other factors, not simply by whether the addressees have good reason to comply. Fifth, a theory of legitimacy should recognize not only that criteria for legitimacy are likely to become more or less demanding over time, depending on how favorable the circumstances are for demanding more of institutions; it should also recognize that legitimacy is not something that is discovered but rather is constructed through the practice of attempting to achieve principled assessment.

An assessment of legitimacy, according to the Metacoordination View, expresses a compromise between the need to have a functioning institution and the desire to impose normative requirements on it.[12] But equally rational individuals may opt for drawing the compromise in different ways, both because of limitations on their knowledge as to what the feasible alternatives are and because they may have different, but not unreasonable attitudes toward the risks and benefits involved. In other words, even the most developed philosophical theory of legitimacy cannot hope to provide fully dispositive criteria for when an institution is legitimate. At most it can provide guidance for those who must together *decide* (not discover) whether an institution is legitimate.

[11] Here Rawls is an exception. For him, the judgment that a state is legitimate has implications for how other states should treat it, in particular, that they should not "interfere" with it.

[12] Note that, as I stated earlier, the need to have a functioning institution may be based on moral considerations, as is the case with the need to have a functioning institution for the promotion of justice. So, it is incorrect to say that on the coordination view, legitimacy assessments reflect a compromise between moral requirements and expediency.

## II. *Assessing the Legitimacy of Key International Human Rights Institutions*

Chapter 1 catalogued the staggering variety of institutions that help to create, interpret, enforce, and in other ways promote compliance with international legal human rights. Clearly, it would not be feasible to try to assess the legitimacy of all or even most of them. Instead, I will focus mainly on three international institutions that figure prominently in the UN-centered international legal human rights enterprise: (i) the Security Council, in its efforts to stop or prevent massive violations of the most basic human rights; (ii) the groups that draft human rights treaties, as they operate within the structure of UN institutions; and (iii) the treaty bodies that monitor states' compliance with treaties they have ratified. With respect to (ii), though for brevity's sake I will simply refer to the treaty-drafting groups, the discussion of legitimacy here will apply to the broader set of institutional processes that encompass the route from the initial proposals for a new convention (which sometimes originate in NGOs), to the process of drafting a declaration, to the discussion and eventual approval of a declaration by the UN General Assembly, to the reformulation of the declaration as a treaty, to the debate over the treaty and consequent revisions, and the submission of the final draft of the treaty for ratification.

There are other institutions, such as the UN Human Rights Council, the General Assembly, and the International Criminal Court (ICC), that are arguably at least as important as the institutions I consider. I do not pretend to have an account of the relative importance of these various institutions. Nor am I trying to achieve an overall assessment of the legitimacy of the complex of institutions that comprise the international legal human rights system. I will not even try to provide a comprehensive legitimacy assessment of the three institutions I do consider, but rather only try to indicate how such an assessment should proceed, while illustrating the fruitfulness of the Metacoordination View of legitimacy set out in the first part of this chapter.

These limitations on my discussion will appear less debilitating once one appreciates a fact that I will emphasize in due course, namely, that the institutional aspect of the system is fragmented, or, in more positive terms, highly modularized. What this means is that even if some particular institutions are of dubious legitimacy, this may not have the negative consequences it would have if the various institutions were more closely integrated. The upshot is that even if there are some important institutions that I have not considered that are of dubious legitimacy, we should not jump to the conclusion that the system as a whole does not deserve our support. For example, some have argued that the ICC is illegitimate because the permanent members of the Security Council can arbitrarily block prosecutions. Given the kind of institution it is—one that is supposed to pursue justice through the rule of law—this is a serious allegation. If, as I believe to be the case, this design feature of the institution does seriously detract from its legitimacy, the effect on the overall international legal human rights system may nonetheless be negligible, because other important parts of the system largely operate independently of the ICC.

The chief conclusions I will reach are as follows: (1) The legitimacy of the Security Council is dubious at best. It certainly does not possess *exclusive* legitimacy with respect to decisions concerning the use of force across borders, mainly because it scores very low on the criterion of institutional integrity, professing to protect human rights while repeatedly failing to authorize interventions to stop genocides and other mass wrongful killings. (2) In contrast, the treaty-drafting groups, or rather the institutionally structured processes through which they operate, may possess considerable legitimacy, once we discard the false assumption that they are a kind of global legislature, to be evaluated according to criteria of legitimacy appropriate for domestic legislatures. (3) The legitimacy of the treaty bodies is questionable, not because, as is commonly said, they lack enforcement capacity, but rather because they are often not sufficiently critical of states. (4) With respect to the treaty drafting groups and the treaty bodies, if we view them in isolation, rather than as elements in a broader network that encompasses international, regional, and national institutions, we will underestimate their legitimacy.

This fourth conclusion will be grounded on an *ecological* view of the legitimacy of international legal human rights institutions that features the concept of reciprocal legitimation. I will argue that the engagement of states with international legal human rights institutions enhances the legitimacy of states, while the legitimacy of international legal human rights institutions is enhanced both by the fact that they contribute to the legitimacy of states and by the fact that they outsource important functions to states, thus overcoming their own lack of capacity. Similarly, the legitimacy of NGOs, another key component of the international legal human rights system, depends on their contribution to the legitimacy of states and international institutions. I will argue that *legitimacy is an ecological concept* in this sense: It is often not possible to determine the legitimacy of an institution in isolation; instead, its legitimacy may be a function of how it fits into a network of institutions.

The aim of this chapter is not to achieve anything approaching a comprehensive evaluation of the legitimacy of the international legal human rights system. Rather, it is to demonstrate that the keys to evaluating the legitimacy of the system as a whole or any important aspect of it are the Metacoordination View of the practical function of legitimacy assessments and the ecological understanding of legitimacy.

I noted earlier that real-world controversies about legitimacy usually proceed on the assumption that any or all of the following considerations can be relevant to assessments of legitimacy: (1) institutional origins (in particular, whether the institution is a usurper, that is, whether it wrongfully displaced a legitimate institution or otherwise came about through seriously unjust actions); (2) comparative benefit (whether the institution does an adequate job of providing the benefits it is designed to provide and in particular whether it provides a substantially greater level of the desired benefits than is obtainable without the institution); (3) minimal moral acceptability (whether the institution operates without perpetrating or contributing to major injustices, including serious, avoidable unfairness in the distribution of the benefits it provides); and (4) integrity (whether the institution avoids serious discrepancies between its professed goals and procedures, on the one hand, and its actual behavior, on the other). All of these criteria are relevant for determining whether the international institutions examined in this chapter are worthy of the standing connoted by the term 'legitimacy,' because they are all relevant to determining whether empowering these institutions by according them the kind of standing that the term 'legitimacy' connotes is reasonable, in the light of the benefits these institutions can provide, on the one hand, and the risk that their power will be used badly, on the other. Because I think it would be difficult to argue that any of the three international institutions have seriously tainted origins or itself engages in serious human rights violations, I will focus on the other criteria.

## The Legitimacy of the Security Council

Perhaps the most persistent complaint about the Security Council, voiced from its inception, focuses on the fact that its permanent members, and only they, have the right to veto proposed resolutions. To many, this arrangement is so morally arbitrary and so unfair in its allocation of power among members as to rob the Council of legitimacy.[13]

In my judgment, this feature of the Council does not deprive it of legitimacy. The best rationale for this feature is that it was necessary if this new institution was to make an effective contribution to international peace and security, which was its original defining mission. In a nutshell, the reasonable assumptions behind this peculiar voting arrangement are (i) that the great powers would cooperate effectively in keeping the peace only if each had assurance that the Council would not be able to undertake actions of which it strongly disapproved and (ii) that their cooperation was necessary for success in peace-keeping. To be sure, this rationale does not provide a justification for the actual list of veto holders, since some of them may not be sufficiently powerful to pose a serious threat if overruled. But it does supply a powerful reason for allocating the veto right to the most powerful states. One might reasonably argue that, in the light of the difficulty of amending the UN charter to withdraw the veto from the weaker permanent members,[14] the current arrangement is

---

[13] My assessment of the legitimacy of the Security Council will be restricted to its role as the authorizer of military intervention (in cases other than individual or collective self-defense), though I recognize that it has other functions as well, including peace-keeping and the authorization of economic sanctions.

[14] Amending the charter requires a Security Council resolution, which any permanent member can veto. It is difficult to imagine circumstances in which any permanent member, and perhaps especially the weaker ones, would refrain from exercising its veto of a resolution to deprive it of the veto.

acceptable, though overinclusive with respect to the possession of the veto, as an attempt to secure the cooperation of the most powerful states (the United States, China, and Russia) in maintaining international peace and security.

Of course, if one assumes that this institution is legitimate only if it is democratic—where this means that all members are to be elected by a majority of all the states in the UN and all members are to have the same rights with regard to decisions to use force—then clearly the Council is illegitimate. But the analysis of institutional legitimacy set out in part I shows why one should not assume that democracy is a necessary condition for institutional legitimacy across the board. It may be the case, as I have argued elsewhere, that, when it is feasible, democracy is a necessary condition for the legitimacy of *the state*, but that is not to say that all institutions, including those, like the Council, that are quite different from states and much more limited in their powers, must be democratic to be legitimate.[15] Having the antidemocratic provision of a veto right for the most powerful states may well be a reasonable price to pay—*if* the institution delivers the benefits it is designed to provide—and if a democratic alternative would be infeasible because it would not reliably garner sufficient support from the most powerful states to make the institution effective.

There are other aspects of the Council, however, that much more seriously impugn its legitimacy. Drawing on a more extensive discussion in an article coauthored with Robert O. Keohane, here I will only mention three.[16] First, the Security Council scores low on accountability, especially accountability for the exercise of the veto. When they exercise the veto, permanent members are not required to provide principled public justifications for doing so or to respond publicly to criticisms of those justifications. More importantly, the most powerful permanent members are not subject to effective incentives for the principled use of the veto. There is no official institutional oversight that is capable of calling them to account for unprincipled uses of the veto. Further, their power largely insulates

[15] Allen Buchanan, "Political Obligation and Democracy," *Ethics* 112:4 (2002): 689–719.

[16] Allen Buchanan and Robert O. Keohane, "The Legitimacy of Global Governance Institutions," *Ethics & International Affairs*, 20:4 (2006): 305–47.

them from a credible threat of economic sanctions by individual states or groups of states, refusals of cooperation on other matters that are important to them, or other informal penalties, including reputational losses. At least in cases where they believe they have important interests at stake, the most powerful permanent members are free to exercise the veto in ways that admit of no credible justification.

The Security Council also lacks transparency, another virtue often quite reasonably thought to be important for legitimacy. Here, as in most cases, transparency is valuable chiefly by virtue of its contribution to accountability—it is hard to hold an institution accountable if its decision-making processes are shielded from public view. Because I think it is clear that lack of accountability for use of the veto is the central problem and lack of transparency relevant mainly because of its contribution to that problem, I will not emphasize the lack of transparency. Further, it would be a mistake to assume that transparency is an unconditional requirement for legitimacy. In some cases, a degree of opacity is necessary if an institution is to work effectively.[17] The central issue is accountability and on that criterion the Security Council fares poorly.

The second and arguably most serious legitimacy deficit of the Security Council is that it scores low on the criterion of institutional integrity. It publicly professes to have extended its role beyond maintaining international peace and security to protecting against major violations of basic human rights, but it egregiously fails to do so. A far from comprehensive list of massive basic human rights violations in which it failed to authorize timely intervention or failed to take action at all includes the following: the mass killings of civilians by the Pakistani army in East Pakistan in 1970, the Cambodian genocide of the mid-1970s, the mass killings of Mayans in Guatemala in the 1970s, the mass killings of Syrian citizens by their own government in the 1980s, the mass killings of Kurds and Shia in Iraq by their own government in the 1980s and again at the end of the First Gulf War, the genocide in Bosnia in the early 1990s (where effective intervention occurred, but three years too late), the Rwandan

[17] David Stastavage, "Open-Door or Closed-Door? Transparency in Domestic and International Bargaining," *International Organization*, 58:4 (2004): 667–704.

genocide in 1994, and the mass murder that the government of Syria is now inflicting on its own citizens.

It would be unreasonable to expect the Council to have authorized timely intervention in all of these cases, but its failure to do so in *any* of them is a serious blow against its legitimacy. As Keohane and I have argued, this record of failure is so dismal that at the very least it undermines the Security Council's assertion of *exclusive* legitimacy—that is, that it is the only body that may rightly authorize military intervention in cases of humanitarian intervention.

Supporters of the Security Council might reply that with all of its flaws it nonetheless scores high on the criterion of comparative benefit and given that the benefit of securing peace is so important, that suffices for its legitimacy. The difficulty with this response is that it is far from obvious that the existence of the Security Council is an important causal factor in the absence of war between major powers for most of the period of its existence. More likely candidates for significant causal factors are the spread of democracy, the nuclear stalemate of the Cold War, the defeat of Nazism and aggressive Japanese nationalism in World War II, and the fact that the German people and their leaders are no longer interested in turning Europe into a German colony, but instead are among the best exemplars of liberal-democratic, rights-respecting political culture.[18]

To say that, given the flaws described above, the Council does not have exclusive legitimacy is not to endorse unilateral humanitarian intervention or even multilateral intervention by a "concert of democracies" of the sort that Anne-Marie Slaughter and John Ikenberry have proposed.[19] Such an alternative would be too risky, given that more responsible substitutes for Security Council authorization are feasible. In cases where the Council fails to authorize intervention to stop a genocide or mass killing, morally credible intervention would have to be undertaken by a group of states that operated

---

[18] This is not to say that the contemporary German record is unblemished. Neo-Nazi groups still exist in Germany and there is considerable political support for the National Democratic Party.

[19] G. John Ikenberry and Anne-Marie Slaughter for the Princeton Project on National Security, *Forging a World of Liberty Under Law, U.S. National Security in the 21st Century* (Woodrow Wilson School of Public and International Affairs, 2006).

under decision-making and implementation processes that were effectively designed to reduce the risk of blundering or opportunistic intervention.[20]

Suppose one goes further and concludes, on the basis of the Council's low scores on the criteria of accountability, transparency, and above all, institutional integrity, along with the lack of clear evidence of comparative benefit, that it is illegitimate, not just that it does not enjoy exclusive legitimacy, when it comes to authorizing military intervention across borders in cases not covered by the right of self-defense. According to the analysis of legitimacy offered in the first part of the chapter, this conclusion would reflect a judgment that, all things considered, the benefits to be expected from the Council do not warrant our according it the sort of standing that institutions generally need if they are to function effectively and without excessive costs.

What would follow from the conclusion that the Security Council is illegitimate, so far as the legitimacy of the international system of legal human rights is concerned? As I have emphasized, that system is exceedingly complex; indeed its various parts are in many cases so disconnected and compartmentalized in their operations as to belie the label 'system.' Or, to characterize the situation in a more positive way, the system is *highly modularized*: Various parts operate with a high degree of independence from one another.

If that is so, then the illegitimacy of even an institution as important as the Security Council need not undermine the legitimacy of other parts of the system. This judgment can be generalized: Given how unsystematic the so-called system of international legal human rights institutions is, the illegitimacy of a particular component is not likely to undermine rest of the system.

Avishai Margalit employs a vivid analogy to distinguish between two types of moral compromises: fly in the ointment compromises and cockroach in the soup compromises. The former are discrete

---

[20] Keohane and I set out the appropriate institutional arrangements in "The Preventive War: A Cosmopolitan Institutional Proposal," *Ethics & International Affairs*, 18:1 (2004): 1–22. This article focuses on the special case of preventive war but much of what is said applies also to humanitarian intervention. See also Allen Buchanan, "Institutionalizing the Just War," *Philosophy & Public Affairs*, 34:1 (2006): 2–38, and Allen Buchanan and Robert O. Keohane, "Precommitment Regimes for Intervention," *Ethics & International Affairs*, 25:1 (2011): 41–63.

and compartmentalized; they need not involve large-scale moral contamination. The latter are pervasively polluting.[21] The same distinction can be applied to illegitimate institutions. In the case of the Security Council, illegitimacy is more like a fly in the ointment than a cockroach in the soup, because the performance of most of the other institutions in the system is not seriously impaired by the Council's failings. Nonetheless, it is a very large and obscenely filthy fly, because the failure to authorize interventions to stop genocides and other mass killings is a great moral failing.

### Are Human Rights Treaty-Drafting Groups Illegitimate Legislatures?

In the past, the International Law Commission played a more prominent role in drafting treaties. The process has become less institutionalized: Ad hoc groups, with memberships that may shift over time as the process unfolds, are now often the mechanism by which human rights treaties are created. This development may be cause for concern. The ad hoc character of the process may make it harder to detect patterns of problems and may impair accountability as well. So, one question is whether the lack of a uniform, institutionalized process for drafting treaties itself creates a legitimacy deficit for the system as a whole. I will not explore that complex issue here, but will merely mark it as an important topic for a more extended inquiry. I will note, however, that some might argue that the fact that the task of drafting human rights treaties is not thoroughly institutionalized makes the process more inclusive and responsive. This may be so if, under current conditions, more thoroughgoing institutionalization would be likely to take the form of bureaucracy in its more negative connotations.

   Instead, I will concentrate on what is perhaps the most potentially serious challenge to the legitimacy of the treaty-drafting process: the charge that the groups involved in it lack some of the important features of legitimate legislative bodies. Their members are not democratically elected through processes that give a vote to all competent individuals who will be affected by the norms they craft, and these

---

[21] Avishai Margalit, *On Compromise and Rotten Compromises* (Princeton, NJ: Princeton University Press, 2010).

norms are not subject to review by an independent judiciary. Presumably, both the democratic character of domestic legislation and its constitutional embeddedness in a system of separation of powers contribute to the legitimacy of domestic legislation. So, the fact that the making of international human rights law through treaties has neither of these characteristics casts doubt on the legitimacy of the treaty-making groups and the treaties they produce.

To criticize treat treaty-drafting groups on the grounds that they lack some of the key features of legitimate domestic legislatures is, however, to misunderstand their nature and function. In fact, they are so unlike domestic legislatures that it is a mistake to apply criteria for the legitimacy of the latter to them. Unlike domestic legislatures, they do not attempt to formulate norms with sufficient specificity for implementation. Nor are the documents they produce legally binding on anyone. Instead, they depend upon domestic legislatures to ratify the abstract norms they formulate, to specify them sufficiently to guide policy, and to incorporate them into domestic law.

Nor do the treaty-drafting groups even attempt, nor should they attempt, to ensure that the norms they produce reflect the preferences of the majority of those to whom they will ultimately be applied. That task is left to states, in the treaty ratification process, so far as treaties must be approved by representative domestic legislative bodies. This division of labor has many benefits, not the least of which is that it allows domestic legislatures to tailor the specification of the norms to the particular circumstances and culture of different societies.

Hence it is a mistake to compare the treaty drafting groups with domestic legislatures and conclude that they are so deficient as to be illegitimate. Instead, it is more illuminating to think of them as outsourcing the task of legislation properly speaking to the legislatures of states that ratify the treaties they produce. They depend heavily on domestic legislatures to do what they cannot and should not attempt to do.

Later, I will argue that the benefits of the division of labor between treaty drafting groups and domestic legislatures go in the other direction as well: Legislatures benefit in several important ways from having international bodies formulate abstract norms that can serve as the starting point for their lawmaking activities. Here I only wish to emphasize that because there is much latitude for different states to specify and implement treaty norms in ways that suit their resource capacities, social practices, and cultural traditions, it is less troubling that the initial, abstract formulation of the norms is by treaty-drafting groups that are not subject to the constitutional checks and balances that exist in well-designed domestic constitutional orders and that these international bodies are much less responsive to the preferences of the global population than democratic legislatures are to their constituencies.

The treaty-drafting groups are certainly not democratic in what might be called the individual-majoritarian sense. They are not designed to produce norms that reflect the preferences of the majority of human beings, though the ultimate goal is to produce norms that are universally binding. (There is nothing troubling about that, if one assumes that morally appropriate international standards for the behavior of states, like other moral standards, cannot be determined by taking a vote anymore than domestic constitutional rights should be determined by majority rule.)

If the treaty-drafting groups imposed laws on people around the world, in the way in which legislatures impose laws on domestic populations, this lack of democracy would be a severe detriment to their legitimacy. But that is not their role. Democratic control over the ultimate product—both the decision whether to ratify human rights treaties and the choice of legislation to realize the purposes the abstract treaty norms are designed to promote—resides in states, not in the treaty-drafting groups.

This fact has an important consequence, given the progress of democracy in the world. If the trend toward democratization continues—if more states become democratic—then the legitimacy of human rights law will be enhanced. As states democratize, the domestic legislatures that ratify treaties and translate their norms into domestic law will become more representative, and the "democracy deficit" of treaty-making groups themselves will become less important.[22] And to the extent that international legal human

---

[22] For an elaboration of the point that increasing democratization at the level of states will help allay worries about the legitimacy of international human rights institutions, see Allen Buchanan, "Human Rights," *Oxford Handbook of Political Philosophy*, ed. David Estlund (Oxford: Oxford University Press, 2012), pp. 279–97.

rights foster the process of democratization, they thereby help create the conditions for enhancing their own legitimacy.

### Does the Treaty Bodies' Lack of Enforcement Capacity Undermine Their Legitimacy?

A human rights treaty typically includes provisions for creating a treaty body to monitor compliance with its provisions. The lack of capacity for enforcement on the part of the treaty bodies might be thought to impugn their legitimacy. After all, their inability to do anything more than issue report cards on states' compliance seems to imply that they fail to satisfy the criterion of comparative benefit mentioned earlier.

Indeed, they appear to fail miserably, *if* one assumes that the chief benefit they are supposed to supply is compliance. Once again, I want to suggest that this is the wrong way to look at the matter. If the enforcement of international legal human rights depended solely, or even chiefly, on the enforcement capacities of the treaty bodies—or, for that matter, on the enforcement capacities of any other *international* bodies, including the Security Council—then one might well conclude that the system is too inefficacious to be legitimate, that it scores too low on the criterion of comparative benefit discussed earlier. But to think in this way is once again to ignore the institutional division of labor.

For the most part, international legal human rights are not enforced by international institutions of any kind, including the treaty bodies. When they are enforced, they are chiefly enforced by domestic institutions. The legitimacy of treaty-drafting groups and the treaty bodies should not be gauged on the assumption that they are supposed to be capable of human rights lawmaking or enforcement on their own, but rather according to whether they play a beneficial role in a larger institutional system that encompasses both international and domestic institutions and that achieves the needed functions through a division of labor.

In trying to assess the efficacy of the system of international legal human rights system, it is also important to remember that enforcement—if by that one means securing compliance by coercion or the threat of coercion—is not the only or the most important way of implementing norms. Even where enforcement thus defined is not available, there are other mechanisms for promoting compliance with international legal human rights. These include both carrots and sticks, running the gamut from appeals to a state's concern about its reputation, to making membership in beneficial alliances or access to credits, loans, and foreign aid conditional on compliance, to economic sanctions.

The treaty bodies produce significant benefits, in spite of the fact that their own ability to hold states accountable for noncompliance is meager. These benefits differ depending upon whether they are interacting with states that care about their human rights performance or those which do not. With respect to the former, queries or negative judgments by the treaty bodies, as well as the simple issuing of requests for reports, can prompt efforts to improve compliance, though this has nothing to do with liability to enforcement. In the case of states that are not committed to human rights, the actions of the treaty bodies provide a focal point for efforts by other parties to increase these states' compliance with treaties. When states fail to deliver compliance reports to the treaty bodies, this is a matter of public record that NGOs and various civil society groups can seize upon to call attention to poor performance on the part of states. The treaty bodies provide highly visible venues in which human rights activists can operate and they are widely regarded as authoritative judges of whether international legal human rights are being realized.

None of this is to deny that the treaty bodies suffer serious defects. They are often extremely slow in their operations, they frequently fail to utilize adequately the expertise of NGOs, and in some cases they include members representing states that routinely engage in major human rights violations.[23] Perhaps the single most serious deficiency, however, is that they tend to be insufficiently

[23] See Navanethem Pillay for the UN Office of High Commissioner for Human Rights, "Strengthening the United Nations human rights treaty body system," June 2012, and Michael O'Flaherty and Claire O'Brien, "Reform of UN Human Rights Treaty Monitoring Bodies: A Critique on the High Commissioner's Proposal for a Unified Standing Treaty Body," *Human Rights Law Review*, 7:1 (2007): 141–72.

critical of states when they persist in violating treaty provisions, fail to submit required periodic reports on their efforts to comply with treaty provisions or do not respond in timely manner to enquiries from the treaty bodies. Although these flaws are significant, they do not undercut the benefits that the treaty bodies provide.

## The Extended Institution

There is a more dramatic way to put my point about the implications for legitimacy of the lack various institutional capacities on the part of treaty-drafting groups and treaty bodies. Earlier I spoke of treaty-drafting groups as outsourcing the tasks of norm specification to states. Similarly, we could say that the treaty bodies and international institutions generally outsource enforcement to states and to other, "softer" mechanisms for promoting compliance to NGOs.

However, if this division of labor is sufficiently entrenched and institutionalized, and if it involves core functions in the international legal human rights enterprise, the term 'outsourcing' may be misleading. Instead, perhaps we should revise our understanding of the boundaries of institutions and say that in these contexts the distinction between international and domestic institutions does not amount to much.

The crucial point is this: *Rather than saying that the international institutions are very limited in their capacities, we should view their capacities as including their ability to utilize the powers of domestic institutions and NGOs.* To take an example outside the human rights domain, instead of saying that the WTO lacks enforcement capacity and has to depend on private enforcement, we might say that when states act on the retaliation permits it issues, they are agents of the WTO, part of the machinery of that institution.[24]

Here I am suggesting an analogy with the Extended Mind Hypothesis, according to which, from a functional point of view, one should regard a person's mind (not her consciousness!) as encompassing the

---

[24] Samantha Besson, "International Legality—A Response to Hathaway and Shapiro," *Opinio Juris Blog*, http://opiniojuris.org/2011/11/15/international-legality-%E2%80%93-a-response-to-hathaway-shapiro.

operations of her computer, if the computer plays an on-going, central role in her cognitive life.[25] Similarly, we might say that in the case of international institutions, deep and persisting functional integration with other institutions warrants a more expansive characterization of the capacities of international institutions or, better yet, a rethinking of our tendency to draw sharp boundaries between international institutions, on the one hand, and domestic institutions and NGOs, on the other.

So far, I have argued that apparent weaknesses in the case of two important international human rights institutions, the treaty-drafting groups and the treaty bodies—do not appear so threatening to their legitimacy once we understand their deep and persisting functional dependence on domestic institutions. Put more positively, this functional dependence contributes to the legitimacy of the international institutions, by compensating for their weaknesses through an institutional division of labor. Given this division of labor, the efficacy and legitimacy of the system of international human rights law is not fatally undermined by the weakness of international human rights institutions considered in isolation. I have also noted that the fragmentary, or, more positively, the highly modularized character of the system of international human rights institutions limits the damage that the illegitimacy of a particular institution does to the legitimacy of the system as a whole (the fly in the ointment point). In the next part, I argue that international human rights institutions perform valuable functions that states cannot perform for themselves—and that this contributes to the legitimacy of states, which in turn contributes to the legitimacy of the international institutions. I show that relationships of *reciprocal legitimation* exist between states, international human rights institutions, and human rights NGOs.

Before proceeding to that discussion, I wish to sketch an idea that I hope to flesh out in some future work. I have noted that the so-called system of international human rights institutions is not very systematic; that it is fragmentary or, more positively, that it exhibits a high degree of modularity. The same can be said for international law generally, both in its doctrinal and institutional

---

[25] Andy Clark and David Chalmers, "The Extended Mind," *Analysis*, 58:1 (1998): 7–19.

aspects. Modularity or, if you will, fragmentation and lack of system, can be a virtue. For one thing, an entity that is modular is more amenable to incremental change: Because it is not thoroughly unified, it is possible to change some parts of it without having to change the whole thing. Cultural selection, like natural selection in organisms, operates incrementally: social structures or organisms that were "seamless webs," that is, that lacked modularity, would be at a lethal disadvantage—they would lack adaptability because they would be incapable of the incremental change that selection produces. In addition, in the case of international law, new norms can be created through the treaty process, by groups of states, without all states having to approve of them, and this fact greatly enhances the opportunities for incremental change that modularity creates.

There is yet another reason why the disunity or modularity of the international legal order has some value: It allows for competition among institutions and norm-entrepreneurs in ways that would not be possible in more unified systems. Disunity or, more positively, modularity, when combined with the capacity for voluntary norm-creation by any like-minded group of states, creates opportunities for competition that can feed a process of incremental change through cultural selection.

This is not to say that the so-called fragmentation of international law in general or the institutional fragmentation of the international legal human rights system are without costs. The point, rather, is that is a mistake to assume that lack of unity is always an evil.

## III. *How International Human Rights Institutions Contribute to the Legitimacy of States and Vice Versa*

In chapter 4, in setting out the first argument for having an international legal human rights system, I identified seven benefits the system provides. Now I want to focus on two of those benefits and explain more fully how they contribute to the legitimacy of states. The two legitimacy-enhancing benefits are (1) providing a backup for the implementation of domestic constitutional rights and (2) mitigating an inherent flaw of democracies, by making government officials accountable for taking the interests and rights of foreigners seriously.

*Backing Up Constitutional Rights*

As I observed in chapter 4, even the most democratic, rights-respecting states sometimes fail to protect the rights that their own constitutions accord to their citizens. This is especially true with respect to women, racial and national minorities, gays, lesbians, and transgender people, but virtually all citizens are vulnerable to rights violations in cases of perceived national emergencies, such as war and when dramatic acts of terrorism occur.

I also noted that there is likely to be a strong congruence between international legal human rights and domestic constitutional rights for two reasons. First, some if not most of the rights included in domestic constitutions are conceived as universal rights—rights that are appropriate for citizens of this particular state because they are appropriate for all human beings. Second, in many cases constitutional bills of rights were consciously modeled on international human rights documents, in particular the UDHR and the ICCPR.

To the extent that there is congruence between international human rights and the rights found in the constitution of a particular state, that state's participation in international human rights regimes can provide a backup for domestic rights protection. Because the protection of citizens' rights is one of the basic justifying functions of the state and because justification is a necessary condition for legitimacy, the adequacy of that protection is an important consideration in assessments of the legitimacy of the state. Stated in terms of the analysis of institutional legitimacy set out in part I of this chapter, whether a state does a creditable job of protecting its citizens' rights is relevant to whether those citizens should regard its laws as providing content-independent reasons for acting, to whether others should refrain from interfering with its operation and adopt other respectful stances toward it, and indeed to whether it is justified in wielding political power. International institutions therefore contribute to the legitimacy of the state when they help ensure the adequacy of its protection of citizens' rights.

Whether participation in international human rights institutions merely enhances a state's legitimacy or is critical to its being legitimate will vary from state to state. If a state has domestic legal institutions that generally do a creditable job of protecting the rights of all its citizens, then its abstention from international institutions that provide a backup for that protection would not render it illegitimate. Thus, Switzerland's refusal to join the UN until 2002 most likely did not significantly impugn its legitimacy.

In contrast, in the case of new states emerging in conditions in which there are powerful threats to the rights of national minorities and there are as yet no domestic institutions capable of providing adequate protections against such threats, refusal to participate in international human rights institutions could deprive a state of legitimacy, not just make it less legitimate than it would be if it participated. This was arguably the case with some of the new states emerging from the breakup of the Soviet Union and Yugoslavia. Participation in the Council of Europe, in particular, appears to have resulted in some newly independent European former Soviet Republics abandoning policies that violated the rights of national minorities within their borders.[26]

Similarly, it has been argued that by ratifying the European Convention on Human Rights, a number of European countries locked in the commitment to liberal constitutional democracy in the decade after World War II, when there were reasonable fears that they might lapse back into authoritarian rule.[27] In this case, too, embracing international human rights law can be seen as enhancing the legitimacy of states.

## Mitigating an Inherent Flaw of Democracies

So far, I have argued that a state's international human rights law can enhance or, in extreme cases, be critical for its legitimacy by virtue of the effect that participation has on that state's own citizens. Now I want to argue for a more ambitious conclusion: Participation in the international legal human rights enterprise can have a positive impact on a state's legitimacy by virtue of the effect it has on the interests of foreigners.

[26] Judith Kelly, *Ethnic Politics in Europe: The Power of Norms and Incentives* (Princeton, NJ: Princeton University Press, 2006).
[27] Andrew Moravscik, "The Origins of Human Rights Regimes: Democratic Delegation in Postwar Europe," *International Organization*, 54:2 (2000): 217–52.

All but the most extreme cosmopolitans acknowledge that it is appropriate, if not obligatory, for the state to show partiality toward its own citizens. But anyone who takes the idea of human rights seriously must acknowledge that there are limits to partiality. Constitutional democracies are designed to ensure that government officials are accountable, ultimately, to their fellow citizens. The democratic commitment to the accountability of government to citizens tends to produce not just accountability, but near exclusive accountability: Democratic processes and the constitutional structure of checks and balances create formidable obstacles to government taking into account the legitimate interests of anyone else. In other words, as I observed in chapter 4, there is an inherent structural bias in democracy toward excessive partiality.

Of course, government officials in a democracy will have incentives to take the rights and interests of foreigners into account *if* a sufficient number of politically active and influential citizens happen to voice a strong preference for doing so. But generally speaking, there is likely to be a considerable discrepancy between the politically effective majority's preferences and what a proper consideration of the rights and interests of foreigners requires. Further, even if a considerable portion of the citizenry genuinely cares about the welfare of foreigners, they may fail to carry through on this when it comes to holding their government accountable. Here, as in many other domains, weakness of the will may undercut good intentions, unless there is some effective way for democratic publics to bind themselves—and their governments—so as to follow through on their cosmopolitan commitments.

International human rights law can facilitate collective self-binding. Participation in international institutions can force domestic government officials to take the rights of foreigners into account and to that extent curb the structural bias toward excessive partiality.

## State Legitimacy and the Treatment of Foreigners

Whether an institution is legitimate depends in part on whether its agents are justified in wielding political power. A state does not merit the sort of respect that legitimacy implies if its agents are not justified in exercising power. States, especially the more powerful ones, wield power not just over their own citizens, but also over others who have no standing whatsoever in domestic political processes.

They do so not only in their foreign policy narrowly conceived, but also through their domestic policies, especially in economic matters. (Think of how the so-called domestic economic policies of the United States can affect foreigners, for example.)

Rights (everyone's rights, not just those of citizens) constrain the justifiable exercise of political power; so whether a state's agents are justified in wielding political power, and hence whether the state is legitimate, depends in part on whether power is wielded in ways that are consistent with respect for the rights of foreigners. Participation in international institutions can therefore contribute to the legitimacy of states (and in extreme cases can even be critical for legitimacy) by preventing them from wielding political power in ways that violate the rights of foreigners.

Earlier, I argued that the term 'legitimacy' connotes a kind of standing and also that, in most contexts, being justified in wielding political power is a necessary condition for legitimacy. I now want to connect these two points in such a way as to add support to my claim that how a state treats foreigners can make a difference to its internal legitimacy, its legitimacy vis-à-vis its own citizens.

The state, at least if it pretends to be anything other than a gunman writ large, claims to act in the name of its people, and this is true for all of its actions, whether they are directed toward foreigners or not. What a state does in the name of its citizens (whatever it does in their name, not just what it does *to them*) can affect whether it is justified in wielding power and whether its citizens ought to treat its laws as authoritative. If a state persistently acts in ways that grossly violate the rights of foreigners, whether through aggressive war or as a predictable result of its domestic economic policies, it imputes these actions and hence the responsibility for them to its citizens. By persistently perpetrating serious injustices against foreigners and imputing them to its citizens, the state can undermine its standing as a justified wielder of political power tout court and the authoritativeness of its laws (all of its laws) for its citizens.

When a state acts in this way, its citizens may still have good reasons to comply with those of its laws that do not violate the human rights of foreigners (for example, because those laws replicate the requirements of morality), but they no longer have content-independent reasons to comply with the state's laws as such. In other words, if the injustice to foreigners is sufficiently severe and persisting, it can undermine the legitimacy of the state across the board, as it were, not just with respect to the particular domain of action in which it perpetrates the injustice.

Given the potential for violating the basic human rights of foreigners entailed by the state's ability to use armed force across borders, participation in international institutions that constrain the use of force can be critical for the legitimacy of the state. States that have powerful militaries and extensive economic and geopolitical interests have a propensity to use force beyond their own borders. If such states do not participate in international institutions designed to constrain the use of military force across borders, they run a serious and avoidable risk that they will abuse their power. This risk is exacerbated, as I have already noted, by domestic institutions that exhibit a structural bias against taking the rights of foreigners seriously. Failure of a state to participate in international security institutions that reduce this risk can detract from a state's legitimacy; participation can bolster it.

Whether such participation is critical for a state's legitimacy (whether the failure to participate would deprive it of legitimacy, as opposed merely to rendering it less legitimate than it would be if it did participate) will depend upon how dangerous the state's unrestrained behavior toward foreigners is. In the case of a single superpower, the potential for excessive partiality to result in egregious harms to foreigners is great indeed.

It is important to keep in mind the distinction between the normative and sociological senses of 'legitimacy.' I have focused on the normative sense of the term. However, it is worth pointing out that there are important connections between the two senses. As I noted in chapter 4, on some accounts of legitimacy, as on some accounts of justice, a publicity condition must be satisfied: An institution is legitimate only if it is possible for competent individuals who are subject to its exercise of power to be able to make a reasonable judgment that it satisfies at least the more basic requirements for being legitimate (or just). This is one reason why transparency may be necessary for legitimacy, in addition to the fact that it facilitates accountability and thereby helps to ensure that the criteria of comparative benefit and integrity are satisfied.

One obstacle to any such publicity condition being satisfied is the marked asymmetry of information about the actual performance of the state that typically exists between the agents of the state and its citizens. To the extent that participation in international human rights institutions can reduce this asymmetry with respect to knowledge that is relevant to making reasonable judgments about the legitimacy of the state, such participation can provide assurance to citizens that their state meets reasonable criteria for legitimacy. When states ratify human rights treaties, their citizens gain access to independent and relatively objective monitoring of their state's performance in respecting their own rights and thereby enhance their legitimacy. I observed in chapter 1 that there is a trend toward greater accountability of states for their violations of the human rights of foreigners and away from the expectation that their human rights-correlative duties are owed only to those under their jurisdiction. If this trend continues, then the international legal human rights system will play a more prominent role in contributing to the legitimacy of states.

## IV. *Reciprocal Legitimation*

Thus far, I have argued (1) that states contribute to the legitimacy of international human rights institutions insofar as the outsourcing of lawmaking and enforcement functions to states mitigates defects of these international institutions that would otherwise undermine their legitimacy, and (2) that international human rights institutions contribute to the legitimacy of states in several distinct ways, and that failure to participate can detract from legitimacy. I have also noted (3) that in extreme cases, whether a particular state is legitimate could depend upon whether it participates in particular international institutions. I now want to complete my account of reciprocal legitimation by showing that (4) an international institution's performing the function of contributing to the legitimacy of states can contribute to its own legitimacy.

Consider an analogy. Within the state, a particular institution can contribute to the state's legitimacy by improving or safeguarding the functioning of other institutions. For example, an independent judiciary, with the power to review legislation, can help ensure that the legislative branch does not violate constitutional rights, and its performing of this function can contribute to the state's legitimacy. The fact that the judiciary functions in this way is part of what makes the state legitimate, because having a judiciary that functions in this way makes the state worthy of our support.

Furthermore, the fact that the judiciary contributes to the state's legitimacy is surely a relevant consideration in assessments of the judiciary's own legitimacy. If the judiciary's exercise of its review powers did not constrain the legislature or achieve some other important result, its exercise of this power would be unjustified. From either of two respondent perspectives (that of the addressees of the court's decisions (that is, the legislators) or that of ordinary citizens), the judiciary's contribution to the legitimacy of the state is a relevant consideration in determining what one's practical stance toward the judiciary should be.

The fact that the relationship between the judiciary and the legislative branch exists within the state is irrelevant. The point is that the contribution that an institution makes to the legitimacy of another institution can be among the considerations upon which its own legitimacy depends, and this holds for international as well as domestic institutions.

### The Legitimacy of NGOs

In part I of this chapter, in laying out the Metacoordination View, I distinguished between criteria and standards of legitimacy. Because institutional outsiders, including those who ought to hold the institution accountable, often lack access to information about its inner workings, they may be unable to judge directly whether the criteria for legitimacy are being satisfied. This problem is not fatal if they can determine whether certain standards are being met that function as reliable proxies for the criteria. Generally speaking, one especially important standard is transparency. Or, to put the point negatively, if an institution refuses to make information about its workings available to outsiders, we have good reason to doubt whether it is satisfying the criteria for legitimacy. The mere availability of information may not suffice, however. Reliable external agents to gather and integrate the information and make it available in understandable form to relevant stakeholders are required—what Robert O. Keohane and I have referred to as external epistemic agents. In the case of international human rights institutions, as with international institutions generally, NGOs often play this role.

The crucial role of external epistemic agents is another illustration of one of the main points of this chapter: *The legitimacy of an institution is an ecological matter. One cannot determine whether a particular institution is legitimate simply by looking at the characteristics of the institution itself. Instead, one must understand how it interacts with other institutions.*

In the case of the international legal human rights system, NGOs are among the most important external epistemic agents. Their legitimacy depends in part on the contribution their activities make to the legitimacy of states and international organizations, such as the treaty making committees and the treaty monitoring bodies.[28]

It is often said, and quite reasonably so, that the legitimacy of NGOs depends in part upon their independence from states. This makes perfectly good sense, once we understand the importance of NGOs as external epistemic agents and appreciate the fact that their legitimacy depends in part on the contribution they make to the legitimacy of states. To serve effectively as external epistemic agents they must be independent; they cannot rely on information provided by states. To contribute to the legitimacy of states they must be sufficiently independent of state policy to make impartial judgments about its human rights performance. When NGOs successfully serve as external epistemic agents, this contributes to their own legitimacy.

## Conclusion

A moral evaluation of the existing system of international legal human rights must include an assessment of the legitimacy of its key institutions, preferably one that is consistent with a general account of legitimacy that applies to a wide range of institutional types. With an adequate general account of institutional legitimacy in hand, it is necessary to consider the particular criteria and standards of legitimacy for various types of institutions. In the case of the international legal human rights system, the large number of institutions involved, their heterogeneity, and the modularized nature of the system, make the task of assessing the overall legitimacy of the system

---

[28] Boyle and Chinkin provide a masterful characterization of international lawmaking, including a valuable discussion of the increasingly important role of NGOs in it. Alan Boyle and Christine Chinkin, *The Making of International Law* (Oxford: Oxford University Press, 2007).

extraordinarily difficult if not impossible. Nonetheless, reasonable legitimacy assessment of particular institutions may be achievable. It may also be possible to conclude that the legitimacy deficits of some institutions are not so severe as to make a qualified support for the system as a whole morally inappropriate.

Theorizing about institutional legitimacy tends to be framed in a way that privileges the legitimacy of the state and makes the legitimacy of international institutions, including human rights institutions, look dubious. It is widely assumed that so far as its internal legitimacy—its legitimacy vis-à-vis its own citizens—is concerned, the state is self-sufficient: All that matters is how it relates to those under its jurisdiction. On some views, the state is internally legitimate if it respects the rights of those under its jurisdiction and is democratic; on others, the consent of those under its jurisdiction is also required. To the extent that it is acknowledged that legitimacy requires the justified exercise of political power, justification is understood solely by reference to the relationship between the state and those under its jurisdiction, in spite of the fact that the state exerts power over other persons as well.

Given this picture, it is not surprising that there is a tendency to think either that the legitimacy of international institutions must be transferred *via* consent to them from legitimate states or, if that is not possible, that their legitimacy must consist in their mimicking those features of the state's relationship to its own citizens (or others under its jurisdiction) that confer legitimacy on it. For those who think that legitimacy is conferred on the state by democratic processes, the natural assumption is that international institutions must be democratic to be legitimate. Because international institutions are not democratic, they are deemed illegitimate.

I have argued that this picture is wrong. The internal legitimacy of a state does not depend solely on how it relates to its own citizens (or others under its jurisdiction); and international institutions, not just domestic political arrangements, can contribute to the internal legitimacy of a state. Further, an international institution can be legitimate even if it is not democratic, if it is properly connected to democratic states in a suitable division of institutional labor.

It is true that the legitimacy of international institutions depends in part on their being endorsed by states; indeed, it is hard to see how it could be otherwise in a world in which global democratic institutions are lacking and individuals' and groups' interests are represented, if they are represented at all, chiefly through their membership in states. But this should not blind us to the fact that legitimation can be bidirectional. International institutions, especially international legal human rights institutions, can contribute to the legitimacy of states, even though they are the creations of states. And their doing this contributes to their own legitimacy.

This chapter has begun the task of determining whether the key institutions of the international human rights system are legitimate, an aspect of the justification of human rights practice that has been neglected by philosophers, who have tended to concentrate more on justifying claims about the existence of moral human rights (on the mistaken assumption that if international legal human rights are justified, it is because they correspond to preexisting moral human rights). Without pretending to have treated this subject exhaustively, I believe considerable headway has been made. I have advanced a conception of legitimacy, the Metacoordination View, which is general enough to apply to a wide range of institutions, including those that are central to the international legal human rights system, yet capable of providing guidance for identifying criteria for making legitimacy assessments.

Unlike accounts that make legitimacy depend solely on the relationship between an institution and those to whom it directs its rules, the Metacoordination View opens the door to an ecological understanding of legitimacy.

The Metacoordination analysis of the general concept of institutional legitimacy, when combined with the ecological view, explains why international legal human rights institutions can be legitimate without themselves being democratic. The Metacoordination View enables us to see that different criteria of legitimacy are appropriate for institutions of different types. On the Metacoordination View, the question is whether these institutions, given the role they play in a larger institutional division of labor, warrant the sort of standing that they need in order to supply their distinctive benefits and do so without excessive costs. The answer to that question is determined by ascertaining whether the institution is worthy of that standing, in light of the risks involved in the empowerment that our giving it standing entails. Where democracy is not feasible, as in the case of international institutions generally at this point in time, but the institutions provide valuable benefits that are not available without them and do so in morally permissible ways, it would be unreasonable to deem them illegitimate simply because they are not democratic. To do this would be to apply a criterion of legitimacy that may well be appropriate for the state, at least under reasonably favorable conditions, but which is ill-suited to institutions of a quite different sort.

In addition, the Metacoordination View facilitates the ecological understanding of legitimacy by making it clear that the considerations that determine legitimacy need not be limited to the character of the relationship between an institution and those to whom it addresses its directives. Other considerations, including the effects of the institution's operations on third parties, where this includes both individuals and other institutions, can be relevant to whether we ought to confer on it the kind of standing that legitimacy connotes.

The single most important point of this chapter is that legitimacy, properly understood, is an ecological concept. Applied to the case of international legal human rights institutions, this insight leads to a much different assessment of their legitimacy. Once we see how the capacities of these institutions are amplified by their reliance on other institutions, and in particular, states, we can better appreciate their legitimacy.

I have also argued that although some key institutions in the international legal human rights system, and in particular, the Security Council, are of dubious legitimacy, others enjoy greater legitimacy than might first appear, once we adopt the ecological perspective and recognize that they are not inferior global analogs of institutions within the state and that they are part of a complex interdependency of institutions in which some of the most important legislative and enforcement functions are allocated to states.

The ecological understanding of legitimacy thus reinforces the Metacoordination View's implication that an institution need not be democratic to be legitimate. An international institution can be legitimate even though it is not democratic, if it is properly connected to democratic institutions in a division of institutional labor.

In the next chapter, I probe the dark side of the interdependency of states and international legal human rights institutions, examining the question of whether, by embracing international human rights law, states may damage their own constitutional orders and wrongly restrict the collective right of self-determination of their peoples, thereby diminishing, rather than enhancing their legitimacy.

# CHAPTER 6

## The Problematic Supremacy of International Human Rights Law

The preceding chapter characterized the positive impact that the system of international legal human rights has on the legitimacy of states and argued that this contributes to the legitimacy of the institutions that comprise the system. This chapter explores the possibility that the system can also have deleterious effects on states. To understand the nature of this concern, it is necessary to place the development of international human rights law in historical context.

### I. *The Emergence of Robust International Law*

The past three decades have witnessed a dramatic increase in the number of democratic states and also the emergence of what might be called robust international law, international law that claims the authority to regulate matters once considered to be the exclusive concern of the state, including the state's treatment of its own citizens within its own territory. International human rights law requires states to abolish long-standing practices regarding punishment, to secure the rights of children in ways that may challenge traditional parenting practices, to change existing political processes to ensure rights of freedom of association and assembly, to provide access for all citizens to basic education and healthcare, and to dismantle patterns of racial or gender discrimination that may be deeply ingrained in a society's culture.

Human rights law is robust international law par excellence, but international criminal law and portions of international environmental and trade law also now impact what were traditionally considered matters reserved for the authority of the state. All international law claims supremacy over the matters to which it applies, but international human rights law, by its very nature, raises the stakes in claiming supremacy because it applies to matters that have hitherto been thought to be solely within the state's prerogative.

## II. *Allegations of Incompatibility*

At first blush, the relationship between democratization and the development of international human rights law seems to be a harmonious one of mutual enhancement: Constitutional democracies have often encouraged the development of international human rights law, which in turn has provided support for democratization. Yet there is a substantial body of thought according to which constitutional democracy and international human rights law are incompatible. The focus of this chapter is on the alleged incompatibility of the commitment to constitutional democracy and the commitment to international human rights law, setting aside other areas of robust international law that are not pertinent to the project of this book.[1]

The allegation of incompatibility should be especially disturbing to liberal cosmopolitans, who tend to assume that democratization at the level of states and the development of a system of international human rights law march hand in hand along the path of moral progress. They are loath to consider the possibility that even if each is progressive in its own right, one must choose one or the other.

Allegations of incompatibility are often unclearly formulated. Five different incompatibilist worries ought to be distinguished.

1. Some who view the growth of international human rights law as a threat to constitutional democracy seem to hold that there is an incompatibility *in principle*. On this view, a state is not

---

[1] Most of this chapter is drawn from the following article, which addresses robust international law in general, not just international human rights law: Allen Buchanan and Russell Powell, "Survey Article: Constitutional Democracy and International Law: Are They Compatible?," *Journal of Political Philosophy*, 16:3 (2008): 326–49.

democratic if its citizens are subject to any political authority that is not exclusively accountable to them.[2] The incompatibility, on this view, is that in recognizing the authority of international human rights law, a state would be accountable to an alien entity—a source of law not within the control of its own people—and hence would not be exclusively accountable to them.

2. Others hold that at least in some cases, including that of the United States, acknowledging the supremacy of international human rights law undermines constitutional democracy (i) by shifting power from the legislative to the executive and judicial branches and thereby damaging the constitution's separation of powers and the system of checks and balances it provides, and (ii) by encroaching on the prerogatives of federal units (in the United States these are called states; in other countries provinces, cantons, etc.) to regulate important matters hitherto recognized as being within their jurisdiction and thereby undermining federalism.[3]

3. Third, there is the worry that international human rights law is not produced by democratic processes and that hence the greater the role for this law, the less democratic a society will be.

---

[2] See Jeremy A. Rabkin, *Law Without Nations? Why Constitutional Government Requires Sovereign States* (Princeton, NJ: Princeton University Press, 2005) and *The Case for Sovereignty* (Washington, DC: American Enterprise Institute Press, 2004). Later I criticize this exclusive accountability argument. Rabkin and some others who have been labeled New Sovereigntists may also hold a related, but distinct view: the Austinian-Hobbesian dogma that any genuine polity or any genuine legal system must have a single "sovereign source," a publicly identifiable agent that is capable of both resolving any possible issue about what the law requires and of effectively enforcing its judgment in this regard. I believe that the dubiousness of this view has been sufficiently exposed and that it is not necessary to consider it here. To think that every legal issue must actually be decidable and be decidable by an agent that is capable in all instances of enforcing its decision is a rationalist fantasy that shows a remarkable ignorance of how successful real-world polities that lack this capacity can be.

[3] For the seminal articulation of this view, see Curtis A. Bradley and Jack L. Goldsmith, "Customary International Law as Federal Common Law: A Critique of the Modern Position," *Harvard Law Review*, 110:4 (1997): 815–76, and "UN Human Rights Standards and US Law: The Current Illegitimacy of International Human Rights," *Fordham Law Review*, 66:2 (1997): 319–69.

4. A fourth concern is the growing tendency of judges in domestic courts to draw on international law in interpreting domestic law.[4] There are two worries here: First, that at least in the area of customary human rights law, but perhaps in treaty law as well, the law is so undeveloped and incoherent that judges may be tempted to "cherry-pick" the norms that yield the answers they prefer; second, that some parts of international human rights law express values that conflict with the values that underlie the domestic law of some countries, with the result that judicial borrowing from international human rights law for purposes of interpreting domestic law or referring to it in order to bring domestic law into line with human rights treaty commitments may disrupt the coherence and integrity of domestic law.

5. Finally, some charge that acknowledging the authority of international human rights law has transferred power from constitutional democracies to international human rights institutions — that is, that there has been a relinquishing of sovereignty — and that this has occurred without appropriate democratic authorization. On this last view, the fact that such institutions are created through treaties or executive agreements according to existing constitutionally specified procedures is insufficient, given that their operations significantly restrict the scope of popular self-government and may also alter constitutional structures.[5] There is a related worry: Even if the processes of incorporating international human rights law are adequate from the standpoint of democratic authorization, a people might relinquish too much sovereignty, thereby diminishing the collective right of self-determination of future citizens, at least so far as unilateral withdrawal from human rights treaties is not an option.

[4] See, for instance, "Transcript of Discussion Between U.S. Supreme Court Justices Antonin Scalia and Stephen Breyer on 'The Constitutional Relevance of Foreign Court Decisions,'" American University, January 13, 2005, available at http://domino.american.edu/AU/media/mediarel.nsf/1D265343BDC2189785256 B8100 71F238/1F2F7DC4757FD01E85256F890068E6E0?OpenDocument.

[5] See, e.g., Jeremy A. Rabkin, *Why Sovereignty Matters*, 2nd ed. (Washington, DC: American Enterprise Institute Press, 1998); John C. Yoo, "Globalism and the Constitution: Treaties, Non-Self-Execution, and the Original Understanding," *Columbia Law Review*, 99: 2 (1999): 1955–2094; Curtis A. Bradley and Jack L. Goldsmith, "Treaties, Human Rights, and Conditional Consent," *University of Pennsylvania Law Review*, 149:2 (2000): 339–468.

In this chapter, I will not address the third incompatibilist concern—the worry about democracy—because I have already done so in the preceding chapter. There I argued that the fact that the processes by which human rights treaties are drafted are not democratic does not itself impair their legitimacy or the legitimacy of international human rights law, because the treaty-drafting groups are not legislatures properly speaking. My point was that treaty-drafting groups merely begin the process by which human rights law, properly speaking, is produced—that human rights legislation is done by states, not international bodies, and that what matters most is whether states have democratic legislative processes. The real issue is whether, in ratifying treaties that have a significant impact on domestic constitutional structures, enough has been done from the standpoint of the democratic authorization in what amounts to constitutional change. The problem here does not lie in the international institutions, but in the domestic political processes by which international human rights law achieves supremacy over domestic law. That is the point of the fifth incompatibilist concern, which I take up in due course.

For convenience, I use the label 'incompatibilist concerns' to cover all of the items listed above, but it should be emphasized that they are quite distinct. The various complaints focus on different ways in which international human rights law can impact domestic law—from the implementation of treaties to serving as a resource for the interpretation of domestic law. Taken together they present a serious challenge to liberal cosmopolitan theorists, most of whom unreflectively assume that their enthusiasm for constitutional democracy and their commitment to international human rights are in harmony.

It is appropriate to label these concerns 'incompatibilist,' because those who voice them do *not* suggest that they are merely pointing out that engagement with international human rights law involves some costs to constitutional democratic values, while acknowledging that the costs might be worth bearing. Instead, they strongly suggest and in some cases explicitly assert that the problems they identify are so serious—and the value of constitutional democracy (or its federal variant) is so obvious and overwhelming—that the proper choice for the citizens and leaders of constitutional democracies is to refrain from acknowledging the supremacy of international human rights law. The fact that the United States has not ratified a number of human rights treaties that the vast majority of other states have ratified (including the Children's Rights Convention, the Women's Convention, and the ICESCR) and has only ratified others decades after most countries did (as was the case with the Genocide Convention) may be due in part to the influence of incompatibilist concerns, especially those that focus on the supposedly damaging effects of international human rights law on domestic constitutional structures, including federalism.

## III. *The Impact of Robust International Law on Constitutional Democracy*

In this part, I first elaborate and then evaluate each of the incompatibilist concerns.

### *The Exclusive Accountability Argument*

Rabkin among others complains that acceptance of robust international law, including international human rights law, can involve a national government's delegation of power over its citizens to entities, namely, international organizations and courts, that are not *exclusively* accountable to those citizens and then seems to conclude that this state of affairs is incompatible with constitutional democracy.[6] Call this the Exclusive Accountability Argument.

It is important to be clear about whether this is an argument about the incompatibility of robust international law with constitutional democracy or as an assertion about its incompatibility with the *US Constitution's* limits on delegation. On the former interpretation, the claim begs the question at issue, by assuming that constitutional democracy requires not only that those who wield power over citizens be accountable to them, but also that they be accountable to them alone. On the latter interpretation, as an assertion about US constitutional law, the claim is perhaps initially more plausible, but does nothing to support the thesis that constitutional democracy and international human rights law, or robust international law generally, are incompatible.

To establish the more general conclusion, one would have to show that any constitution that did not require delegated powers to be

---

[6] Rabkin, *Law Without Nations?* and *The Case for Sovereignty.*

230 The Heart of Human Rights

exclusively accountable to the domestic citizenry is not a genuine democratic constitution. That would require showing either that such delegation is incompatible with democracy or that it is incompatible with constitutionalism. It is hard to know even how one would begin to make such an argument, either conceptually, by trying to show that nonexclusive accountability is inconsistent with the core ideas of democracy or of constitutionalism, or empirically, by trying to show that nonexclusive accountability causes the destruction or malfunctioning of democracy or of constitutionalism. Simply to assume that constitutional democracy per se bars any delegation of political power to agencies that are not exclusively accountable to the citizens of the democracy begs the question of whether constitutional democracy and international human rights law are compatible.[7]

Furthermore, there is an obvious reply to the more restricted claim that delegation of authority to agents not exclusively accountable to the citizens of the United States is incompatible with the American form of constitutional democracy. The US Constitution authorizes the president, with concurrence of two-thirds of the Senate, to ratify treaties. In some cases, treaties set up mechanisms for dispute resolution, through arbitration by third parties who are not accountable to the citizens of the contending states or at least not accountable exclusively to them. The clause of the Constitution that authorizes treaty-making includes no suggestion that such treaties are prohibited.

## The Unprincipled Borrowing Argument

The concern here is that domestic judges will abuse their office, picking and choosing from various bodies of international law in order to get the outcomes they prefer, if international law is regarded as a legitimate resource for the interpretation of domestic law.

---

[7] Note that my claim here is *not* that democracy precludes a constitution that requires exclusive accountability, but only that there seems to be no reason to assume that a democratic constitution must require exclusive accountability. Hence I am not committed to the view that if the US Constitution requires exclusive accountability, then this shows that it is defective. For a detailed defense of the view that robust international law, including human rights law, is not in principle incompatible with either the idea of constitutionalism or with that of democracy, see Allen Buchanan and Russell Powell, "Fidelity to Constitutional Democracy and to International Law," *The Routledge Handbook of International Law*, ed. David Armstrong (Cambridge: Cambridge University Press, 2010), pp. 249–67.

There are really three distinct concerns, though they have not been clearly distinguished in the literature. The first is that judges will undermine the rule of law by making decisions according to their preferences rather than according to principles of law. The claim is that the incoherence or underdeveloped character of international law, or of certain areas of international law, and in particular customary human rights law, facilitate unprincipled borrowing.

Second, some incompatibilists, including Rabkin and Supreme Court Justice Scalia, gesture rather sketchily toward what might be a communitarian version of this objection.[8] Their idea is that in some cases (the United States being one of them) the cultural values that undergird a system of domestic law may be at odds with the values that are expressed in international human rights law and that, when this is the case, judicial borrowing for purposes of interpreting domestic law can result in law that does not fit the people to whom it is applied and which does not cohere with preexisting domestic law. For example, Justice Scalia and others have criticized judges' recourse to international human rights law in interpreting the US Constitution's ban on cruel and unusual punishment on these grounds.[9]

The third concern is that judges will pick and choose from international law in a way that encroaches on the proper authority of the legislative branch, thwarting legislative purpose by interpreting laws in the light of international law that runs contrary to that purpose.[10] Because there are additional ways in which engagement with international human rights law might derange internal constitutional structures, I will take the third version up under that general heading

---

[8] See Scalia-Breyer, note 4 supra. See also Atkins v. Virginia, 536 US 304 (2002) (Justice Scalia, dissenting); Rabkin, *Law Without Nations?* and *The Case for Sovereignty*.

[9] Justice Scalia, for instance, maintains that the only legal and moral standards relevant to US constitutional jurisprudence are "the standards of decency of American society—not the standards of decency of the world, not the standards of decency of other countries that don't have our background, that don't have our culture, that don't have our moral views." Scalia-Breyer, ibid., p. 2.

[10] In the US case, on the assumption that customary international law has the status of federal common law, all of these worries are exacerbated. And because federal common law takes precedence over conflicting states' laws, there is the additional concern that judge's recourse to international law undermines federalism by encroaching on the proper domain of the states' lawmaking authority.

below. For now, let us consider the first and second versions of the complaint about unprincipled judicial borrowing: the worry that judges will use recourse to international law as an interpretive resource so as to substitute their preferences for principles and the concern that such borrowing will disrupt the normative coherence of domestic law (the communitarian concern).

Here the distinction between in principle incompatibility and incompatibility under current conditions and practices, a distinction which I introduced at the beginning of this chapter, but which has been neglected by both sides of the debate, is again pertinent. Whether domestic judicial reliance on international law as an interpretive resource runs an unacceptable risk of excessive judicial discretion or of undermining the normative coherence of domestic law will depend on (a) how coherent the relevant international law is and on (b) the degree of continuity between the two bodies of law.

According to some Incompatibilists, lack of coherence is especially pronounced in the case of customary international human rights law, because of lax or at best rather indeterminate standards for what counts as this kind of law.[11] If these critics are correct, it does not follow that domestic judges should forswear all reliance on international human rights law as an interpretive resource, but rather that they should be especially cautious about relying on customary human rights law. So, this particular incompatibilist concern is not an in principle objection to treating international human rights law as a resource for interpreting domestic law. Moreover, it would dissipate entirely if international human rights law matures into a more coherent and determinate system of law, as European human rights law is already well on its way to doing.

Nor does the existence of discontinuities between domestic law and international human rights law provide a conclusive reason for rejecting the latter as a resource for interpreting domestic law. In some cases, the degree of continuity may be rather high, precisely because the domestic legal system has been consciously shaped in

---

[11] One worry is that an overly-permissive conception of what it takes to satisfy the *opinio juris* condition for the emergence of a customary norm has begun to take root—in particular, that mere pronouncements by state officials can suffice to demonstrate the subjective belief that the practice is consistent with or required by the prevailing law.

the light of international legal norms, especially in the area of human rights law. This is the case, for example, in some countries that have recently emerged from authoritarianism and in some developing countries: Their constitutions deliberately seek to harmonize domestic and international law, at least so far as human rights are concerned.[12] Deliberate efforts to harmonize domestic and international law have occurred in other areas as well, including trade law, intellectual property, and the regulation of communications.

How well robust international law and domestic law cohere is a contingent matter and may vary across different areas of international law. So the risk that acceptance of robust international law will result in unprincipled judicial borrowing cannot be a reason for thinking that constitutional democracy and robust international law are incompatible in principle. Further, for the Incompatibilist to say that where coherence is lacking we should reject robust international law would be to beg the deeper question as to whether the citizens and leaders of constitutional democracies have good reason to support the development of robust international law, even if doing so comes at some cost to the coherence of their own legal order. If they do have good reason, then to that extent they also have reason to try to achieve greater coherence between domestic and international law, even if it means modifying domestic law. In chapter 4, I set out

[12] Attempts to harmonize domestic and international law are varied. In some countries, human rights conventions and other aspects of international law are accorded a supreme status above all domestic law including the Constitution (see, e.g., the Netherlands, Belgium, and Luxembourg). For instance, under Article 91(3) of the Netherlands' Constitution (adopted in 1983), treaties that conflict with the Constitution may be approved by the Chambers of Parliament by a two-thirds vote; as per Article 94, statutes that are inconsistent with treaties are not applicable. In other countries (such as Austria and Finland), treaties that derogate from or are otherwise inconsistent with the domestic constitution may be approved by a super majority in parliament, rendering them equal or superior to the Constitution. In many states, international treaties preempt both earlier and subsequent domestic statutes (see inter alia France, Portugal, Spain, Switzerland, and Greece), although a few countries only accord this status to international law concerning human rights (see, e.g., Russia, Romania, and the Czech Republic). In other states, however, the major human rights conventions have the status of ordinary domestic law, applying a "later-in-time" rule to resolve conflicts between domestic and international law (see, e.g., Germany, Ireland, Italy, Norway, Poland, Turkey, United Kingdom, and the United States, inter alia).

a number of weighty reasons why states should support international human rights law. The key point is that it is wrong to assume that where international law and domestic law do not cohere, we must accept this as an unalterable fact and cleave to the supremacy of domestic law as it now is.

The charge that, because of deep differences in cultural values, judicial recourse to international law as a resource will produce domestic law that does not fit the people to whom it is applied has limited force as an argument against acknowledging the authority of international human rights law for two reasons. First, those who advance it do not clearly identify the supposed deep differences in cultural values and more importantly they do not even begin to show that such differences are relevant to *all* areas of international human rights law that judges may treat as a resource for interpretation. Second, they do not consider the possibility that in some cases cultural differences in values may diminish over time, in part through the development of international human rights law. Instead, they beg the question by assuming that if there are cultural differences, the proper response is always to uphold the supremacy of the domestic law that expresses one side of the cultural divide.

It is no doubt true that in some cases international human rights law runs contrary to cultural values present in some of the countries. This is perhaps most evident in the case of human rights norms prohibiting gender and religious discrimination: Some societies contain cultural values that are extremely sexist and intolerant of religious diversity. In such cases, the fit between international human rights law and (some) domestic cultural values may be considerably less than perfect. And *if* domestic law reflects the cultural values in question, then recourse to the latter by domestic judges may introduce some incoherence into domestic law.

What exactly is supposed to follow from this? It does not follow that those countries should deny the authority of the international norms in question or that the project of developing international human rights law ought not to be pursued. That would only follow if congruence with domestic cultural values or the coherence of domestic law in the short term were overriding values. Because there is no reason to believe they are (and a number of good reasons to think they are not, including the importance of protecting human rights), the most that follows is that considerations of cultural fit and legal coherence can provide *some* reason for not accepting international human rights law in those cases in which those considerations are relevant.

In chapter 7, I explore in depth the claim that international human rights law expresses values that are incompatible with those included in *reasonable* collectivistic moralities. At present, the point I wish to emphasize is that the mere fact of incompatibility between local cultural values and international human rights law is in itself no reason whatsoever to deny the supremacy of the latter.

## The Constitutional Derangement Argument

This incompatibilist argument focuses on the damage that acknowledging the supremacy of international human rights law can do to the internal constitutional structures of a constitutional democracy. The potential damage is of two sorts: the undermining of the constitutional allocation of power among the branches of the government, and the undermining of federalism by robbing federal units (states, cantons, provinces, etc.) of some of their proper authority. This argument has been most actively advanced in the case of the United States, so I will use that case to illustrate it.

International human rights law, like international law generally, can become binding domestic law in the United States chiefly in two ways: through the ratification of treaties and when international customary law is regarded as federal common law. Some US constitutional scholars charge that in either case the incorporation of international law into domestic law diminishes the rightful authority of the legislative branch.[13]

---

[13] The tripartite separation of powers is allegedly vitiated by the federal incorporation of international law in several ways. The judicial branch is said to exceed its constitutional mandates by incorporating customary international law into federal common law and by invoking foreign precedent as persuasive authority in US constitutional jurisprudence. The executive is claimed to exceed its constitutionally enumerated powers by entering into "self-executing" treaties, which regulate subject matter reserved to Congress and/or to the several states. Finally, the entire federal government is held to exceed its legitimate authority by incorporating into US law international norms that regulate content constitutionally reserved for state regulation. See, respectively: Bradley and Goldsmith, "Customary International Law as Federal Common Law"; Yoo, "Globalism and the Constitution"; and Rabkin, *Law Without Nations?* and *The Case for Sovereignty*.

According to the US Constitution, international law created through treaties automatically becomes the law of the land: When the United States ratifies a treaty, its provisions take precedence over both the law of the states (federal units) and prior federal law with which it is inconsistent, without the requirement of federal legislation (unless the treaty is "nonself-executing"). The executive's power to make treaties is not unlimited of course, because ratification requires Senate approval; but this is arguably a weaker form of legislative control—and less democratic—than in the ordinary creation of federal law, which requires majorities in both the Senate and the House.

Constitutional scholars who take this form of the Constitutional Derangement Argument seriously point out that the US constitutional provision that makes treaties federal law without federal legislation was drafted in a world in which international treaties did not impinge on the core of the protected sphere of state sovereignty, as is the case with modern human rights law.[14] (There is considerable irony in the fact that many of these scholars tend to be "originalists" who decry the idea that the Constitution should be reinterpreted in the light of new developments, while in this case saying, in effect, that what the treaty clause actually says has to be disregarded because times have changed.)

Given that the US Constitution declares the supremacy of treaty law over states' laws and inconsistent prior federal law and given the clarity of its provisions for the ratification of treaties, it is implausible to argue that law created by treaty is contrary to the US Constitution.[15] For one thing, the first treaty the United States ratified, the Treaty of Paris, ceded considerable control to bodies it created for settling issues between the United States and Britain, in concluding the American War of Independence. Nonetheless, even if it is implausible to argue that the treaty clause does not mean what it says, it might still be the case that the acceptance of international

[14] Yoo, "Globalism and the Constitution" (arguing that self-executing treaties are unconstitutional); Rabkin, *The Case for Sovereignty*.

[15] This case is persuasively made by David M. Golove, "Human Rights Treaties and the US Constitution," *DePaul Law Review*, 52: 2 (2002): 579–635; "Treaty-Making and the Nation: The Historical Foundations of the Nationalist Conception of the Treaty Power," *Michigan Law Review*, 98:5 (2000): 1075–319.

human rights law through treaty ratification effects a reallocation of power away from the legislative branch that is suboptimal from the standpoint of constitutional design and perhaps contrary to the intentions of the framers of the constitution as well.

Similarly, it can be argued that human rights treaty law reallocates power from the legislatures of the states (federal units) to the federal executive and the Senate, when the treaties are ratified and take precedence over the states' laws. The charge here is that acknowledging the supremacy of international human rights law changes the constitutional structure of the federal union, by weakening self-government in the federal units. The same sort of structural change could be effected by according customary international human rights law the status of federal common law. For example, acknowledging the authority of international human rights treaties or of customary human rights law could result in a diminution of federal units' control over the nature of punishments within their jurisdictions by prohibiting the death penalty.

Fortunately, for present purposes it is not necessary to penetrate any farther the thicket of US constitutional interpretation. Instead, it will suffice to make two general points, whose significance is not limited to the peculiarities of the US context. First, for states whose constitutions were drafted prior to the era of robust international law generally and of human rights law in particular and which have not been modified in the light of these developments, the possibility that domestic legal acknowledgment of the supremacy of international human rights law may alter such a state's constitutional structures cannot be dismissed. The introduction of new legal norms that regulate matters previously assigned by the constitution to various branches and levels of government may well be at odds with existing constitutional design; to assume that they will be harmonious would be unduly optimistic. Second, when acknowledgment of the supremacy of international human rights law does impair the functioning of existing constitutional arrangements, the proper conclusion to draw is not that constitutional democracy is incompatible with international human rights law, but rather that acknowledging the supremacy of the latter is incompatible with the optimal functioning of *the particular form of constitutional democracy that includes those constitutional structures.*

Showing that this or that existing constitutional structure is impacted negatively by acknowledging the supremacy of international human rights law is a far cry from establishing that constitutional democracy and international human rights law are incompatible, because there is a plurality of forms of constitutional democracy. Further, constitutional structures rarely if ever work either optimally or not at all; instead, they do the jobs they were designed to do with greater or lesser effectiveness. So, even when acknowledging the supremacy of international human rights law does have a negative impact on the constitutional structures of a particular state, the impact may be of greater or lesser seriousness. In cases where the impact is limited, accepting some detriment to the functioning of constitutional arrangements may be a reasonable trade-off, if this is the only way to secure the important benefits that international human rights law provides.

For example, some loss of legislative authority on the part of the units of a federal constitutional democracy might be a reasonable price to pay, under certain circumstances, if this is necessary for achieving better protection of basic human rights (the backup function I described earlier as one of the benefits of participation in the international legal human rights system). It is a further question, of course, as to when a diminution of legislative authority counts as an infringement of the constitution, as opposed to a departure from previous practice regarding legislative functions, and still another as to whether, when a constitution is being infringed, it is always obligatory either to change it or to eliminate the infringement.

## *The Loss of Collective Self-Determination Argument*

As I have already noted, it is common in some quarters to lament the "democratic deficit" of global institutions generally, including those that are central to the system of international legal human rights. There are two distinct problems to be sorted out. The first is the democratic deficit problem properly speaking: the fact that the international institutions through which international human rights treaties are crafted and compliance with them is monitored are not democratic. That problem, I argued in the preceding chapter, does not look so grave once we understand the division of labor between international institutions and state institutions. Further, this first problem would be solved if the international institutions in question became democratic. But a second problem would remain even if the daunting task of achieving global democracy were completed: Even if they were democratic, international institutions might impose unjustifiable limitations on the exercise of the collective political self-determination.

Suppose that all of the international institutions involved in the drafting and monitoring of human rights treaties were democratic in a very strong sense: Suppose, that is, as Richard Falk and others have proposed, the existence of a global legislature whose members fairly represented everyone or better yet a global direct "virtual" democratic assembly in which all competent persons vote on legislation.[16] There might no longer be a democratic deficit, but a second problem would persist: If the global legislature makes human rights law, and that law reaches into what had been the domains hitherto controlled by constitutional democracies, then the citizens of those democracies will suffer a diminution of self-governance; their political self-determination will be reduced. The point is that regardless of whether international human rights law is created through democratic processes or not, it constricts the domain of self-government in constitutional democracies (and in other types of states as well).

By itself, this does not imply that international human rights law and constitutional democracy are incompatible; to think so would be to beg the question by assuming that in constitutional democracies self-determination must be *unlimited*. Nor does it imply that international human rights law's claim to supremacy should be rejected; to think so would be to assume that the preservation of the largest possible domain of self-determination in constitutional democracies takes precedence over all other considerations, including the benefits that international human rights law can bestow. The critical issue is this: When does the diminution of self-determination in a constitutional democracy become so great as to be incompatible with it warranting the title of a democracy, a polity whose members are in some meaningful sense self-governing?

To answer this question we have to delve deeper into the basis of the commitment to constitutional democracy. So far, I have

---

[16] See Richard Falk and Andrew Strauss, "On the Creation of a Global Peoples Assembly: Legitimacy and the Power of Popular Sovereignty," *Stanford Journal of International Law*, 36:2 (2000): 191–219.

emphasized only some of the values upon which the commitment to constitutional democracy rests, but there are others. One of the most important is the value of political self-determination. Constitutional democracy can enable the people of the state as a whole and, in the case of federal constitutional democracies, also territorially concentrated groups within the state, to exercise political self-determination.

## PROPER SELF-DETERMINATION

Political self-determination is valuable for a number of reasons that it is unnecessary to rehearse here. Because some of these reasons will have greater weight for members of different groups, and because self-determination is not an all or nothing matter, but rather comes in many forms and degrees, there is no single or easy answer to the question: How much self-determination is enough for a constitutional democracy?

An intuitively plausible reply is that we can appeal to the value of self-determination itself and simply say that the citizens of constitutional democracies should decide how much self-governance they will relinquish to global governance institutions.[17] But even if we grant that the decision to relinquish some dimensions of self-determination to a robust international legal order ought itself to be viewed as a matter of self-determination, we still need to know *how* this choice ought to be made. And even if the case could be made that it is permissible or even obligatory to relinquish a great deal of self-governance to the international legal human rights system, it would not follow that *just any way* of transferring political power is appropriate. More precisely, we need to ask whether the same values that undergird the commitment to constitutional democracy also place constraints on *how* powers of self-government can be transferred to international institutions.

One cannot assume that the ways in which international human rights law is actually being incorporated into domestic legal systems satisfy reasonable constraints on the relinquishing of

---

[17] On reflection, this intuition may not stand scrutiny, because, at least in principle, it seems that the citizens of a democracy could (mistakenly) cede authority beyond the point at which it could be said that they are self-governing.

self-determination. To gain a sufficiently critical perspective on current practice, an analogy may be useful.

## ROBUST DEMOCRATIC AUTHORIZATION

There is much to be said for the idea that when existing political units come together to form a federal state, as occurred in what became the United States, or when a centralized state devolves into a federal state, or when secession occurs, these are such significant constitutional changes as to require some form of democratic authorization that is more robust than the ordinary legislative process. In brief, for such major changes in the character of a polity, *broad public deliberation and popular choice* seem to be required.[18] Similarly, if the development of international human rights law continues to reduce the domain of self-determination for a constitutional democracy, the point may be reached at which proper appreciation of the value of self-determination requires broad public deliberation and popular choice, that is, some sort of authorization that is more directly democratic than an ordinary legislative act or the ratification of a treaty.[19]

I now want to suggest a parallel point with respect to another incompatibilist concern discussed earlier: the negative impact of international human rights law on existing constitutional structures, including the allocation of power among the branches of

[18] In order to ratify treaties of major importance, such as those that establish robust supranational organizations, many nations require special majority legislation (e.g., Greece, Austria, Finland, Croatia, inter alia) or constitutional revision (e.g., France), while others hold referenda (e.g., Denmark, Sweden, and Switzerland).

[19] James Nickel has suggested to me that in some cases of acknowledging the authority of robust international law what might be called tacit democratic authorization would suffice—that none of the mechanisms for public deliberation and choice we list would be required. For example, if citizens do not "punish" those officials who signed the relevant treaties by voting against them in the next election, this could count as a kind of democratic authorization. In my view, the notion of tacit democratic authorization is problematic in general, but perhaps especially problematic when it comes to such significant political changes as secession, accession, and devolution. Accordingly, I believe that there should be a presumption of a requirement of public deliberation and choice, at least for cases in which acknowledging the authority of Robust international law is likely to produce constitutional changes or changes in the scope of self-determination that are comparable to secession, accession, and devolution.

government and between federal units and the federal government. If the alteration of existing constitutional structures is significant, then some especially robust form of democratic authorization is required here also.

Let us call international law that can reasonably be expected to either (a) significantly restrict a polity's self-determination or (b) significantly alter its internal constitutional structures Robust international law (with a capital R). Now consider three ways in which a constitutional democracy might come to be subject to Robust international law. The first, to which I have already alluded, is through broad public constitutional deliberation and popular choice: processes that give more weight to the popular will than ordinary legislative processes and which are preceded by special public deliberations designed to reflect the fact that constitutional changes are at stake. Here the mechanisms for accepting Robust international law would be a new constitutional convention, constitutional amendment, or a referendum in which all citizens could vote. The second alternative is some form of special supermajority national legislation: recognition of the supremacy of international law that qualifies as constitutional change would require approval from the national legislature (including both houses, in bicameral systems) by considerably more than a bare majority. The distinction between this alternative and the first is perhaps less than clear: If a special national legislative act were preceded by extraordinary public deliberation, it might be sufficiently democratic. The third alternative is a *process of accretion* in which no public constitutional deliberation or popular choice occurs and no special legislative approval is required—a process that might be characterized rather uncharitably as a constitutional democracy's slow death by a thousand cuts.

In the US case, the accretion can occur through a combination of congressional-executive agreements ("fast-track" processes that bypass the usual Senate supermajority requirement for approval of trade agreements), automatic inclusion of ratified treaties in "the law of the land," the recognition of international law as federal common law, judicial borrowing from international law, and the development of more robust global governance institutions that increasingly create legally-binding policies through their own bureaucracies, without specific consent from states.

The third process, that of accretion, is deeply problematic from the standpoint of the commitment to democracy: There are alterations of a constitutional democracy that could properly be called constitutional changes, but there is no point at which there is public deliberation about them that recognizes that they are constitutional changes and no process of the sort that is ordinarily thought to be appropriate for constitutional choice is invoked to determine whether to make them. Nor is there even any special national legislative act to signal that this is not just lawmaking or traditional treaty-making as usual.

The processes by which European Union law has evolved have included, at several critical junctures, something approaching the first model for accepting Robust international law, the public constitutional deliberation and popular choice model.[20] But for most states, including the United States, the process of accepting international law, including human rights law, has been one of accretion: Public constitutional deliberation and popular choice have been conspicuously absent.

Whether or not this process of accretion has in fact *already* subjected the United States and other states to Robust international law—that is, whether the acceptance of international law has caused significant changes in constitutional structures or in the scope of political self-determination of sufficient magnitude to require public constitutional deliberation and choice—is perhaps open to reasonable disagreement. To make a sound judgment on this matter one would need to do two things, neither of which those who worry about the impact of international law on constitutional democracy have done. First, one would have to tell a convincing *causal* story about the actual, not just the potential, negative impact of the ratification of human rights treaties on the constitutional powers of federal units, or on the allocation of powers between the federal, legislative, and judicial branches of government, or on the scope of the country's self-determination. Second, one would also have to provide a normative account of *which* alterations of constitutional structures and which limitations on self-determination warrant

---

[20] The record here is mixed. The introduction of the Euro currency and the ratification of the Lisbon Treaty have been criticized as falling far short of deliberative democratic authorization.

public constitutional deliberation and popular choice. Beyond that, one would also need a normative account of the proper mechanisms for public constitutional deliberation and popular choice. In brief, one would need normative accounts of both self-determination and of constitutional change that cohere with the principles and values that ground constitutional democracy.

## A PRINCIPLE OF ROBUST DEMOCRATIC AUTHORIZATION

My objective here is not to try to provide either the causal or the normative accounts. Instead, I simply want to advance a rather commonsensical principle: Where the acceptance of international law by a constitutional democracy can be reasonably expected to result in significant alterations in constitutional structures or in significant diminutions in political self-determination, then, as with other profound changes (such as consensual secession, accession to a federation, or devolution from a centralized state to federalism or consociationalism), there is a strong presumption that public constitutional deliberation and popular choice are required. The intuition that grounds this meta-constitutional principle, call it M, is both simple and robust: Some political changes are so momentous that the ordinary processes for making political decisions are inadequate, and in such cases the decision ought to be made by the ultimate source of political authority, the people.

Although principle M is intuitively plausible, to my knowledge it has not been advanced by either party to the debate about the compatibility of constitutional democracy and international human rights law. Compatibilists have not considered it because they have ignored the impact of international human rights law on constitutional structures and self-determination. Incompatibilists have not considered it because they have assumed that the existing constitutional order is sacrosanct and have not been willing to take seriously the possibility that it might require modification for the sake of accommodating international human rights law. If states satisfied principle M in their processes for incorporating international human rights law, then the most serious incompatibilist concern, the worry that acknowledging the supremacy of international law can relinquish sovereignty or alter the constitution without proper democratic authorization, would dissipate.

## IV. *Reframing the Debate*

### *Gaps in the Arguments*

It should be clear at this point that even the best arguments on both sides of the debate on the compatibility of constitutional democracy and international human rights law are fundamentally incomplete. Once we set aside the unconvincing arguments that purport to show that international human rights law and constitutional democracy are incompatible in principle, we are left with the claim that international human rights law can alter constitutional structures and diminish self-determination without proper democratic authorization, and that there are risks involved when judges treat international law as a resource for interpreting domestic law. But unless one assumes (implausibly) that *any* change in constitutional structures or *any* reduction in the scope of self-determination is unacceptable, or that international human rights law cannot be made more coherent and determinate or that lack of coherence in the law is never a price worth paying, it does not follow that those committed to constitutional democracy should reject the supremacy of international human rights law. On the other side of the ledger, it is not enough, in order to allay worries about the impact of international human rights law on constitutional structures or on the scope of self-determination for enthusiasts of international human rights law to point out that there are weighty reasons why citizens of a constitutional democracy ought to value international human rights law. The three justificatory arguments for an international legal human rights system advanced in chapter 3 should resonate with the friends of constitutional democracy, but they do not address the concerns about constitutional change and loss of self-determination.

### *Trade-Offs, Not Incompatibility*

Because Compatibilists have not addressed these two most serious incompatibilist concerns, they have not been forced to confront the question of *trade-offs* between their commitment to constitutional democracy and their commitment to promoting cosmopolitan values through international human rights law. In other words, Compatibilists have not considered the possibility that the commitment to constitutional democracy may have to be compromised for the sake of building a robust international legal order or *vice versa*. Incompatibilists have not faced the question of trade-offs either, because they assume that the existing constitutional order and democracy as they understand them are so important that no other values can compete with them.

The idea of trade-offs warrants elaboration. The recognition that trade-offs may be required rests on a kind of value pluralism, the reasonable idea that the commitment to international human rights law and the commitment to constitutional democracy can both be high moral priorities, without either trumping the other across the board. Once we see that both the commitment to constitutional democracy and the commitment to international human rights law rest on a plurality of values, it should not be surprising that tensions between the two commitments could arise.

The first step in reframing the debate between Compatibilists and Incompatibilists in a more fruitful way is to dispense with the assumption that the question is whether constitutional democracy and international human rights law are compatible. Instead, we should begin with a thorough understanding of the various tensions between the commitment to constitutional democracy and the commitment to international human rights law and then ask how we can best honor both commitments. To determine whether and in what way one commitment ought to be compromised for the sake of the other, however, it will be necessary to answer questions about the relative importance of a plurality of values that can only be provided by a more comprehensive political philosophy.

### Global Justice, Human Rights, and Constitutional Democracy

A political philosophy that gives priority to a substantive conception of global justice over democratic process and that accords a significant role to international human rights law in promoting global justice might prescribe one trade-off between the commitments to constitutional democracy and to international human rights law. A theory that gives greater weight to democratic processes and has a more modest conception of the demands of global justice might prescribe another. On the former sort of theory, some damage to domestic democratic processes might be a price worth paying for the sake of better realization of international legal human rights, understood as an important component of global justice.

Compatibilists are appreciative of the weighty moral reasons in favor of acknowledging the supremacy of international human rights law. Incompatibilists have shown how acknowledging the supremacy of international human rights law can alter constitutional structures or diminish self-determination, and, more importantly, do so without proper democratic authorization. Neither kind of consideration provides *practical conclusions* concerning the supremacy issue in the absence of a more comprehensive political philosophy than either party to the debate has even begun to outline.

I have suggested that principle M above is an important element of a response to the problem of resolving tensions between the commitment to international human rights law and to constitutional democracy. But principle M is unsatisfyingly indeterminate, without a background theory to determine what counts as a "significant" diminution of self-determination and what counts as a change in constitutional structures versus a shift in practice within existing structures.

### A Neglected Issue in Liberal Cosmopolitan Theory

I will conclude this chapter with an observation on the bearing of the debate about the compatibility of constitutional democracy with international human rights law on the current state of liberal cosmopolitan political philosophy. Mainstream liberal cosmopolitan theory accepts the persistence of states, while at the same time advocating the development of international human rights law to prune back state sovereignty in the name of human rights. As liberals, liberal cosmopolitans advocate constitutional democracy at the level of the state;[21] as cosmopolitans, they advocate international human rights law. What they have failed to realize is that these two commitments can be in tension, in at least two ways: First, acknowledging the supremacy international human rights law may derange internal constitutional structures; and second, depending upon the process by which its authority comes to be accepted, it may constitute an *undemocratic* diminution of self-determination. To resolve these

---

[21] . . . unless they advocate the abolition of the state system in favor of world government—a position which few cosmopolitans advocate these days.

tensions, liberal cosmopolitan theorists must expand significantly the domain of their theorizing. They must develop mutually consistent accounts of human rights and of constitutionalism, including a normative theory of constitutional change, and of the proper scope of self-determination in a world of states; and they must do so in a way that is consistent with their basic values as cosmopolitans.

# CHAPTER 7

---

# The Challenge of Ethical Pluralism

The basic idea behind the international legal human rights project, I have argued, is to provide universal standards, in the form of international law, for regulating the behavior of states toward individuals under their jurisdiction, considered as social beings, for the sake of those individuals themselves. The aim of this chapter is to articulate in its most cogent form and then to evaluate the allegation that the international legal human rights project is radically misconceived because there are no valid universal standards or at least not any of the sort the international legal human rights system contains. To put the allegation more precisely: Because of the fact of ethical pluralism, it is unjustifiable to ascribe the same set of individual legal rights to all human individuals or in some other way try to regulate the behavior of states according to one set of standards applicable to all of them. The Ethical Pluralist challenge strikes at the heart of the human rights enterprise, including its legal core. Accordingly, it deserves careful consideration.

Ethical Pluralism, as I shall understand it, is the view that there is a plurality of valid moralities, none of which is uniquely rational. My aim in this chapter is to determine whether valid nonindividualistic, or more positively, collectivistic moralities pose a serious challenge either to the existing international legal human rights regime or to the project of having such a regime. In part I, I characterize Ethical Pluralism in more detail and explain why it is an attractive view—sufficiently attractive, at least, to take seriously the challenge it purports to pose to the human rights enterprise. Then I draw a distinction between individualistic and collectivistic moralities and use it to state more clearly the most common and serious form of the ethical pluralist challenge to human rights: The charge that an international legal regime of individual rights is incompatible with some valid moralities, because not all valid moralities are sufficiently individualistic as to acknowledge individual rights. In the first part, I also distinguish Ethical Pluralism from Ethical Relativism and explain why I take Ethical Pluralism, rather than Ethical Relativism, to be the more serious challenge to the international legal human rights regime. In part II, I set out and critique arguments designed to show that the justification for an international legal human rights regime is inconsistent with valid collectivistic moralities. My main conclusion will be that while some particular international legal human rights—depending on how their content is interpreted—may be inconsistent with some aspects of some valid collectivistic moralities, the existing international legal human rights regime as a whole, and the project of having such a regime, can be justified from the perspective of valid collectivistic moralities.

I will argue that, contrary to what many have assumed, the international legal human rights regime does not rest on moral foundations that give short shrift to the sorts of values that are distinctive of valid collectivistic moralities. I will show that even those who espouse collectivistic moralities that deny the existence of individual *moral* human rights have powerful reasons to support a regime of international *legal* human rights. I will also suggest that even if it is true that some aspects of the international legal human rights regime disadvantage some collectivistic moralities, the protections the regime provides for collectivistic values are so substantial that the proper course of action for those who espouse collectivistic moralities is to strive to reform the regime to make it more congenial to their values, not try to destroy it or regard it as illegitimate.

## I. *Ethical Pluralism and Valid Moralities*

### *Valid Moralities*

According to Ethical Pluralism, there is a plurality of valid moralities, none of which is uniquely rational. The qualifier 'valid' is important. Ethical Pluralism, as I shall understand it is not a purely descriptive view according to which there is a plurality of moralities. That descriptive view, in which 'moralities' simply refers to the moral codes various groups happen to have, is compatible with moral nihilism, understood as the thesis that no morality is rationally defensible. If no moralities were valid in the sense of being rationally defensible—that is, if moral nihilism were true—then it would follow trivially that no particular morality is uniquely rational.

Moreover, showing that dysfunctional or otherwise clearly defective moralities are inconsistent with the idea of human rights or the justification for having an international legal human rights regime would not be of much interest. The interesting question concerns valid moralities. The worry is that there are some valid moralities whose core values or norms are somehow at odds with the human rights enterprise—or, more specifically, with the claims to universality that are distinctive of it.

Ethical Pluralism, as I shall understand it, then, is a normative view: It holds that there is a plurality of valid, that is, rationally defensible moralities, but that none of them is uniquely rational. Thus, if individuals or a group opt for one valid morality rather than another, they do not thereby make a mistake—their allegiance to that morality rather than another is not unreasonable.

Obviously, the notion of validity, as applied to moralities, is both controversial and ambiguous. To side-step irrelevant controversies, the notion of validity I shall be operating with is rather weak. As a first approximation, we can say that a morality is valid if it is not unreasonable to espouse it. For our purposes, a rather rough and relatively undemanding characterization of a set of necessary conditions for a morality being valid in this weak sense will suffice. To begin with, we can say that in order to count as valid, a morality must do an adequate job of performing the most important characteristic functions of a morality: providing social cohesion, facilitating productive cooperation, contributing to the relatively peaceful resolution of commonly occurring conflicts, and providing useful guidance to individuals in their pursuit of a good life.[1]

Even as a characterization of necessary rather than sufficient conditions, this may appear to be too undemanding, however. Several suggestions for supplementing it immediately come to mind. The first, and most intuitively plausible in my judgment, is that to

---

[1] One might add the caveat: at least in not extremely unfavorable circumstances.

qualify as valid, a morality must be able to perform the functions listed above without depending upon high levels of violence to secure compliance with its norms. This additional requirement makes sense, given that part of what is distinctive and distinctively valuable about moralities is that they achieve coordination, facilitate productive cooperation, and provide resources for the peaceful resolution of conflicts largely by functioning as a system of *internalized* controls. According to this way of thinking, we would not view something as a morality, or at least not as a valid morality, if it were simply a set of rules enforced by coercion, without internalization.

Additional requirements for validity, either epistemic or normative, may be more controversial. A minimal epistemic requirement would be that a morality is valid only if it does not rely *importantly* on *easily* falsified factual beliefs or on *patent and gross* inferential errors. The rationale for this requirement is simply that to be valid a morality must not rely importantly on egregiously irrational beliefs. A morality grounded in egregiously irrational beliefs would qualify as unreasonable and hence would not be valid.

Normative requirements might be more controversial. One might hold that a morality is valid only if it includes some notion of impartiality or some requirement of universality for moral reasons. Or one might think that to be valid a morality must be consistent with some version of the idea that all human beings or all normal human beings have moral standing (though perhaps not equal moral standing).

Ethical Pluralism, as I understand it, does not deny that moralities are subject to rational criticism. Instead, it holds that there is a plurality of valid moralities in this sense: There is more than one morality that does a reasonable job of performing the characteristic functions of morality and also satisfies other appropriate epistemic and normative conditions, and there is no rational basis for saying that one morality among those that fit this description is *superior overall*. That is compatible with every valid morality being subject to rational criticism—to being rightly judged to be deficient in some way or other. It is also compatible with some—perhaps many—moralities not being valid because they fall below whatever the standards of adequacy for morality are (perhaps by failing egregiously to perform one or more of the characteristic functions listed above).

I do not pretend to have established the truth of Ethical Pluralism understood in this way; nor do I need to establish it. I only need to have said enough about the idea of a plurality of valid moralities to show that Ethical Pluralism is a plausible doctrine. Hence, to object that I have not given a full account of what it is for a morality to be valid would be off target. My strategy is neither to provide a comprehensive definition of Ethical Pluralism nor to defend it but rather to give it the benefit of the doubt and then determine whether it poses a serious threat to the human rights enterprise.

I would like to note, however, that showing that there is no morality that is superior overall to all others, while at the same time acknowledging that moralities are subject to rational criticism, would be no easy matter. Instead of undertaking this task, the savvy Ethical Pluralist will try to shift the burden of argument to her opponent, first making the case that there is a plurality of moralities that do a creditable job of performing the characteristic functions of morality and satisfy other reasonable and relatively uncontroversial conditions, and then demand an account of why some particular morality among these is uniquely rational, in the expectation that one is not likely to be forthcoming.

What makes the idea that there is no uniquely valid morality attractive, and thereby lends credibility to this attempt to shift the burden of argument, are two rather commonsensical notions. The first is that a morality expresses a commitment to some set of values. The second is that there is a plurality of objective, or at least not unreasonable values, and that there is no one uniquely valid comprehensive ranking or weighing of them. Keeping this plausible notion of value pluralism in mind, the next step in my argument aims to make equally plausible the idea that there can be valid collectivistic, as well as individualistic moralities, because both individualistic and collectivistic ways of living are objectively valuable or at least not unreasonable.

## Valid Collectivist Moralities

The most serious and frequently voiced version of the ethical pluralist challenge to human rights assumes that there are valid *collectivistic* moralities. One prominent instance of this line of criticism is the claim that human rights are somehow incompatible with "Asian values."[2] Because I think the notion that Asians have a distinctive morality is unpromising (given the enormous diversity of cultures and the diversity of values within particular cultures found in Asia), and because I think it is also unlikely that moralities correlate neatly with geographical boundaries, I will use instead the idea of a collectivistic morality.

Empirical research indicates that moralities can be ranged along a spectrum from more individualistic to more collectivistic.[3] Collectivistic moralities are often said to be those that highly value groups, including the family and the larger society, while tending to be more critical of the pursuit of individual self-interest and less approving of assertions of individual autonomy. David Wong has suggested to me that a more apt characterization of collectivistic moralities is that they tend to value highly certain *relationships* among individuals, rather than features of individuals characterized independently of their participation in relationships.[4]

Understood in this way, collectivistic moralities need not deny the value of the individual, condemn all expressions of self-interest, or fail to recognize that some degree of individual autonomy is generally an important ingredient of human good. Nor need they assume metaphysically robust views about groups or attribute moral qualities to groups that are not reducible to qualities of relationships. Rather, the basic point is that collectivistic moralities preeminently

[2] Joanne R. Bauer and Daniel A. Bell, *The East Asian Challenge for Human Rights* (Cambridge: Cambridge University Press, 1999); Daniel A. Bell, *Beyond Liberal Democracy: Political Thinking for an East Asian Context* (Princeton, NJ: Princeton University Press, 2006), and *East Meets West: Human Rights and Democracy in East Asia* (Princeton, NJ: Princeton University Press, 2000); David B. Wong, "Rights and Community in Confucianism," in *Confucian Ethics: A Comparative Study of Self, Autonomy, and Community*, eds. Kwong-loi Shun and David B. Wong (Cambridge: Cambridge University Press, 2004), pp. 31–48.
[3] Daphna Oyserman, Heather M. Coon, and Markus Kemmelmeier, "Rethinking Individualism and Collectivism: Evaluation of Theoretical Assumptions and Meta-analyses," *Psychological Bulletin* 128:1 (2002): 3–72; Eun Rhee, James S Uleman, and Hoon Koo Lee, "Variations in Collectivism and Individualism by In-group and Culture: Confirmatory Factor Analysis," *Journal of Personality and Social Psychology*, 71:5 (1996): 1037–54; Harry C. Triandis and Michele J. Gelfand, "Converging Measurement of Horizontal and Vertical Individualism and Collectivism," *Journal of Personality and Social Psychology*, 74:1 (1998): 118–28; Harry C. Triandis, *Individualism and Collectivism* (Boulder: Westview Press, 1995).
[4] Personal communication, November 2, 2001.

value relationships and do not weigh individualistic values as heavily as other moralities do. To make the idea of a collectivistic morality more concrete, consider Confucianism. It is plausibly viewed as a collectivistic morality—that is to say, it falls somewhere on the collectivistic side of the collectivist-to-individualist spectrum.[5]

Relying on the distinction between individualistic and collectivistic moralities, we can now formulate more precisely the ethical pluralist challenge to the international legal human rights system and to the human rights practice that is grounded on it. The claim is that, because the system of international legal human rights accords a prominent role to individual legal rights, it must rest on individualistic moral foundations—normative assumptions that are inconsistent with some important tenets of valid collectivistic moralities. Before evaluating this claim, it will be useful to make clearer why it ought to be taken seriously.

## The Attraction of Ethical Pluralism, from a Broadly Evolutionary-Functionalist Perspective

An appreciation of the distinction between individualistic and collectivistic moralities adds considerable force to my initial effort to make Ethical Pluralism plausible enough to take seriously the challenge it appears to pose for the human rights enterprise. If one thinks of moralities as human creations, the idea that there is a plurality of valid moralities seems natural enough. One would expect that different groups would develop somewhat different ways of solving the problems to which moralities, as human creations, are a response. It would be surprising if there were only one way of creditably performing the distinctive functions of morality, and there is no reason to expect that there is one uniquely best way. Some moralities might do a better job with respect to some functions, other moralities better with respect to other functions. Even if it were possible somehow to determine an aggregate score for each morality across performance levels for the various functions, there might well be no overall winner.

Further, it would not be surprising if the set of moralities that do reasonably well at performing these functions varied somewhat

---

[5] Confucian Ethics; David B. Wong, *Natural Moralities: A Defense of Pluralistic Relativism* (Oxford: Oxford University Press, 2006).

along a spectrum from more collectivistic to more individualistic, if one assumes, quite reasonably, that both individualistic and collectivistic ways of living have their merits, within limits. This prospect becomes even more cogent if one appreciates *path dependency*. If, for whatever reason, a society develops a set of moral norms and practices that are located on the collectivistic segment of the spectrum of possibilities, then the opportunities for good available to people growing up in that society will be shaped accordingly. For those people, it will tend to be true that relationships and the flourishing of the group will not only be especially valued, but also especially valuable objectively speaking. A collectivistic morality, as it is embodied in social practices and institutions, will shape their capacity and opportunities for good, in ways that make their good depend more heavily on their participation in groups and relationships. Similarly, if a society has, for whatever reason, taken the path of a more individualistic morality, this will influence not only what is valued but also what is valuable for its members. Because they are shaped by an individualistic morality and live in a society that provides opportunities for living well in a more individualistic way, individual autonomy will be more valuable for them objectively speaking. Their psychologies will be attuned to a more individualistic way of living and they will find that way of living more satisfying and worthwhile. The key point is that although moralities are presumably constrained by basic psychological capacities that are universal or at least very widespread among all humans, particular moralities help realize that capacity in different ways, with the result that there is no one right or optimally good way for humans to live.

My choice of the terms 'individualistic' and 'collectivistic' (versus individualist and collectivist) has been deliberate. Empirical research suggests that most if not all societies or cultural groups value both individuals and groups and relationships. It is not a matter of one or the other, but rather a matter of relative weights.[6]

The virtue of Ethical Pluralism, then, is that it can accommodate the reasonable notion that good human lives and good human societies include room for both individualistic and collectivistic values, while recognizing that the relative weights of these two types of values can vary, within limits. After all, even within a relatively homogeneous

---

[6] Triandis, *Individualism and Collectivism*, note 3 supra.

group, different individuals may exhibit different weightings, and it would be difficult to defend the view that only one weighting is rational.

To summarize: A plausible understanding of Ethical Pluralism will include not only the idea that there is a plurality of valid moralities, but also a recognition that the set of valid moralities will include both collectivistic and individualistic moralities, and will not include either purely individualist or purely collectivist moralities. Equipped with this understanding of what the range of valid moralities is likely to span, we can now turn to the task of specifying more carefully what the ethical pluralist challenge to human rights is.

To do this, we need to distinguish two different claims that might be made about the relationship between valid collectivist moralities and the international legal human rights regime. According to the Inconsistency Claim, the fundamental tenets of valid collectivistic moralities are inconsistent with the justification for having an international legal human rights regime. According to the Disadvantage Claim, valid collectivistic moralities are disadvantaged by the international human rights regime—that is, the international legal human rights regime interferes significantly with efforts to realize the values that this type of morality espouses.

It is necessary to distinguish these two claims, because it is conceivable that even if there were no inconsistency between the beliefs or commitments that constitute a collectivistic morality and the justification for a regime of international legal human rights, nevertheless, the implementation of that regime might make it harder to realize that morality's values. The Inconsistency Claim is potentially the more serious challenge, however, because it asserts a fundamental conceptual incompatibility between collectivist moralities and the international legal human rights regime. In contrast, even if the Disadvantage Claim is true, it need not constitute a conclusive objection to the regime, from the standpoint of collectivistic moralities, because it is compatible with such moralities being favorably disposed to the regime all things considered. This would be the case, if the advantages that the international legal human rights regime confers on valid collectivistic moralities outweigh the disadvantages. Because it is the more serious challenge, my focus in part II will be on the Inconsistency Claim. But what I say about it will have important implications for the Disadvantage Claim as well.

Before unpacking and scrutinizing the Inconsistency Claim, I want to explain why I think it is better to frame the challenge in terms of Ethical Pluralism rather than Ethical Relativism. Ethical Pluralism, as I have characterized it, is a metaethically modest thesis. It avoids taking a stand on whether ethical beliefs are true or false and on whether there are moral facts. I should also emphasize that thinking of moralities as human creations is compatible with there being some objective moral truths, or if, you will, some moral facts. Looking at moralities as human creations leaves open the possibility that there is such a thing as moral truths and that some moralities track them better than others.

In contrast, on an antiobjectivist interpretation of validity, valid moralities might simply be those that perform the characteristic functions of morality creditably and are motivationally or emotionally coherent. This characterization of validity is compatible with the view that moral judgments are neither true nor false. The key point is that neither my characterization of Ethical Pluralism, nor my suggestion that it is a plausible view to hold if one thinks of moralities as human creations, commit me one way or the other on the question of objectivity. While a *full* explication of the notion of a valid morality would presumably require taking a stand on that question, I do not need a full explication in order to frame the Ethical Pluralist challenge. I only need to say enough to make credible the idea that there is a plurality of valid moralities but no good reason to think that one morality is uniquely rational. My characterization of Ethical Pluralism, then, is intended to leave open a range of metaethical positions.

Nevertheless, I suspect that the most plausible version of Ethical Pluralism will hold that there are some moral truths and that to be valid in any interesting sense a morality must do a decent job of recognizing them or at least be compatible with them. In other words, the most likely alternative, as I see it, is that there are some (perhaps very few) moral truths, that a valid morality must recognize or at the very least not contradict, but that beyond that there are differences among valid moralities that are not rationally resolvable. This understanding of Ethical Pluralism readily accommodates the intuitively plausible idea that both individualistic and collectivistic modes of living are both, within limits, objectively valuable.

Ethical Relativism, as it is usually understood, is the claim that the truth of a particular ethical belief is determined by the morality of which it is a part and that because different groups (cultures, societies, etc.) have different moralities, one cannot speak of an ethical belief being true or false *simpliciter*. Instead, one must say that ethical belief B is true relative to (or for) Group G. Because Ethical Pluralism carries considerably less metaethical baggage, I will stick with it.

## II. *Evaluating the Ethical Pluralist Challenge*

In the analysis that follows, it will prove useful to distinguish two distinct targets of the Ethical Pluralist challenge: the commitment to having *an* international legal human rights regime and the commitment to *the particular international legal human rights regime we actually have*. For it might turn out that there is no incompatibility between valid collectivistic moralities and the justification for having that type of regime, even though the particular regime we have has features that are unacceptable from the standpoint of such moralities.

Let us first consider the generic version of the challenge: the claim that valid collectivistic moralities are inconsistent with the justification for having an international legal human rights regime. One might think that this claim is true if one thought that a system of individual legal human rights is justifiable only if there are corresponding moral individual rights and also thought that individual moral rights are incompatible with some valid collectivistic moralities. But that line of reasoning is mistaken because, as I argued in chapter 2, legal individual rights, including international legal human rights, can be justified without appeal to corresponding moral individual rights. In chapter 4, I developed sketches of justifications for representatives of each of the major categories of international legal human rights that did not rely on premises about corresponding moral individual rights. Further, I showed that a number of prominent individual legal human rights can be adequately justified without appealing to moral rights at all.

Why else might one think that there is an inconsistency? The most obvious answer is that one thinks that even if legal individual rights can be justified without appeal to corresponding moral individual rights or to some moral individual rights or other, any justification for legal individual rights must nonetheless appeal to individualistic values of some sort and therefore be unacceptable from the standpoint of collectivistic moralities. To put the same point differently, one might assume that a regime of individual rights could only be justified from the perspective of moralities on the individualistic side of the spectrum of valid moralities.

One might think this if one assumed that individual rights are simply protections of individual interests or individual autonomy — that they only serve to shield the individual from various threats or to carve out a domain of autonomy for the individual. That is clearly mistaken, however. Many individual rights included in international human rights law provide valuable protections for groups, and in doing so allow groups to exercise autonomy through their collective decision-making processes. For example, the right to freedom of religion provides protections for individuals to participate in the life of religious communities, affording them a secure space within which they can determine together the character and direction of their common life. In fact, the hard-won struggle for legal rights to freedom of religion emerged in the context of mutually destructive conflicts among religious groups.

Other international legal human rights protect important relationships by safeguarding the individual's capacity to participate in them, as is the case with the right to marry and to have a family, the right to freedom of association, and the right to a nationality. Further, the major modern human rights documents, including the Universal Declaration of Human Rights (UDHR) and the two covenants that together with it constitute the so-called International Bill of Rights, explicitly characterize humans as social beings and acknowledge the importance of the rights they declare in enabling individuals to flourish as social beings.[7] In doing so, they unambiguously reject any suggestion that human rights are valuable only for isolated individuals, abstracted from the relationships that give shape and

[7] UN General Assembly, *Universal Declaration of Human Rights* (1948), available at www.un.org/en/documents/udhr; UN General Assembly, *International Covenant on Economic, Social and Cultural Rights* (1966), available at www2.ohchr.org/english/law/cescr.htm; UN General Assembly, *International Covenant on Civil and Political Rights* (1966), available at www2.ohchr.org/english/law/ccpr.htm.

meaning to their lives and contribute fundamentally to their good. So, to the extent that international human rights protect groups and individuals qua members of groups or qua participants in relationships, and also conceive of human beings as essentially social, it is false to say that they are the expression of an individualistic morality.

There is a second, equally spurious reason why one might think that individual rights are highly individualistic and therefore worry that they give short shrift to collective values. One may have confused the concept of an individual right with a particular conception of individual rights that currently enjoys great popularity, at least in liberal thinking. Ronald Dworkin invokes this conception of a right when he says that rights "trump" appeals to social utility.[8] If one thinks of rights in this way, one is likely to regard them as somehow *essentially opposed to the common good and hence to collectivistic values.*

There are three reasons why this would be an error. First, as utilitarians have long pointed out, sometimes more utility is gained by recognizing individual rights than by attempting to maximize utility directly. So it might turn out that having an international legal regime of individual rights would be justified on utility maximizing grounds. This would be more likely to be the case if such a system allowed for exceptional cases in which rights could be infringed for the sake of avoiding massive disutility. The existing system has just such a provision: Most international human rights are "derogable"—they may be infringed in national emergencies, for example.[9]

Second, and much more important, *when individual rights block appeals to what would maximize overall utility, they thereby protect a wide range of collectivistic values.* In brief, human rights shield

---

[8] Dworkin himself does not say that this trumping feature is included in the very concept of a right, but it appears that the popularity of his view has led some to embrace that further conclusion. See Ronald Dworkin, "Rights as Trumps," in *Theories of Rights*, ed. Jeremy Waldron (Oxford: Oxford University Press, 1984), pp. 153–68.

[9] For example, Article 4 of the International Covenant on Civil and Political Rights allows States "in times of public emergency which threatens the life of a nation" to temporarily derogate from some of their obligations but only to the "exigencies of the situation." Nonderogable rights include the right to life, freedom from genocide, freedom from torture, freedom from slavery and forced labor, the right of all individuals to be recognized as persons under the law, the right not to be prosecuted under ex post facto law, and freedom of thought, conscience and religion.

many different kinds of plausible collectivistic values from one extremely implausible collectivistic value, namely, unlimited state power. The assumption that individual rights are fundamentally opposed to collectivistic values betrays ignorance of the historical context in which the regime was created and the evils to which it was a response. Historians of the modern human rights movement agree that its founding was in large part a response to the horrors perpetrated in the name of Fascism during World War II.[10] The Holocaust and the general brutality of occupation by the forces of Nazi Germany and Imperial Japan revealed the unparalleled threat that the modern state posed to a wide range of collectivistic values, all in the name of the dubious claim that the nation is of supreme value—or even that it is the only thing of intrinsic value. According to this ideology, all groups and relationships were to be subordinated to the state, acting supposedly on behalf of the nation. Groups and relationships the state did not value or was not able to remold in its own image were ruthlessly destroyed. The most obvious examples were Jewish communities and national minorities, but any religious or political groups unwilling to give their unconditional allegiance to the state, as well as the family itself, suffered grievously as the result of the unbridled exercise of state power. When the nation-state claims to be the ultimate source of value, all other groups and all relationships other than that of abject obedience to it are imperiled. Therefore, it is profoundly mistaken to say that the only purpose or even the primary purpose of the international legal human rights regime is to protect *individuals* from the state. A regime of international legal human rights would be of great value even if all actual moralities were collectivistic. Individual rights, legal or moral, are not essentially opposed to collectivist values, even if one assumes that they are essentially opposed to maximizing overall utility. They protect collectivist values from supposed utility maximization and they reduce the risk that some one set of collectivist values will drive out all the rest.

[10] Mary Ann Glendon, *A World Made New: Eleanor Roosevelt and the Universal Declaration of Human Rights* (New York: Random House, 2002); Johannes Morsink, *Inherent Human Rights: Philosophical Roots of the Universal Declaration* (Philadelphia: University of Pennsylvania Press, 2009); Johannes Morsink, *The Universal Declaration of Human Rights: Origins, Drafting, and Intent* (Philadelphia: University of Pennsylvania Press, 1999).

Third, human rights are generally understood to be or to include claim-rights, and there is nothing in the concept of a claim-right, at least if it is understood according to the standard Hohfeldian analysis, that requires a right to be an extraordinarily weighty consideration, much less a trump, against utility maximization or, for that matter, against the pursuit of collectivistic values of any sort.[11] It is true, of course, that claim-rights have corresponding duties. But even if a duty is understood as an exclusionary reason for acting or refraining, this only means that it preempts *some* considerations or other that would otherwise count as reasons to act contrary to the duty. It does not imply that what is excluded, or all that is excluded, are appeals to social utility or collectivist values. Particular conceptions of rights may emphasize the exclusion of these considerations, but it is not part of the concept of an individual claim-right that this be so. So one cannot argue that the concept of an individual claim-right is opposed to collectivistic values.

## The Distinctive Value of Individual Rights

I now want to return to a question I posed in chapter 1: Why, if a primary goal of those who attempted to "make the world anew" amidst the devastation of World War II and the Holocaust was to protect groups from the power of the state, did the protection take the form of a system of *individual* rights? Why should those who subscribe to collectivistic moralities endorse individual rights rather than rights for groups? I made substantial headway on answering this question in chapter 4 and will elaborate on that discussion here.[12]

There is a historical reason: The League of Nations relied on group rights (of national minorities), and its failure to avert the war appears to have encouraged the conclusion that individual rather than group rights should be the centerpiece of the new order. Quite

---

[11] Gopal Sreenivasan, "Duties and Their Direction," *Ethics* 120:3 (2010): p. 469.

[12] Here it is important to note that the term 'group right' is ambiguous. It can refer to special individual rights ascribed to members of a group, which might be more clearly designated as 'group specific individual rights.' Or, it could mean rights that are exercisable, not by individuals but either collectively by a group or by their supposed representatives. In the discussion that follows, it is the latter understanding of 'group right' that is relevant.

apart from that, there are several weighty advantages of individual rights.[13]

First, to be able to secure the protections provided by a group right, a group must have some institutional structure that provides the capacity to invoke or exercise the right. Usually, this will mean that there must be some officials who are authorized to exercise the right on behalf of the group, though in some cases (as in referenda on self-determination) collective exercise may be achieved through a majority voting procedure in which all competent members of the group can participate. But many of the groups that are potential targets for the harmful use of state power do not possess such a structure—they lack the requisite organization. This is true of many religious groups, and in some cases being politically organized in such a way as to exercise group rights can even be contrary to their own conception of their values and identity. In other cases, as with sexual preference minorities, there may be no reasonable prospects for the group to create an institutional structure that would enable the exercise of group rights. For groups of either sort, it may be much more effective if rights are ascribed to individuals. That way, any individual, by invoking the right, can activate the protection the right provides to the group.

Second, for group rights to be exercised effectively, it is not only necessary that the group have the requisite political organization, it is also necessary that those in power recognize the group as a legitimate candidate for having group rights. But of course in many cases in which a group within the state needs the protection that group rights would afford, the state withholds recognition. Individual rights avoid making the protection of a group dependent upon the recognition of the existence of the group by those who wield social or political power. This is an important advantage, because the modern state not only has the power to destroy or remold recognized groups, but also the power to determine which collections of individuals are groups that are suitable candidates for having group rights. The ascription of international legal rights to all human individuals can be viewed as an attempt to provide protections to groups

---

[13] For a more comprehensive survey, see Allen Buchanan, "What's So Special About Rights?" *Social Philosophy and Policy* 2:1 (1984): 61–83.

in a way that prevents the state from being able to deny protections to them by refusing to recognize them. Further, entrenched legal rights for individuals can protect groups whose emergence could not even have been predicted at the time the legal individual rights were enacted.

Protections for groups that are officially ascribed to individuals are thus advantageous from a collectivistic standpoint. In addition, depending upon the political conditions, if the members of a hitherto unrecognized group have individual rights, they can exercise them to exert pressure on the state to grant recognition. In other words, individual rights can be valuable means for political mobilization aimed at achieving the recognition needed for securing group rights. Without individual rights to physical security, to freedom of expression and association, and to political participation, politically unrecognized groups may be unable to achieve the sort of recognition that is a first, necessary step toward securing group rights. Individual rights may also be crucial for enabling the group to build the institutional structure needed for the exercise of group rights, if it succeeds in achieving recognition.

None of this is to say that a system of protections that consists exclusively of individual rights provides the *best* protection for groups within the state. Will Kymlicka and many others have argued that in multicultural societies systems of individual rights need to be supplemented with group rights.[14] That point is well-taken, but it should not blind us to the fact that the international legal human rights regime, while consisting largely of individual rights, provides valuable protection to groups or, more accurately, to collectivist values, against the potentially lethal power of the state.

There is no need to belabor the protection that individual rights provide for individual well-being and autonomy. The point, rather, is that individual legal rights protect *both* individuals and groups and hence ought to be attractive to both collectivistic and individualistic moralities. It is not clear that the same can be said for group rights. They may protect groups, but they run the risk of neglecting individuals' interests and autonomy, especially in cases where the individual does not share the preferences of those who are exercising

---

[14] Will Kymlicka, *Multicultural Citizenship: A Liberal Theory of Minority Rights* (Oxford: Clarendon Press, 1996).

the group's right (supposedly) on its behalf. As I have already noted, where there is a system of individual rights, groups that are being harmed or disadvantaged by the exercise of their larger society's group rights can do something to defend their interests, even if they are not recognized by the powers that be as legitimate groups and even though they lack any group rights of their own. But where individual rights are lacking, group rights may be unattainable, as I have just argued, and, if attained, may be very risky to some individuals within the group. Thus, there appears to be an interesting asymmetry: Individual rights without group rights can be highly valuable, but group rights without individual rights may carry unacceptable risks.

There is yet another reason why those who espouse collectivistic moralities should value legal individual rights: They contribute to the flourishing of the group. If individuals are to be in a position to work together effectively to redirect group goals or reform aspects of the group's shared life, individual rights may be essential. Where a system of legal individual rights does not protect and empower individuals who dissent from the status quo, the development of new goals and the achievement of reforms may not be possible, at least without violent revolution, because those who control the exercise of the group's rights may refuse to exercise them for these purposes. Or, if development occurs, it will reflect the interests and values of an elite, not of the group as a whole.

Of course, these problems may not arise if those who exercise the group's rights are accountable to all members of the group—as would be the case where the exercise of group rights was the result of democratic processes. But for democratic processes to function reasonably well, there presumably must be individual rights to freedom of expression and association. Otherwise, there is the risk that if those who exercise the group's rights are accountable at all, they will only be accountable to some, not all of the individuals and groups within society, for example, those whose interests are recognized as being strategically important or legitimate by the people in power. Legal individual rights perform two valuable functions vis-à-vis group rights, then: They place limits on the exercise of group rights, providing protection for individuals whose interests and values are not fully congruent with those of the people who control the exercise of the group's rights (whether that be the majority or an elite), by putting some aspects of the individual's life beyond the reach of the exercise of group rights; and they facilitate improvements in the group's goals or to reform its defective practices and do so in a way that helps ensure that some will not be excluded from helping to determine the direction of change.

The argument so far can now be summarized. There is nothing in the concept of legal individual rights that biases a system of legal individual rights against a proper appreciation of collectivistic values. In a number of cases, legal individual rights are not justified exclusively or even primarily by showing that if realized they protect the individual right-holder's interests or autonomy. Instead, the justification for the right depends on showing how its realization serves collectivistic values. Legal individual rights do typically serve to protect individuals, but they often protect them qua members of groups. It is simply a confusion to think that even in those cases when individual rights do block appeals to overall utility maximization they express an exclusive concern with individualistic values; rather, they serve to protect groups within society from harms that would be inflicted on them in the name of a supposed greater social good.

Finally, international legal human rights are not best conceived as the legal embodiment of timeless natural rights of abstract, isolated individuals, but rather, inter alia, as a deliberate and eminently reasonable response to the threats posed by the modern state—including protection against the threats the modern state poses for the flourishing of valuable relationships and groups. For all these reasons, it is wrong to say that international legal human rights are the expression of an individualistic morality and are only acceptable from an individualistic moral perspective.

My refutation of the ethical pluralist challenge to human rights comes with a bonus: In showing why a system of individual legal rights is valuable across the spectrum of moralities from individualistic to collectivistic I have at the same time explained that there are good reasons for the prominence of individual rights norms in the project of using international law to regulate the behavior of states toward those under their jurisdiction. The special advantages of individual rights, as opposed to group rights, which I have just noted, strengthen the case for a prominent role for individual rights norms in this system of law that I began to make in chapters 1 and 4.

## The Official Justification of the Existing International Legal Human Rights Regime

So far I have cast doubt on the view that an international legal regime of individual rights must rest on moral foundations that are so individualistic as to make the justification for having such a system unavailable to those who espouse valid collectivistic moralities. In doing so, I have focused on rather abstract characteristics that define a type of legal regime: one that ascribes rights to individuals in international law. Suppose that I have made the case that it is possible to justify *a system of this sort* without appealing to moral views that are so individualistic as to be at odds with valid collectivist moralities. It might still turn out to be the case that the existing international legal human rights regime, *as it is conceived in its own official justifying discourse*, is highly individualistic—too individualistic to be palatable from the standpoint of a collectivistic morality.

To the extent that the existing international legal human rights regime has an official justification, it is found in the preambles of the major human rights documents, including the UDHR and the two covenants. Drawing on the meticulous scholarship of Hans Morsink, I have argued in an earlier paper that so far as these documents speak to justification at all, they appear to conceive of international legal human rights as an attempt to realize certain individual moral human rights in international law, and view these individual moral human rights as grounded in the equal worth, or dignity of the human individual.[15] On the surface, at least, this official justificatory rhetoric sounds highly individualistic and therefore might be thought to be inconsistent with collectivistic moralities.

In that same paper I also argue, however, that there is a historical explanation for why the major documents employ this justificatory discourse: The documents were developed as a reaction to the horrors wrought by Fascism during the Second World War, including,

---

[15] Allen Buchanan, "Human Rights," *The Oxford Handbook of Political Philosophy*, ed. David Estlund (Oxford: Oxford University Press, 2012), pp. 279–97; Morsink, *Inherent Human Rights* and *Universal Declaration of Human Rights*.

preeminently, the Holocaust, and therefore understandably proceeded on the assumption that two essential features of Fascist ideology were largely responsible for these great evils, namely, radical collectivism and radical basic status inegalitarianism. Radical collectivism is the view that individuals have no worth on their own account, independently of the contribution they make to the life of the nation (or some other group). Radical basic status inegalitarianism is a denial of the principle that all human beings have an equal basic moral status. The idea that there are certain fundamental moral rights that all individuals possess simply because they are human beings, that are unearned and not dependent upon social contribution or social or legal recognition, was quite reasonably thought to be an apt way of repudiating both radical collectivism and radical basic status inegalitarianism. In other words, the founders of the international legal human rights regime apparently believed that the best justification for the system of law they were creating would include an emphatic repudiation of what they considered to be the ideological roots of the worst abuses of state power and they employed the language of the inherent dignity of the individual to accomplish this.[16] In taking this path, the founders may have unwittingly suggested that the justification for the international legal human rights regime was *exclusively* individualistic, despite repeated references in the major documents to the essentially social nature of human beings and the fact that many international human rights clearly provide valuable protections for groups and relationships.

If this historical interpretation of the official, founding justification of the actual international legal human rights regime is accurate, then it is obvious that that justification is incompatible with *the most extreme* collectivist moralities—those that deny that individuals have any significant value on their own account, independently of their contribution to valued relationships and groups. It does not

---

[16] The word "include" is important here. It can be argued that from the very beginning, the conception of international legal human rights was more expansive, that in addition to serving as protections against the extreme harms wrought by the implementation of ideologies of extreme status inegalitarianism and extreme collectivism, they were also thought of as standards for achieving a decent life for all or perhaps even as transnational standards of justice.

follow from that, however, that the official justification is inconsistent with *valid* collectivistic moralities, so long as we assume, as I have argued that we should, that valid collectivistic moralities will acknowledge that individuals have *some* significant value on their own account. Valid collectivistic moralities do not recognize only collectivistic values; they merely give some of them greater weight vis-à-vis individualistic values.

Nonetheless, perhaps there are some collectivistic moralities that are not so extreme as to repudiate the independent value of individuals entirely, but that are nonetheless sufficiently collectivistic to be incompatible with the apparently very high degree of independent value that appears to be attributed to individuals in the official justification of the international legal rights regime. Let us grant, *arguendo*, that there are such collectivistic moralities and that they are valid. It may still be the case that *other* justifications for the actual international legal regime are available to them even if the official justification is not—justifications of the sort that I have outlined above, which appeal to various ways in which a regime of individual legal rights protects groups and relationships.

This last stage of the argument can now be summarized. A valid collectivistic morality will give some weight to individualistic values— it will not deny that individuals have some independent worth, nor will it deny that individual autonomy and the pursuit of individual interests have a significant place in a good human life—and it will be strongly committed to protecting groups and relationships from the unbridled exercise of state power. Such a morality can provide ample support for the international legal human rights regime, without embracing the notion that international human rights are grounded *solely* in the dignity of the individual, considered apart from her relationships to various groups.

### *Does the Actual International Legal Human Rights Regime Disadvantage Valid Collectivistic Moralities?*

Suppose, as I have argued, that it is not the case that the international legal human rights system, simply because it prominently features individual legal rights, is only justifiable from the perspective of individualistic, as opposed to collectivistic moralities. It still might be true that, as a matter of fact, the system seriously disadvantages some valid collectivistic moralities. If that is so, then surely it calls the system's justification into question, at least from the standpoint of those who are adherents of these moralities. The system could be said to disadvantage collectivistic moralities if it made it harder for those who espouse these moralities to live in accordance with them or to realize their distinctive values.

It seems clear that the implementation of some rights in the existing system does work to the disadvantage of some elements of some collectivistic moralities. For example, the right to freedom of religion, understood as including the freedom of adults to choose their own religious affiliation, may make it hard for some religious moralities to flourish or in extreme cases even to survive under modern conditions in which individuals are exposed to a variety of opposing religions and to secular viewpoints as well. Similarly, the right of the individual to choose a marriage partner, if effectively implemented everywhere, would presumably disadvantage moralities that view the choice of a marriage partner as a decision for the family or for the village elders, rather than the individual.

Suppose we grant, for the sake of the argument, that such collectivistic moralities are valid. Does that entail that the international legal rights regime is unjustifiable from their standpoint? Obviously, the answer is "no." The advantages that the regime provides overall might outweigh the disadvantages. This would be true, if a group whose morality would be disadvantaged by the implementation of some particular international legal human right would be even more vulnerable were it not for the protections that the regime provides.

Moreover, as Hart emphasized in his response to Devlin in the enforcement of morality debate, there is no reason to assume that moralities, whether collectivistic or individualistic, are fragile, seamless webs.[17] Recent work on the evolution of moral norms lends support to Hart's claim: A change in one norm can often occur without the whole system falling apart.[18] Indeed, unless this were the case, it would not be possible for selective pressures to mold moralities any more than biological natural selection would be possible in an

[17] H.L.A. Hart, *Law, Liberty, and Morality* (Stanford: Stanford University Press, 1963), pp. 51–52.
[18] Kim Sterelny, "Snafus: An Evolutionary Perspective," *Biological Theory* 2:3 (2007): 317–28.

organism that could not develop a new trait at the expense of an old one without disintegrating. Viable moralities, like viable organisms, must have the capacity to adapt to new challenges, and adaptation as a result of selective pressures is generally incremental, not wholesale.[19] So we should not assume that if some aspect of the international legal human rights regime negatively impacts some feature of a collectivistic morality, its adherents are faced with a stark choice between the survival of their morality and support for the international human rights project. Given the significant protections that international legal human rights provide for groups and relationships, and given the costs and risks of scrapping the regime in favor of some other mode of achieving a comparable level of protection, the best alternative for those whose collectivistic moralities are disadvantaged by some aspects of the existing regime may be to lobby for more reform rather than to discard the baby with the bathwater.

This counsel of prudence seems all the more reasonable if we keep two points in mind: First, there appears to be no coherent, systematic alternative to an international legal regime of individual rights on offer; and second, even if there were, the transition costs of institutionalizing might well be prohibitive. In the six and a half decades since the UDHR was ratified, an impressive, though admittedly flawed institutionalization of international legal human rights has developed.

One way in which reform of the existing system might be achieved would be to strive for recognition of the legitimacy of interpretations of individual legal rights that more adequately reflect the social embeddedness of individuals and the importance of collectivistic values. An actual example of this strategy at work is the ruling of the International Committee for Human Rights (ICHR), the treaty body for the International Covenant on Civil and Political Rights (ICCPR), in the famous *Lubicon Lake Band Case*. The ruling interpreted the *individual's* right to culture (in Article 27 of the ICCPR) as implying *collective* land rights for an indigenous group whose culture was said to depend heavily on the ability to continue to pursue traditional hunting and fishing activities on their ancestral lands.[20]

[19] Allen Buchanan, *Beyond Humanity? The Ethics of Biomedical Enhancement* (Oxford: Oxford University Press, 2011).

[20] Lubicon Lake Band v. Canada, Communication No. 167/1984 (1990), U.N. Doc. A/45/40, Supp. No. 40 (1990), at 1.

There is another reason not to exaggerate the implications of the claim that the international legal human rights regime disadvantages reasonable collectivist moralities. Even if the claim is true, its significance is considerably reduced by the fact that in international law the system of individual rights is increasingly being supplemented with group rights. Perhaps the most conspicuous case is the growing recognition in international law of indigenous peoples' rights, which are understood to include group rights and to acknowledge the collectivistic character of indigenous peoples' cultures; but it is arguable that the notion that other minorities, especially national minorities, have group rights has also taken hold in international law.[21] These developments soften the negative impact of some international legal human rights on collectivistic values. Their addition should make the overall international legal order of which the individual human rights system is a part more congenial from the standpoint of collectivistic moralities.

It is one thing to say that some international legal human rights, if implemented, disadvantage some valid collectivistic moralities, quite another to say that the international legal human rights regime is only justifiable from the standpoint of individualistic moralities. The former statement is no doubt true, but the latter, as I have shown, is false. Given the valuable protections that the international legal human rights regime provides to collectivistic values, and the costs and risks involved in scrapping the existing system for the sake of developing a new one that excluded individual rights, the most reasonable stance for those who espouse reasonable collectivist moralities is to try to reform and if necessary supplement the existing system, not to fundamentally oppose it.

---

[21] S. James Anaya, *Indigenous Peoples in International Law* (Oxford: Oxford University Press, 2004), at note 20; Cindy Holder and Jeff Corntassel, "Indigenous Peoples and Multicultural Citizenship: Bridging Collective and Individual Rights," *Human Rights Quarterly*, 24:1 (2002): 126–51.

# CHAPTER 8

——

## Conclusions

The system of international legal human rights is the core, or, one might also say, the heart of modern human rights practice. The basic idea upon which this practice was founded is that international law should be used to develop universal standards to regulate the behavior of states toward those under their jurisdiction, for the sake of those individuals themselves.[1] In refuting the ethical pluralist challenge to the human rights enterprise, I have shown that even though the system's moral foundations include the idea that individuals are morally important on their own account, it is not inappropriately individualistic, because the rights it contains recognize the social nature of human beings and the role that community plays in their good.

I have also argued that the best interpretation of the system of international legal human rights presents it as having the functions of requiring all states to affirm and protect basic equal status for all (the status egalitarian function) and to ensure that all have access to the conditions for leading a decent or minimally good life (the well-being function), where this includes both protecting individuals from serious harms and providing them with the resources and services characteristic of the modern welfare state. This interpretation is superior, I have argued, to those according to which the function of the system is to protect normative agency or individual autonomy or to secure basic interests (or needs) or to help realize a set of corresponding moral rights.

---

[1] Here, for brevity, I will omit the qualifier 'considered as social beings,' but hope that the reader will keep it and my explanation of its importance in mind.

Neither the normative agency/autonomy interpretation nor the basic interests (or needs) interpretation can explain the prominent status egalitarian element in the system; yet there are, as I have argued, weighty reasons in favor of retaining it. Ensuring that all have some adequate threshold of opportunities for autonomous living or for "normative agency" is compatible with patterns of discrimination that do not prevent all from reaching the threshold. Ensuring that all have the opportunity for a minimally good or decent human life or achieve satisfaction of their basic needs is compatible with gender or racial discrimination that is not so severe as to undercut this opportunity. Similarly, a system of international legal standards for states, even one that gave a prominent role to a set of rights ascribed to all individuals, could help ensure that all have the opportunity for a minimally good or decent life and yet lack the other status egalitarian features the existing system exhibits. Such a system would not prohibit states from discriminating among groups of individuals within their jurisdiction as to the scope or weight of their rights, the conditions for under which their rights are derogable, or the remedies provided to them in cases in which their rights were violated.

The existing international legal human rights system, in contrast, does more than require that states protect and promote the good of all under their jurisdiction—it does more than ensure "membership" in a political community for all in that anemic sense. Promoting the good of everyone is compatible with systematic formal and informal discrimination that consigns some to an inferior status. In addition to helping to ensure that states promote the good of all, the existing system affirms and protects equal basic status for all.

The same is true for decent domestic legal systems. They too include features that cannot be explained on the hypothesis that they function only to ensure that everyone's good is promoted and protected, if this means that all are to have the opportunity for a minimally good or decent life. They not only ascribe a set of rights to all—which might be sufficient for achieving the well-being function—they also prohibit any discrimination with regard to the scope and weight of the rights, set the same conditions for derogation of the rights, and require effective remedies—the same remedies—for all. In doing so they encompass both the well-being function and the status egalitarian function.

The autonomy (or normative agency) interpretation suffers from two additional liabilities: It gives a roundabout and unpersuasive grounding for many rights that are more readily explained as protecting well-being against serious harms, as in the case of the right against torture; and it is also subject to the charge of parochialism, since there are reasonable moralities that do not place such a high priority on autonomy. The third interpretation, the Mirroring View, according to which the function of the system is to realize a set of corresponding preexisting individual moral human rights, cannot account for some prominent international legal human rights that are appropriately included in the system, because moral human rights, by virtue of the fact that their corresponding duties are morally owed to the individual right-holder and hence must be grounded solely in the moral importance of features of the individual right-holder, do not have the broad scope of some highly plausible international legal human rights. Nor can the Mirroring View account for the fact that collective rights, including the right of political self-determination, are included in the international legal human rights system.

If we reject the Mirroring View, a more secure grounding for international human rights can be achieved by the pluralistic approach to justification that I have outlined. Such an approach allows us to keep in center-view the idea that every individual is of moral significance on his own account while at the same time appealing to moral arguments that are less constraining than those that are based on corresponding individual moral rights. Sound arguments for having various international legal human rights can appeal to the need to achieve the efficient fulfillment of imperfect duties and to the need to secure morally important public goods, and can invoke the moral importance of the interests of large numbers of persons, not just those of the right-holder.

Arguments that appeal to more than the interests of the individual right-holder do not collapse into consequentialism, because the commitment to status egalitarianism ensures that no individual will be denied protection for the sake of maximizing overall good. In other words, the status egalitarian commitment requires that whatever rights are justified by appealing to the interests of large numbers of people are ascribed to all individuals, that they have the same weight and scope for all, are subject to the same derogation conditions, and that all have rights to effective remedies for their violation.

I have also argued for a more radical conclusion: Once we appreciate the instrumental character of legal rights, it becomes evident that a system of international legal human rights can have quite different moral groundings. More specifically, there is good reason to think that an adequate justification for all or most of the rights included in the existing system of international legal human rights can be achieved without relying on premises about the existence of moral human rights. Such a system can be justified instead on the vocabulary of basic moral values and (mere) moral duties to promote and protect them.

Without restating the often complex arguments for them, I will now simply list the most important results of my investigation in this book. (A much more complete list is provided in appendix 2.) After that, I will identify what I take to be the major challenges for the further development of international human rights law.

1. Because international human rights law is central to the modern practice of human rights, an assessment of that practice must include a determination of whether the international legal human rights system is justified.

2. Even in cases in which international human rights law does not impose legal obligations on states or other entities, it serves as a politically potent, widely accepted moral standard to which various actors can appeal in their efforts to uphold human rights. That is, the practice of human rights includes political techniques by which states and other entities (non-state groups such as Hamas, international organizations such as the WTO, and corporations) are held accountable for international legal human rights violations even in the absence of the violation of a legal duty. Thus the moral and political power of international human rights law exceeds its legal power. This fact must be taken into account in assessing the value of the international legal human rights system; ignoring it makes the system look less potent than it is.

3. There are at least three basic justifications for a system of international legal rights like the existing one. The first appeals to seven important benefits that participation in the system provides to a wide range of actors. The second is that without the system of international legal human rights, the international order would be unjustifiable, because the powers it confers on states would impose unacceptable risks on human beings, both

as individuals and as members of communities. The third is that states and the governments that act on their behalf have a special obligation to support the system of international legal human rights, because they are the chief beneficiaries of the sovereign powers that the system functions to constrain and are in the best position to shape the character of the international order.

4. The most basic idea of the international legal human rights system is to use international law to set standards for how all states are to treat individuals under their jurisdiction, for the sake of those individuals themselves, considered as social beings, rather than for the sake of promoting state interests. The best interpretation of the existing system of standards, so far as they constitute a distinctive new development in international law, is that they function primarily to affirm and protect the equal basic status of individuals and to help ensure that they have the opportunity to lead a minimally good or decent life, where this encompasses both protection from serious harms and abuses that states can inflict and, more positively, the provision of the basic goods and services of the modern welfare state. Although these functions can be formulated in terms of moral rights, they need not be.

5. In approaching the question of justifying the international legal human rights system, it is a mistake to assume the Mirroring View, according to which international legal rights (so far as they are justified) correspond to preexisting moral rights. Contrary to the Mirroring View, international legal human rights can be justified even if there are no corresponding, preexisting moral human rights, because legal rights can have a number of different moral groundings, of which the need to realize corresponding individual moral rights is only one. Further, a number of important and justifiable international legal human rights cannot be justified as realizations of preexisting moral human rights, because there are no corresponding moral human rights, that is, none with the same broad scope. A full justification for these rights requires more than showing that they realize a corresponding moral human right.

6. There are powerful reasons to adopt a pluralistic justificatory strategy, one that allows for grounding international legal human rights on a number of distinct moral considerations.

7. The system of international legal human rights, though it prominently features individual rights-norms, provides valuable protections for groups and communities.
8. An ecological view of institutional legitimacy is essential: As with many other institutions, the legitimacy of international legal human rights institutions depends on how they fit into a network of institutions characterized by a division of labor that allows for reciprocal legitimation.
9. Conceptions of legitimacy tailored to the special case of the state are ill-suited for assessing the legitimacy of most international institutions, including those that play a key role in the system of international legal human rights. Once we adopt the more comprehensive understanding of institutional legitimacy supplied by the Metacoordination View and understand that legitimacy is ecological, it becomes clear that international legal human rights institutions can be legitimate even though they are not democratic and lack some of the other characteristics of legitimate states, if they are appropriately connected to other institutions, and in particular democratic states and NGOs, in a workable division of institutional labor.
10. A legitimate system of international legal human rights provides crucial benefits for states, including enhancement of their legitimacy, and does not fundamentally threaten state sovereignty or the commitment to constitutional democracy. The supremacy of international human rights law over domestic law does not itself undermine democracy or constitutionalism; what matters is whether a state's procedure for engaging with international human rights law is sufficiently democratic and pays sufficient attention to the impact of this law on domestic constitutional structures and the exercise of collective self-determination.

## I. *Limitations of the System of International Legal Human Rights*

On the basis of the characterization I have provided of the existing international legal human rights system, we may conclude that it has at least five chief limitations or, more negatively, deficiencies. First, because treaty law best serves the goal of providing a relatively clear, authoritative standard for the behavior of states, the effectiveness of the international legal human rights enterprise depends largely on states ratifying treaties. Yet states are free, under current international law, to refrain from ratifying treaties or to ratify them with "reservations and understandings" that nullify some of the legal duties in their own case.

This is a serious limitation on the efficacy of the system. Hence, one fundamental question is whether it would be justifiable, or could become justifiable, to make the system less voluntary, by limiting further the right to use the reservations and understandings option or, more radically, by introducing a new norm of international law according to which some specified supermajority of ratifiers can impose legal obligations on nonratifiers. Such a norm could apply to all international legal human rights or, more plausibly, to an especially vital subset of them.

It would a mistake to dismiss this proposal as being contrary to the nature of international law. International law is not and never has been a fully voluntary matter. Jus cogens norms are legally binding regardless of state consent, and customary norms are legally binding on states that did not even exist when these norms were being created.[2] *The question is not whether, but rather to what extent, it is justifiable to depart from the requirement of state consent.*

In the domestic case, it is appropriate to enforce laws on citizens regardless of whether they consented to them or not, but on some accounts only when domestic political institutions are democratic. The crucial issue, on this view, is whether international human rights institutions must be democratic if human rights law is to be justifiably enforceable in the absence of state consent. It is one thing to say that enforcement of legal norms is justifiable only when law results from democratic processes *under conditions in which democracy is feasible,* another to say that democracy is an unconditional requirement for justifiable enforcement. If democracy is not

---

[2] It is assumed that norms are "accepted" by the community of states. If this means that all states do in fact accept them, then the question arises as to how one knows that this is the case. It will not do to say that acceptance can be inferred in the absence of explicit rejection of a norm. Weaker states might refrain from explicitly rejecting a norm out of fear of retaliation, not because they accept the norm in any sense that would be normatively potent enough to justify holding them accountable for compliance with it.

presently feasible at the global level, the question is whether there are other, second-best normative requirements which, if met, would make it justifiable to enforce a substantial set of international human rights obligations on states without their consent. To frame the question differently: Under what conditions would an expansion of the class of jus cogens norms to include more human rights norms than those prohibiting slavery, torture, and genocide be justifiable? To be justified, would this expansion require improved institutions or would a more robust consensus on the moral importance of the norms in question suffice? What would count as a more robust consensus and how would one know when it has been achieved?

In attempting to answer these questions, the results of chapter 3 should not be taken lightly. There I argued that all states and the governments that claim to act as their agents have an obligation not only to support but to participate in the system of international legal rights. That argument did not rely on consent. Consequently, it opens the door to the possibility of modifying the system so that a supermajority of states ratifying a treaty could impose the treaty's obligations on nonratifiers.

Whether such a modification would be justified, all things considered, is another, more complicated matter which I cannot pursue further in this work. Here I will only repeat what I said earlier. If the rationale for such a supermajority norm is that international legal human rights obligations can be imposed on states without their consent if the norms in question enjoy a very robust consensus, then introducing a new norm according to which a supermajority of ratifying states could impose international legal human rights obligations on nonratifying states would be problematic under current conditions. The consent of nondemocratic states could not reasonably be taken as evidence for a robust consensus, because it could not be assumed that the representatives of the state genuinely represent the majority of their peoples. Quite apart from that, there is something troubling, on the face of it, in the idea of a majority imposing duties on a dissenting minority in the absence of a constitutional framework aptly designed to check abuses of majority decision-making. Nothing resembling such a constitutional framework exists at the global level.

The possibility of creating a new supermajoritarian norm should not be dismissed, however. Current thinking about the European

Union may provide a model. Some have advocated a constitution for that regional entity that would allow new laws to be binding on all members states if a supermajority voting requirement were satisfied. The idea is that if the European Union became a genuine federation, such a provision could be appropriate. Some have proposed this idea as a response to the current debt crisis the European Union is grappling with. But one might well extend the model to the case of human rights treaties. If, for reasons not directly having to do with human rights, the European Union evolves into a federation with provision for binding majority rule with respect to some laws, it might eventually extend this provision to human rights law. Whether a similar move is ever likely to occur at the global level is much more problematic.

The second limitation of the system is that while it does a reasonably good job of specifying the primary obligations of states, that is, their obligations toward those under their jurisdiction, it does not assign clear default obligations, that is, obligations for states (or international organizations) to act when a state fails to fulfill its primary obligations. The most dramatic instance of this shortcoming is the lack of a clear legal obligation to use military intervention to stop large-scale wrongful killings when no other means will suffice. Moreover, the permanent member veto in the Security Council, taken together with the UN Charter's requirement of Security Council authorization for intervention, poses an obstacle to states assuming such an obligation. But there is also no clear assignment of default obligations when a state doesn't kill its people but instead fails to prevent their avoidable deaths from malnutrition and disease. This deficiency is perhaps even more serious than the limitations on state obligations that result from the voluntary nature of treaty law noted in the preceding paragraph.

There is some movement in the direction of remedying this deficiency or at least ameliorating its negative effects. In particular, the Responsibility to Protect (R2P) movement is an attempt to encourage states to step into the breach when a state fails in its human rights obligations vis-à-vis those under its jurisdiction, but so far it has stopped short of creating a new legal obligation.

I suspect that most state leaders and international relations experts would say that a proposal to modify international human rights law that imposed clear and robust obligations on states that go beyond their primary obligations to those under their jurisdiction is not feasible. They would predict that states would not ratify treaties that imposed such obligations on them. Nor does it seem likely that a new norm of customary international law that imposes default obligations is likely to emerge. For one thing, the behavior of states would have to alter remarkably for there to be the clear pattern of behavior in accordance with such a norm that is a necessary condition for the emergence of a new customary norm. At present, the clearly discernible pattern is that states generally do not act as if they had a genuine legal obligation to secure human rights when a state defaults on its obligations.

Apart from that practical worry, there is at least one serious principled objection. Under prevailing conditions, such a new norm of international law would be subject to serious abuses. It would provide states with a legal pretext for inappropriate interference in the internal affairs of other states. This objection would be all but conclusive if it were left up to individual states to decide unilaterally when the relevant duties were in play and what mode of acting on them was appropriate.

The risk of abuse would not be so great if the new norm was properly institutionalized, however. In particular, the requirement of *collective* action to fulfill the duties, *if operationalized in a set of sound institutional processes designed to reduce the risk of abuse and error*, would be especially valuable. The current arrangement, under which the human rights-correlative duties of states are primarily only toward those under their jurisdiction makes sense, given the limitations of existing institutions; but a more expansive conception of states' duties might be not only acceptable, but morally mandatory, if greater institutional resources became available. A major challenge for the system of international legal rights is to develop institutional resources that would make a more expansive conception of duties not only feasible but also morally acceptable.[3]

The third limitation of the existing system is that international human rights law does not assign clear obligations to nonstate actors, in particular, global corporations and international organizations that

---

[3] For an explanation of how greater institutional resources can make more ambitious norms appropriate, see Allen Buchanan, "Institutionalizing the Just War," *Philosophy & Public Affairs*, 34:1 (2006): 2–28.

partially control the global economic and financial structure, such as the International Monetary Fund (IMF) and the World Trade Organization (WTO). Yet these entities have a tremendous impact on human rights worldwide. One obstacle to remedying this deficiency is that the international human rights system was devised on the assumption that the primary problem was the behavior of states toward their own peoples and that, consequently, the primary duty-bearers should be states, considered as independent actors. To achieve a meaningful assignment of human rights duties to nonstate actors such as global corporations and international financial and economic organizations would require an institutionalized sharing of responsibilities among states for seeing that these duties were fulfilled, since no state acting independently could be expected to hold these powerful nonstate actors accountable.

In principle, there appears to be no barrier to modifying the system of international legal human rights in this way. States can create international legal obligations and if they choose to they can impose human rights obligations on global corporations and key economic and financial international organizations. They have already assumed international legal responsibilities regarding the behavior of corporations operating within their territories. Whether they are likely to use human rights treaties to impose obligations directly on corporations is another question altogether.

One reason why such an innovation will be hard to come by is that states are often so dependent on particular global corporations or view their own interests as so closely aligned with these entities' interests that they would be reluctant to subject them to common control. The most powerful states, whose cooperation would be essential for imposing human rights duties on global financial and economic organizations, already exert disproportionate control over them and will be reluctant to subject their operations to collective international control, whether in the name of human rights or for any other reason.

As with the Responsibility to Protect, there are recent developments that may turn out to be the first steps toward the emergence of new legal norms that would remedy this deficiency. The *Guiding Principles on Human Rights and Business* are not legally binding norms, but they are an attempt to extend the political force of human rights to corporations.

A fourth serious limitation is that the system of international human rights law, as it currently exists, is not designed to provide any direct assistance for coping with the problem of damage caused by features of the global basic structure. Because it primary function is to regulate states in their behavior toward those under their jurisdiction, it is not geared toward mitigating the effects of the extreme power disparities among states or the unfairness that this inequality produces in the global basic structure. In particular, international human rights law has nothing directly to say about the problem of the unfair bargaining advantage that powerful states enjoy in their dealing with weaker states, and the domination and exploitation that it facilitates, not only in particular transactions, but in the shaping of the very nature of the global basic structure within which they occur.

International human rights law does provide something that is directly relevant to these structurally-grounded injustices: the idea that it is a matter of international concern that all human beings should have the opportunity for a decent or minimally good life and live in a social environment that affirms and protects their equal basic status. It is true that the basic idea of the system is to regulate state behavior toward those under its jurisdiction and that those who created the system were, for historical reasons, especially concerned with human damage that can occur at the hands of particular states. But from the beginning it was assumed that states should positively provide for the welfare of those under their jurisdiction, not merely refrain from abusing them. The moral rationale for this requirement relied on the idea that all human beings ought to have the opportunity for a decent or minimally good life simply by virtue of what human beings are. As the system of international law developed, it also came to embody more forcefully the commitment to protecting the equal basic status of all persons, and this came to be understood as requiring more than that the state itself refrain from discrimination. That is, some human rights treaties obligate states to protect individuals under their jurisdiction against private actions, including those that occur within deeply entrenched cultural practices that deny their equal basic status.

If all humans ought to have the opportunity to lead a minimally good or decent life and to be treated as having equal basic status, and if this imperative is of sufficient moral weight that it should be a matter of international concern that takes the form of international law, then in principle human rights law should not be limited to efforts to addressing only one factor that prevents these requirements from being met, namely, the bad behavior of states toward those under their jurisdiction. If features of the global basic structure result in some human beings lacking the opportunity for a decent or minimally good life or create such extreme material inequalities that some are vulnerable to denials of their equal basic status, then the wrong is of the same nature as the wrongs states perpetrate against those under their jurisdiction and that were the original target of the international legal human rights project. They are preventable adverse departures from the conditions of life that are appropriate for all human beings by virtue of the kinds of beings they are. In that sense, they are proper objects of international human rights law.

A fifth limitation is that the international legal human rights system currently lacks the resources for achieving appropriate constraints on the proliferation of international legal human rights. Since the beginning of the project of developing international human rights law, the number of human rights conventions has risen from the original two covenants to twenty-seven (thirty-seven in the case of the European human rights regime), while the number of norms in the total collection of conventions has swelled to six hundred and sixty-seven.[4] That is a remarkable increase over the number in the Universal Declaration of Human Rights. Rights inflation can occur, however, without any new conventions. Rights in existing conventions can be given overexpansive interpretations. The worry is that unbridled proliferation damages the very idea of international human rights by abandoning the notion of extraordinarily high priority norms in favor of an ever-expanding list of protected interests, and that the political effectiveness of the enterprise is likely to be compromised by dispersing energies in the pursuit of the realization of so many norms.

Early in this book, I noted that with respect to welfare rights the risk of proliferation seems especially high because of the inherent

[4] For an excellent characterization of the extent of international human rights proliferation and a critique of this tendency, see *Draft Report: Human Rights Proliferation*, by Guglielmo Veridrame and Jonathan Mchanghama prepared under a grant from the Templeton Foundation (2013).

vagueness of the notions of ensuring basic welfare state functions or providing the opportunity for a minimally good life. The worry is that there will be an imposition of ever more demanding obligations on states regarding welfare state functions, so that instead of merely helping to ensure that everyone has the opportunity to lead a minimally good or decent life, international law will be directed toward the much less credible goal of ensuring full human flourishing for all.

Does the international legal human rights system have the institutional, doctrinal, and cultural resources needed to achieve the needed restraint? More specifically, does it have what it takes to ensure that the pursuit of overdemanding standards of justice does not give short shrift to the legitimate claims to self-determination on the part of collectives, whether they be states or groups within states? Will international human rights law reach the point—or has it reached the point already—at which it unduly constrains proper collective self-determination as to what justice requires at the domestic level?

Even if states voluntarily subject themselves to an increasingly more demanding set of international legal human rights obligations and do so in ways that are compatible with the requirements of democratic authorization outlined in chapter 6, there is still another worry: namely, that the resulting costs and burdens that individuals and groups will have to bear if the state is to be able to fulfill these expansive obligations will be morally indefensible. Here we encounter a familiar problem: How extensive should welfare state functions be, given that discharging them means limiting liberty and diminishing the resources available to individuals and groups for pursuing their own vision of the good? Will the proliferation of welfare rights in international human rights law push states toward unjustifiably robust welfare functions?

Whether or not welfare rights are especially prone to inflation, it would be hard to deny that there is a more general problem of international legal human rights inflation. Without attempting to provide anything like a comprehensive analysis of the general problem— much less an adequate solution to it—I will now explore a way of framing the issues that I hope will be helpful for further inquiry. Before doing so, however, I want to emphasize that the enormous increase in the number of treaties and human rights norms is not itself conclusive evidence of inflation. For one thing, duplication of existing conventions' provisions in new conventions is not always a bad thing. For example, the creation of a special convention on torture was arguably a good thing, even though the right against torture was already included in several existing conventions. Nonetheless, the transition from a couple of dozen rights to several hundred and from two conventions to more than two dozen should at the very least prompt serious concerns about inflation.

I will begin by noting that proponents of the Mirroring View might argue that even if it is true, as I have argued, that there is no reason of principle to require that all international legal rights mirror preexisting moral human rights, observing this stricture would do much to curb international legal human rights inflation. On this interpretation, the Mirroring View is not a claim about a conceptual connection between moral human rights and international legal human rights; nor is it a claim about what is required in principle for justifying international legal human rights. Instead, it is a practical proposal for how to curb international legal human rights inflation: namely, include in international law only those legal rights for which there are corresponding moral human rights.

There are two problems with this proposal. First, as I argued at length in chapter 2, respecting this stricture will result in a very truncated list of international legal human rights, or at least in a list of rights that have very lean content. In other words, the scope of duties correlative with the rights will be so limited that the legal rights simply will not achieve what we reasonably expect them to achieve. This is too high a price to pay, at least if there are other effective ways of curbing inflation. Second, it is far from clear that appealing to moral human rights would do much to curb international legal human rights inflation, because there is not sufficient agreement on what moral human rights there are and there is no sign that there will come to be. As I noted in chapter 1, the problem is not just that there is disagreement among philosophical theories of moral human rights and that there are no philosophical accounts that merit the title of theories—that is, none of the present contenders provide convincing arguments for constructing a list of moral human rights. Instead, they all seem to be afflicted with the same malady: they identify certain morally important interests and then slide—rather than argue—to the conclusion that the interests are of the proper character and importance to ground directed duties. Even if (by some miracle) philosophers came to converge on one theory of moral human rights, there is no reason whatsoever to think that it would be adopted by those agents who create international legal human rights.

My suggestion, then, is that resurrecting the Mirroring View as a practical proposal for constraining the list of international legal human rights is not promising. Instead, I want to begin what I hope will turn out to be a more fruitful discussion by offering a taxonomy of other options for achieving the needed constraint, and then make a preliminary assessment of which options look most attractive.

Constraint can be achieved by several different agents, at different junctures along the standard path from the initial decision to try create a new convention, to the drafting of a declaration, to the approval by the General Assembly of the declaration, to the ratification of the convention by the number of states required for it to go into effect, to the implementation of the convention's provisions by domestic institutions. In principle, constraint could be exercised at any stage of this process. There are three main modes of constraint: (1) doctrinal constraints (determinate legal principles that, if followed by relevant agents, achieve constraint); (2) informal internal constraints on the part of the agents who are in a position to exercise constraint (a stable psychological predisposition against the proliferation of rights, but one that is not a reflection of determinate legal principles of constraint); and (3) institutional mechanisms for constraint, designed to counterbalance the incentives various agents have for inflation.

First, one could rely on internal informal psychological constraint on the part of the treaty-drafters, but so far, there is little evidence that this would work. At least some of these agents operate under strong incentives for excessive proliferation. For example, among those who most ardently agitate for a new special convention on the rights of the elderly, those who expect to provide health and social services that will become mandatory if the treaty goes into effect, as well as lawyers who will help the elderly exercise their new rights, are predictably well-represented. I hope I will not be judged to be cynical if I surmise that merely imparting a clearer philosophical account of what international legal human rights are for is not likely to sap the force of these incentives. In my judgment, attempting to create informal internal dispositions to constraint on the part of those who seek to create new human rights treaties is not likely to be fruitful, unless it incorporates tangible incentives or effective institutional mechanisms aptly designed to transform the existing culture of treaty-makers. In other words, I doubt that requiring a moral philosophy course followed by an admonition to these people to pull up their moral socks and limit their demands would be effective.

A second approach would be to require some credible expert body, endowed with appropriate authority, to determine whether a proposal to *start* the treaty-drafting process was acceptable. The idea here would be to impose a filter at the outset, rather than try to introduce constraints after the treaty-making process has gotten started. One of the considerations such a body would need to take into account is whether a new treaty is needed, or whether it would be more cost-effective to direct resources toward achieving better compliance with existing treaties.

A third alternative would involve a similar institutional innovation, but this time at the next stage in the process. A kind of devil's advocate could be appointed to interrogate those who are proposing a draft declaration to the General Assembly. The role of this individual or committee would be to provoke a serious discussion in the General Assembly's deliberations about a draft declaration as to whether a new treaty was really needed or whether, even assuming that it is, it should include all the proposed rights. For example, the devil's advocate could require evidence that the creation of a new treaty would be more effective than better implementation of the relevant provisions of existing treaties.

A fourth alternative would be to rely on constraints being imposed at the ratification stage. This already occurs in two ways: groups that formulate new human rights treaties have to produce something that will be ratified by the minimum number of parties needed for the treaty to go into effect; and any state can constrain the content of the rights in a treaty, as they apply to itself, by exercising its right to invoke reservations and understandings. However, qualification of the state's obligations must not be contrary to the main purposes of the treaty, and that places limitations on how effective this strategy for coping with inflation can be. Moreover, states may find it hard to refrain from ratifying because they are subject to pressure from concentrated, vocal interest groups.

A fifth option is restraint on the part of international and domestic judges in the interpretation of international legal human rights.

In the case of states whose constitutions acknowledge the supremacy of international (or regional) human rights courts' interpretations, restraint by domestic judges may have little effect if international (or regional) court judges indulge in overexpansive interpretation. My sense is that the worst overly expansive interpretations have tended to occur at the international (and European regional) level, not at the domestic level. If that is the case, then what we might otherwise view as a progressive development—namely, an increasing acknowledgment of the supremacy of international human rights law—may exacerbate the problem of inflation. Curbing overexpansive judicial interpretation is particularly difficult, because the independence that is conferred on judges to help insulate them from political pressures makes it difficult for other agents to impose effective incentives for restraint. Yet without altering the tangible incentives under which they work, it may be very difficult to produce a shift in judicial culture toward less expansive interpretation. In brief, efforts to install internal constraints, without a change in insentives, are likely to be insufficient.

A sixth option would be to try to introduce into international human rights law a distinction that is already present in the more developed domestic legal systems: that between legal rights and administrative directives designed to give them effect. If one examines human rights conventions, one is struck by the fact that an awareness of this distinction is conspicuously absent. Assertions about rights are mixed together with assertions that also use the terminology of rights but that are more plausibly construed as directions to officials as to how to realize the rights. If this distinction were better observed, the result would be a shorter list of rights. Perhaps it would be beneficial to develop a new practice whereby human rights treaties were divided into two distinct parts: statements of rights and statements of administrative directives. Even better, perhaps some authorized independent body should be charged with the task of demanding of the treaty-drafters why each item listed in the rights part of the document should be there rather than in the administrative directives part.

A seventh alternative for achieving constraint is to filter the kinds of cases that reach international human rights courts, in order to shield judges from the temptation to give overexpansive interpretations of existing rights. The European Court of Human Rights, which is often said to be guilty of overexpansive interpretation of the rights included in the European Convention on Human Rights, currently lacks some of the opportunities for refusing to hear cases that are available to courts in some domestic systems, including the US Supreme Court. Although this mechanism of constraint does require the cooperation of judges, since it is typically they (or their subordinates) who apply the criteria that determine which cases are heard, it may nonetheless be an effective self-binding mechanism. In other words, judges may find it easier to avoid overexpansive interpretation if they can prevent themselves from being in a situation in which the temptation will occur.

My surmise is that all of these options should be utilized, but that the second (an institutional filter for proposals for starting a treaty-making process), the sixth (employment of a distinction between rights and administrative directives for their realization), and the seventh (principled refusal to hear certain types of cases) are the most promising. They do not rely on success in radically changing the culture of treaty-makers or international judges or on achieving convergence on substantive views about what the proper function of international legal human rights are.

My aim in this section has not been to provide a solution to the problem of international legal human rights inflation. Indeed, I have not even attempted to make a conclusive case that there is such inflation. Instead, I have tried to make two points. First, the standard philosopher's response to the problem of inflation—the attempt to make international legal human rights mirror moral human rights—is not promising. Nor is it plausible to think that philosophical clarification of any sort is likely to do much to solve the problem. Second, a more promising approach will not rely on the relevant agents internalizing the same understanding of the moral point of the international legal human rights system; instead, it will rely chiefly on new institutional mechanisms (like a filter for treaty-making projects) and existing legal resources (like the distinction between rights and administrative directives for realizing them and the notion that judges may sometimes refuse to hear cases).

## II. *Intrasocietal or Global Equal Basic Status?*

Once we come to understand the formidable influence that the global basic structure exerts on human lives, we are forced to be more critical about the very meaning of the commitment to affirming and protecting basic equal status that I have said is central to the international legal human rights enterprise. So far, international human rights law has focused on what I have called the *intrasocietal*, as opposed to the *global* interpretation of this commitment.[5] According to the intrasocietal interpretation, international human rights law should only concern itself with ensuring that every individual enjoys basic equal status vis-à-vis the other members of his or her own society, where the term 'society' here means the group of people subject to the authority of a particular state. To the extent that international human rights law has mainly concerned itself with regulating the behavior of the state toward those under its jurisdiction, the requirement to affirm and protect equal basic status can only be understood according to the intrasocietal interpretation.

According to the global interpretation, international human rights law should perform a much more ambitious function: ensuring equal status for each individual vis-à-vis all other human beings. This more ambitious function cannot be cashed out in terms of the duties a state has toward those under its jurisdiction, because other factors, including the character of the global basic structure, can affect whether a person is treated as having equal basic moral status vis-à-vis all other individuals.

Whether their plight is the result of their own wretched governments or the workings of the global basic structure or some combination of the two, people who are barely surviving at the margin of subsistence, illiterate, suffering from preventable or treatable diseases, unable to compete in modern labor markets, and cut off from access to much of what makes modern life valuable (and makes its burdens tolerable) are at the very least in danger of being regarded by others and perhaps even by themselves as passive, unfortunate victims. Simply as a matter of psychological fact, it may be hard to treat other human beings whom we think of in this way as being genuinely our equals. Instead, we may succumb to patronizing and unjustifiably paternalistic attitudes toward them.

Be that as it may, there is another worry about the connection between the global basic structure and global basic equal status. I noted earlier that under modern conditions, in which the state plays such a huge role in human life, the presumption is that for competent

---

[5] I am indebted to Julian Culp for pressing me to explore this ambiguity.

adult citizens, proper public recognition of equal basic moral status requires the right to equal political participation. There is no world state. There is, however, a global basic structure and a rapidly growing set of global governance institutions that partly constitute it and increasingly come to shape it.

So far, those who occupy positions of power in global governance structures are disproportionately from the richer states. If global governance becomes more robust, then the fact that access to positions of power in global governance institutions is largely restricted to individuals from the wealthier countries will raise very serious questions about global equal basic status. Whether international human rights law can cope with the problem of structural impairments to equal basic status on the global interpretation is a neglected but important issue that I hope to address on a future occasion.

Even if international human rights law is and remains restricted to the effort to affirm and protect equal basic status only in its intrasocietal dimension, that is something of great value. One difficulty with the proposal that it should go beyond this to embrace a commitment to global equal basic status is that it is far from clear what this would amount to. In other words, in some respects at least, the ideal of intrasocietal equal basic status is clearer than that of global equal basic status. My point is not to endorse unequivocally such an expansion of the function of international legal human rights law in the absence of a sound analysis of what global equal basic status would involve, but rather to make two much more modest claims.

First, if intrasocietal equal basic status is a fundamental moral requirement, it is hard to avoid the presumption that global equal basic status is as well, at least in principle. It is a truism to say that we live in an increasingly globalized world. This means, among other things, that people are increasingly aware, not only of how they are regarded and treated by others in their own society, but also of their status vis-à-vis other human beings more generally. Globalization also means that how one's life goes depends, not only on whether one is regarded as an equal within one's own society, but whether, or how much one's well-being and one's values count in the decisions that shape the global basic structure. Under these conditions, the same moral considerations that underwrite the commitment to intrasocietal equal basic status also speak in favor of global equal basic status. And this is true even if, as one might argue, the priority for human rights law should be affirming and protecting intrasocietal equal basic status. Second, the existing international legal human rights system does not appear to be well-equipped to promote global equal basic status.

## III. *Diagnosis Versus Remedies*

It is important to emphasize that the moral roots of international human rights law I have tried to uncover in this book are not to be identified with natural rights doctrine. There is no assumption that international legal human rights norms are simply legal embodiments of corresponding preinstitutional moral rights, much less rights that are deducible a priori from the concept of human nature or from the fact of human rationality. Instead, international legal human rights, as I understand them, are valuable instruments, given the nature and limitations of international law, for promoting equal basic status and well-being in the light of contingent assumptions about the standard threats to them that exist in the modern world.

The key point is that this conception of what international legal rights are and what they are for can accommodate the idea that it is important to provide protection against threats posed by the global basic structure, not just by the behavior of states toward those under their jurisdiction or indeed by any other particular agents. In other words, it is clear that the contentful understanding of the conditions of living that all humans ought to enjoy that has been developed in international human rights law can serve the *diagnostic* function of characterizing the damage done to them by the global basic structure: Harms due to the global basic structure can be conceptualized in terms of the failure to realize international legal human rights. The question is whether international human rights law can also provide effective *remedies*.

So far, it is fair to say that modern human rights practice has had more success in its diagnostic function than in its remedial function, at least when it comes to alleviating the severe poverty and ill health of hundreds of millions of people in less economically developed countries. A philosopher who reviewed a draft of this volume concluded from this sad fact that the Practice and by implication international human rights law is guilty of a serious parochialism: It focuses on threats to the world's best off individuals, rather than those that cast a shadow over the lives of the worst-off. It is striking, he said, that there is no human right to clean water, considering that hundreds of millions of people lack clean water and suffer grievously as a result.

I see the matter rather differently. International human rights law has no need of a right to clean water, because it contains other legal rights that subsume it. The right to health, the right to an adequate standard of living, and some other social and economic rights, if realized, would ensure access to clean drinking water. (In fact, in some contexts, merely respecting peoples' economic liberties would enable them to secure clean water and other resources needed for leading a decent life.) So, the problem is not lack of legal coverage. The problem is that so far the Practice has not developed adequate mechanisms, whether legal or political, for ensuring that the most basic social and economic rights (and economic liberties) of people in the less economically developed countries are realized. The Practice has done too little to alleviate severe deprivation.

To the extent that the charge of parochialism voiced by the reviewer is valid, the problem is not that the content of international human rights law reflects the needs of those in affluent countries rather than those of the world's worst off. Instead, it may be that the founders of the international legal human rights system were subject to a different sort of parochialism: They overgeneralized from the experience of economic prosperity in the West. They may have not appreciated how difficult it would prove to be for many countries to achieve the adequate standard of living to which the system says each individual has an international legal human right.

The Practice has failed to make much headway on the problem of severe deprivation for at least four reasons. First, it has not been able to ensure that poorer states fulfill their primary duties to those under their jurisdiction; second, it has not assigned clear default duties, much less provided mechanisms for ensuring their fulfillment; and third, it has not had much impact on the contribution of the global basic structure to deprivation. (Note that I include here the way in which aspects of the global basic structure, including the norms of sovereignty discussed in chapter 4, continue to facilitate corrupt governments and therefore to sustain the obstacles to overcoming deprivation that they erect.) Finally, even though the trade policies of some countries—including preeminently the United States, Japan, and the members of the European Union—include tariffs and subsidies that clearly contribute to deprivation in poorer countries, little has been done to change this. Trade barriers and subsidies are not usually regarded as a human rights issue, but they ought to be.[6]

The problem of reforming the global basic structure is arguably the most daunting. It appears to be much easier to harness the power of international law to mitigate threats directly posed by state actions that affect primarily their own peoples, than threats posed by features of the global basic structure, in part because the assignment of responsibility in the former case seems much more straightforward. If a state treats those under its jurisdiction in ways that undercut their opportunities for a decent or minimally good life or engages in or tolerates practices that relegate them to an inferior basic status, then the state may rightly be held accountable. Contentful legal duties not to act in those ways can be formulated and incorporated into international law.

The situation is much more difficult in the case of threats to well-being or equal basic status that result from features of the global basic structure, because the connection with particular acts by particular states is much more tenuous and complex. Because these are harms that emerge from the operations of a diverse set of institutions that exist because of the actions (and omissions) of a large number of different agents, assigning responsibility for the harms they cause is difficult. A legal duty ascribed to all states not to contribute to sustaining a global basic structure that undercuts individual welfare or equal basic status would be much less useful as a device for holding states accountable than a duty not to interfere with freedom of expression or even a duty to provide basic education.

The crucial question—perhaps the most fundamental question for the future of human rights practice—is whether the international human rights system can be developed in such a way as to go beyond diagnosing the nature of the wrongs of severe deprivation, including those caused by features of the global basic structure, to developing better political and legal resources for helping to remedy

[6] Fernando Teson and Jonathan Klick, "Global Justice and Trade," *Global Justice and International Economic Law: Opportunities and Prospects*, eds. John Linarelli, Frank J. Garcia, and Chius Carmody (Cambridge: Cambridge University Press, 2010), on the importance of lowering trade barriers.

them. In the case of damage done by the global basic structure, it would be necessary to conceptualize unfair bargaining practices among states and other structural injustices of the international order as violations of legal human rights, and then go on to devise contentful duties to be ascribed to states that would prohibit them. In addition, it would be necessary to embed these new duties in appropriate institutions and practices that would promote a significant degree of compliance.

Whether this innovation would be feasible or advisable, or whether, instead, a distinct new body of international law would be a better alternative is an interesting and hard question. The alternative might be a body of law whose fundamental moral vocabulary was that of fairness, rather than individual rights. This new body of law and human rights law would promote different aspects of global justice comprehensively understood.

My surmise is that the discourse of legal individual rights, geared as it is toward regulating how states treat individuals, rather than how states treat each other and how the global basic structure should be made to conform to the requirements of justice, is not likely to be suitable for the remedial, as opposed to the diagnostic task. If I am right about this, it is not a condemnation of the project of international human rights law or of the modern human rights practice that is grounded on it. There is no reason to think that this type of law, or any one type of law, should solve all the moral problems of global concern. Instead, what it indicates is that there is a need for a new type of international law that addresses questions of global justice not readily dealt with by human rights law. It is gratuitous to assume that international human right law can or should encompass the whole of global justice.

My purpose in this book has been to provide an accurate characterization of the international legal core or heart of modern human rights practice, to explain how central it is to the Practice, and then to explore the question of whether the system of international legal human rights is justified. I have also argued that the legitimacy of the processes by which states incorporate international human rights law can be at least as problematic, if not more problematic, than the international legal institutions themselves. If that is the case, if the justificatory arguments I have advanced are cogent, and if, as I have argued, there are no countervailing reasons capable of defeating them, then future philosophical theorizing should have two main foci: developing a principled account of how states can embrace international human rights law through proper processes of democratic authorization, and exploring the possibilities of overcoming the limitations of the system identified above. With respect to the first limitation—the system's commitments to voluntariness with respect to positive human rights law—the question is whether either the urgency of improving states' accountability for how they treat their peoples or the development of better international human rights institutions, or a combination of both, would make it justifiable for a strong majority of states to impose legal human rights obligations on states that do not voluntarily assume them. Making headway on that issue will require a more basic inquiry into the extent to which international law should depend on state consent.

## IV. *The Reciprocal Influence of Morality and Law in the Practice*

I began this book by explaining how central international human rights law is to the practice of human rights. I have argued that we greatly underestimate the value of international human rights law if we think of it as a kind of replication, in legal form, of preexisting moral norms. International law—like law generally—is both more powerful and more creative than that. It provides a lever for changing state behavior that can be more effective than direct appeals to morality, as I explained in chapter 1.

In addition, the processes by which the norms of international treaty law are formulated and interpreted constitute a mode of institutionalized practical reasoning that can actually add to our moral knowledge, not just clarifying the values we seek to further through international law, but also helping us to see that our initial understanding of the moral problems that international law can help solve was arbitrarily limited. That is precisely what is happening, I have just suggested, in the case of our growing understanding of the wrongs people suffer as a result of some features of the global basic structure. We have begun to understand that the same concerns for human well-being and equal basic status that underpinned the project of international human rights law from the beginning now require us to try to mitigate the deleterious effects of the global basic structure and that it is indefensible simply to assume, without argument, that the role of international human rights law is limited to regulating the behavior of states toward those under their jurisdiction.

It is true, of course, that the founders of the international legal human rights system drew on ideas from the philosophical tradition of moral human rights. This is abundantly clear in the justificatory rhetoric of the major documents and in the historical record of the processes that led to the drafting of the UDHR. It is also true, however, that the development of international human rights law has given more determinate content to the fundamental moral idea that human beings, by virtue of the kind of being they are, are morally entitled to certain conditions of living. This gain in moral understanding, so far as I can tell, did not come about primarily through advances in contemporary moral philosophy (though ideas from that discipline may have exerted some limited influence). Instead, so far, at least, improvements in our understanding of the basic moral values that underlie the system of international legal human rights have resulted from the on-going development of the legal heart of the human rights enterprise itself. Law is guided by morality and distinct from it, but legal developments can cause us to reflect on our moral principles and to revise them.

I have argued against the view that international legal human rights, so far as they are justified, must mirror an antecedently knowable list of moral human rights. This is not to say that I think that the idea of moral human rights will play no role in sound justifications for international legal human rights. It might turn out that the best justification for having a body of international law that has as its chief functions ensuring that all have the opportunity to lead a minimally good or decent human life and affirming and protecting the equal basic status of all will ultimately rely on the premise that there are moral human rights to basic well-being and equal status.

It might also be the case that the best justification for the system will also appeal to a few other, more specific moral human rights. (Suppose, for example, that according to the best theory of moral human rights, there is a relatively small set that includes a right to life, a right to lead a life, and perhaps a few other rights.) It might be the case that a theory of moral human rights of that sort will, as it were, point the way toward the sorts of rights that ought to be included in a system of international legal human rights, the idea being that the latter will contain a much larger set of legal rights needed to realize the small set of moral human rights. On this account, international legal human rights would not mirror moral human rights, but statements about the existence of moral human rights would play an important role in justifying the legal rights. Suppose that account is correct. Nonetheless, if my argument about the difference between moral and legal claim-rights is correct, these moral human rights will only be starting points—they will not supply anything approaching the full content of a set of international legal human rights, because, being solely subject-grounded, their corresponding duties will be too austere. Hence it will be inaccurate to say that international legal rights are justified only so far as they help realize a smaller set of preexisting moral human rights. The moral duties that correlate with the moral human rights will be less extensive than the legal duties that correlate with the international legal human rights.

I am not convinced, however, that much is to be gained by appealing to a short list of moral human rights. Instead, it may suffice to ground the system of international legal human rights on the more basic idea that all human beings are morally entitled to being provided with the opportunity to lead a minimally good or decent life and to the public affirmation and protection of their equal basic moral status. Or it might suffice simply to begin with the premise securing well-being and equal status for all people is a fundamental moral priority and not invoke the language of moral rights even at this most fundamental level. In either case, one may be able to develop the complex set of argumentative steps necessary to justify a system of international legal human rights without relying on premises about more specific moral human rights, as I argued in chapter 4. But whether I am right about that is irrelevant to the truth of everything else I have said in this book.

## V. *The Contingency and Fragility of Success*

When reflecting on the tone of critics of the human rights enterprise, it often seems to me that their concerns are, if not exaggerated or misconceived, at least somewhat lacking in perspective. The harsher critics seem to me to be unaware of both what a radical and unlikely moral reform the development of a system of international legal rights was and how fragile its admittedly limited success may turn out to be.

The first prerequisite for a reasonable evaluation of anything of value is to appreciate that it might not have been—and that it may not continue to exist. (That, I believe, is the fundamental insight of conservative thought.) I believe that once this appreciation is achieved in the case at hand, the complaint that international human rights law is not equally effective in binding strong as well as weak states and provides opportunities for stronger states to wield it as a weapon or lever for achieving their own ends, like other complaints about the system, looks much less damning.

At any time prior to the founding of the modern human rights enterprise, most people with even a modicum of knowledge about world politics and existing international law would have thought it extremely unlikely that the vast majority of states would use international law to bind themselves in ways that greatly restricted their sovereignty, even in its exercise within their own territories. Such a prospect was almost as unlikely as the abolition of slavery was at the end of the eighteenth century. The smart money would have wagered heavily against the success of both of these momentous moral improvements—and lost.

The unlikely creation of a system of international legal human rights was contingent on the confluence of a number of factors. It is often said, quite reasonably, that the will to create the system was stimulated by the horrors of World War II and the Holocaust—that the utter moral bankruptcy of existing international order had to be conclusively demonstrated before such a major reform would be undertaken. That is only one causal precondition, however. Another was that the victors of World War II included states that were, if not enthusiastic about the creation of the system, at least unwilling to block its creation or seriously subvert its operations. In particular, the world's most powerful state, the United States, has generally supported, and overall has not seriously hindered the development of the system of international legal human rights. Even though the US government has been less than a full participant in the system (refusing to ratify some of the most basic human rights treaties and resisting the creation of the International Criminal Court), it has supported the application of international human rights law to other states and has not seriously undermined the system's key institutions. Perhaps just as importantly, its relatively good protection of human rights domestically, combined with the wealth and education of its population and the strength of its civil society institutions, have created a situation in which US-based human rights NGOs have flourished and provided valuable support for the system as a whole.

All of this could change and there is a significant probability that it will, if the influence of the United States declines and China becomes the world's one superpower — without changing its stance on human rights. China is perhaps unique among the powerful states in explicitly repudiating the basic idea that undergirds the system of international legal human rights, namely, that it is proper and indeed morally necessary for international law to regulate the internal affairs of states.[7] China instead seems to view human rights documents simply as public pledges by states to conform to the norms they list, while denying that external agents have even the right to criticize states for noncompliance, much less to take actions to ensure that they comply. Moreover, China's behavior toward NGOs that try to operate within its borders is not a favorable portent for how its policies will impact the human rights enterprise if it becomes globally dominant. Perhaps instead of focusing exclusively on the flaws of the modern human rights enterprise, including the deficiencies of its legal core, those who are committed to human rights should question their confidence that the system is stable and that the only change to be anticipated in the future is further progress. Thus the image on the cover of this book is ambiguous. The sun could be rising or it could be setting.

[7] China, Information Office of the State Council, *Human Rights in China* (Beijing: Information Office of the State Council, 1991).

# APPENDIX 1

———

## Nonrights Norms in Major Human Rights Documents

The Universal Declaration of Human Rights (UDHR) and various human rights treaties contain a large number of items that are not phrased in terms of rights. Included are (a) instructions to states for how various listed rights are to be implemented, (b) statements about the conditions under which listed rights may be limited or abrogated, and (c) statements aimed at ensuring that listed rights are realized equally for all. However, there are also many items in the UDHR and major treaties that appear to be neither assertions of rights nor instances of (a), (b), or (c). They are what I shall call "nonrights norms." These nonrights norms in most cases are assertions of duties on the part of states—"mere" duties; not duties stated as correlatives of rights of individuals.

The presence of these nonrights norms in the major human rights documents reinforces two points made in chapter 1. First, in principle, the basic idea of the system of international legal human rights—setting international legal standards for how states are to treat those in their jurisdiction, for their own sakes—could be realized by a set of mere legal duties, without any reference to individual legal rights. Second, it is a mistake to assume that the function of international human rights law is to realize moral human rights. The following is a list of nonrights norms in the UDHR, the International Covenant on Civil and Political Rights (ICCPR), and the International Covenant on Economic, Social, and Cultural Rights (ICESCR).

## *Universal Declaration of Human Rights (UDHR)*

Article 4. No one shall be held in slavery or servitude; slavery and the slave trade shall be prohibited in all their forms.

Article 9: No one shall be subjected to arbitrary arrest, detention, or exile.

Article 11(2): No one shall be guilty of any penal offence on account of any act or omission which did not constitute a penal offence, under national or international law, at the time when it was committed. Nor shall a heavier penalty be imposed than the one that was applicable at the time the penal offence was committed.

Article 12: No one shall be subjected to arbitrary interference with his privacy, family, home or correspondence, nor to attacks upon his honour or reputation. Everyone has the right to the protection of the law against such interference or attacks.

Article 15(2): No one shall be arbitrarily deprived of his nationality nor denied the right to change his nationality.

Article 16(2): Marriage shall be entered into only with the free and full consent of the intending spouses.

Article 17(2): No one shall be arbitrarily deprived of his property.

Article 20(2): No one may be compelled to belong to an association.

Article 21(3): The will of the people shall be the basis of the authority of government; this will shall be expressed in periodic and genuine elections which shall be by universal and equal suffrage and shall be held by secret vote or by equivalent free voting procedures.

## *International Covenant on Economic, Social, and Cultural Rights (ICESCR)*

Article 1(2): All peoples may, for their own ends, freely dispose of their natural wealth and resources without prejudice to any obligations arising out of international economic cooperation, based upon the principle of mutual benefit, and international law. In no case may a people be deprived of its own means of subsistence.

Article 10(1): The widest possible protection and assistance should be accorded to the family, which is the natural and fundamental group unit of society, particularly for its establishment and while it is responsible for the care and education of dependent children. Marriage must be entered into with the free consent of the intending spouses.

Article 10(2): Special protection should be accorded to mothers during a reasonable period before and after childbirth. During such period working mothers should be accorded paid leave or leave with adequate social security benefits.

Article 10(3): Special measures of protection and assistance should be taken on behalf of all children and young persons without any discrimination for reasons of parentage or other conditions. Children and young persons should be protected from economic and social exploitation. Their employment in work harmful to their morals or health or dangerous to life or likely to hamper their normal development should be punishable by law. States should also set age limits below which the paid employment of child labour should be prohibited and punishable by law.

Article 15(3): The States Parties to the present Covenant undertake to respect the freedom indispensable for scientific research and creative activity.

## International Covenant on Civil and Political Rights (ICCPR)

Article 1(2): All peoples may, for their own ends, freely dispose of their natural wealth and resources without prejudice to any obligations arising out of international economic cooperation, based upon the principle of mutual benefit, and international law. In no case may a people be deprived of its own means of subsistence.

Article 6(2): In countries which have not abolished the death penalty, sentence of death may be imposed only for the most serious crimes in accordance with the law in force at the time of the commission of the crime and not contrary to the provisions of the present Covenant and to the Convention on the Prevention and Punishment of the Crime of Genocide. This penalty can only be carried out pursuant to a final judgment rendered by a competent court.

Article 6(5): Sentence of death shall not be imposed for crimes committed by persons below eighteen years of age and shall not be carried out on pregnant women.

Article 7: No one shall be subjected to torture or to cruel, inhuman or degrading treatment or punishment. In particular, no one shall be subjected without his free consent to medical or scientific experimentation.

Article 8(1): No one shall be held in slavery; slavery and the slave trade in all their forms shall be prohibited.

Article 8(2): No one shall be held in servitude.

Article 8(3a): No one shall be required to perform forced or compulsory labour.

Article 9(2): Anyone arrested shall be informed, at the time of the arrest, of the reasons for his arrest and shall be promptly informed of any charges against him.

Article 9(3): Anyone arrested or detained on a criminal charge shall be brought promptly before a judge or other officer authorized by law to exercise judicial power and shall be entitled to trial within a reasonable time or to release. It shall not be the general rule that persons awaiting trial shall be detained in custody, but release may be subject to guarantees to appear for trial, at any other stage of the judicial proceedings, and, should the occasion arise, for execution of judgment.

Article 10(1): All persons deprived of their liberty shall be treated with humanity and with respect for the inherent dignity of the human person.

Article 10(2a): Accused persons shall, save in exceptional circumstances, be segregated from convicted persons and shall be subject to separate treatment appropriate to their status as unconvicted persons.

Article 10(2b): Accused juvenile persons shall be separated from adults and brought as speedily as possible for adjudication.

Article 10(3): The penitentiary system shall comprise treatment of prisoners the essential aim of which shall be their reformation and social rehabilitation. Juvenile offenders shall be segregated from adults and be accorded treatment appropriate to their age and legal status.

Article 14(7): No one shall be liable to be tried or punished again for an offense for which he has already been finally convicted or acquitted in accordance with the law and penal procedure of each country.

Article 15(1): No one shall be held guilty of any criminal offence on account of any act or omission which did not constitute a criminal offence under national or international law, at the time when the criminal offense was committed. If, subsequent to the commission of the offense, provision is made by law for the imposition of the lighter penalty, the offender shall benefit thereby.

Article 17(1): No one shall be subjected to arbitrary or unlawful interference with his privacy, family, home or correspondence, nor to unlawful attacks on his honour and reputation.

Article 18(2): No one shall be subject to coercion which would impair his freedom to have or to adopt a religion or belief of his choice.

Article 18(4): The States Parties to the present Covenant undertake to have respect for the liberty of parents and, when applicable, legal guardians to ensure the religious and moral education of their children in conformity with their own convictions.

Article 20(1): Any propaganda for war shall be prohibited by law.

Article 20(2): Any advocacy of national, racial or religious hatred that constitutes incitement to discrimination, hostility or violence shall be prohibited by law.

Article 23(3): No marriage shall be entered into without the free and full consent of the intending spouses.

# APPENDIX 2

---

## Results of the Investigation

(1) No philosophical theory of human rights can succeed in providing a sound critical perspective on human rights practice unless it takes seriously the fact that international human rights law plays a central role in the Practice.

(2) Given the centrality of international legal human rights in the Practice, a philosophical theory of human rights that sheds light on the moral assessment of the Practice must determine whether the existing system of international legal human rights is justified or, if it is not, whether it can be modified so as to make it justifiable. Whether it is justified depends upon whether the functions it performs are morally sound, the means it employs to achieve them are morally permissible, its institutional implementation is legitimate, and upon whether the system of law has the resources for improving itself over time.

(3) Attempts to justify particular individual legal human rights must be indexed to the type of system of international legal rights in which the particular right is to be included. A characterization of the system type requires a specification of the roles in political discourse and action that the legal rights are to play, the functions they are to serve, the authority they are to possess vis-à-vis other bodies of law, including domestic constitutional law, and the capacities of the institutions through which the rights are to be interpreted and implemented.

Even if one assumes that the sole function of international legal rights law is to realize a set of preexisting moral human rights, it would not follow that the former should mirror the latter. Even if all international legal human rights are grounded in some way in moral human rights, their content should reflect the roles they are to play in the practice of human rights and the authority they are supposed to possess.

(4) In approaching the question of justification, it is a mistake to assume the Mirroring View, according to which a sound justification for an international legal right typically includes an appeal to the existence of a corresponding, preexisting moral right. Contrary to the Mirroring View, international legal human rights can be justified even if there are no corresponding, preexisting moral human rights, because international legal human rights can have a number of different moral groundings, of which the need to realize a corresponding moral right is only one. More specifically, international legal human rights can be justified (in part) by appeal to the moral importance of individuals on their own account, without mirroring a set of moral human rights. In addition, once we understand that legal rights can serve several distinct kinds of moral purposes, and that the realization of moral rights is only one of these, we should acknowledge that a sound justification for international legal human rights need not refer to moral rights at all.

(5) The duties that correlate with moral human rights are directed: morally owed to the right-holder. But the duties that correlate with legal rights, even though they are, as a matter of legal obligation, owed to the right-holder, need not be morally owed to the right-holder. Justifying moral (claim-)rights requires showing how some aspect of the right-holder's autonomy or interests or some other features of the individual are morally important enough to ground the corresponding duty, in order to make sense of the idea that the duty is owed to the right-holder. In the case of legal rights, the corresponding duties need not be grounded so narrowly; they can also be grounded in the importance of the interests of others than the right-holder, for example. What this means is that the scope of moral human rights, that is, the extent of the duties they ground, generally will be narrower than the scope of legal human rights. This is true for the right to democratic government, the right to basic education, the right to health, the right to due process under the law, the right to freedom of expression, and perhaps other rights as well.

Appealing to the existence of a corresponding moral human right is in these cases not sufficient for justifying the legal human right.

(6) Assuming the Mirroring View not only arbitrarily constrains inquiry into the justification of international legal human rights, it also encourages fallacious assessments of the existing international legal rights system. Recurrent complaints by philosophers that there is human rights inflation—that some items on the lists of rights found in prominent human rights conventions are not really human rights—are not cogent to the extent that they simply assume the Mirroring View. For example, even if there is no moral human right to periodic holidays with pay, there may still be sufficient reason to enact an international legal human right of this sort. Whether or not there is depends on what functions a system of international legal rights should serve, and it cannot be assumed that the sole function is to realize preexisting, corresponding moral rights. Instead of assuming that legal human rights that do not correspond to moral human rights or serve to realize moral human rights are instances of inflation, we should recognize that a list of moral human rights is too narrow a basis for justifying a system of international legal human rights.

(7) Rejecting the Mirroring View and adopting instead a Pluralistic Justificatory Strategy does not mean that anything goes. Any sound justification for a system of international legal human rights must satisfy certain constraints. In particular, it must be compatible with the chief functions that international legal human rights perform in human rights practice, on the best interpretation of the Practice. The two chief functions are (i) helping to ensure that each individual has the opportunity to lead a minimally good or decent life (the well-being function) and (ii) affirming and protecting the equal basic moral status of each individual. Both the well-being function and the status egalitarian function impose morally plausible limitations on sovereignty. In addition, a justification must be compatible with the idea, arguably central to the Practice, that (iii) international legal human rights are rights individuals have "simply by virtue of their humanity" on a reasonable interpretation of that idea.

(8) Moral arguments that do not appeal to preexisting, corresponding moral human rights can provide a powerful justification for a

system of international legal human rights that satisfies these three constraints ((i)-(iii) in (7)).

(9) Adopting a pluralistic methodological strategy for justifying international legal human rights makes it possible to deflect one important version of the complaint that international human rights law and the human rights practices that rely on it are incompatible with a proper appreciation of Reasonable Ethical Pluralism. If the justification of international legal human rights presupposes the existence of moral human rights, and if some reasonable moralities are incompatible with moral rights generally or with moral human rights, then this is a serious problem. But if there are other modes of justification— including some that are accessible from the standpoint of reasonable moralities that reject moral individual rights generally or moral human rights—then that problem disappears.

(10) A pluralistic methodological strategy also clears the way for explaining—and justifying—certain features of existing human rights law and practice that are problematic if we assume the Mirroring View. Included here are the fact that the UDHR and the ICCPR include collective rights of self-determination, with no hint that they are reducible to individual rights, and the fact that the Genocide Convention is not framed in terms of individual rights, even though it is considered a core element of international human rights law. These features are not anomalies, once we take seriously the possibility that international human rights law can serve purposes other than the realization of preexisting moral rights of individuals.

(11) Once we adopt the pluralistic justificatory strategy we are free to consider more impartially the various functions that a justifiable system of international legal human rights could perform. We are also able to consider the possibility that even if, as Hans Morsink has argued, the founders of the modern human rights practice thought that the main purpose of having a system of international legal human rights was to realize a corresponding set of preexisting moral human rights, the practice may also perform other functions. Further, we are able to consider whether the system ought to or may rightly develop new functions, including the creation of standards of global justice comprehensively considered. In other words, even if,

at the founding or even up to the present, international human rights law has only served to help realize a part of the domain of global justice, what I have referred to elsewhere as transnational justice, that could change and perhaps should change. (By the phrase 'transnational justice' I mean standards of justice that it is appropriate for international society to expect every state to observe internally.) If international human rights law could be modified to mitigate, in a direct and effective way, the huge disparities of power among states and the injustices of the global basic structure that they facilitate, it would address issues of global justice on which it is now largely silent.

(12) Whether or not human rights practice exhibits an individualistic bias cannot be determined simply by noting that for the most part the items in human rights conventions take the form of individual rights, because individual legal rights can and do serve a number of different moral values, including nonindividualistic ones. What matters most is whether the rights serve moral values that are not distorted by individualistic biases and whether the institutions through which human rights norms are formulated, interpreted, and reinterpreted over time have the resources to correct for such biases. Existing institutions in fact have considerable resources for doing this, though there is room for improvement.

(13) Those who are sincerely concerned about the risk that legal standards are distorted by biases should be supportive of international legal human rights, so far as the latter serve to affirm and protect equal basic moral status, because some of the worst moral biases consist of mistaken beliefs about natural differences between different types of humans (men and women, blacks and whites, etc.) that ground judgments of inferiority, and false beliefs of this sort are more likely to be sustained in societies in which equal basic moral status is not publicly affirmed and protected. In brief, where international legal human rights are respected, we have more reason to be confident that our moral views, laws, and institutions are unbiased than under conditions in which human rights are not respected, because violations of human rights typically contribute to social conditions that are epistemically defective in ways that encourage mistaken beliefs about basic moral status.

(14) To justify a system of international legal human rights it is not sufficient to provide in principle justifications for various international legal human rights, considered simply as legal norms in the abstract. It is also necessary to address the moral status of the institutions that create, interpret, and implement these norms. Conceptions of legitimacy tailored to the special case of the state are ill suited for assessing the legitimacy of most international institutions, including those that play a key role in the system of international legal human rights. Once we adopt the more comprehensive understanding of institutional legitimacy supplied by the Metacoordination View, it becomes clear that international legal human rights institutions can be legitimate even though they are not democratic and lack some of the other characteristics of legitimate states.

(15) It is frequently said that international law generally, including international human rights law, suffers a legitimacy deficit because of the relatively primitive character of international legal institutions—in particular, the lack of representative legislative institutions and a developed, independent judiciary operating within a context of constitutional constraints on legislation. This standard picture of the legitimacy-impairing deficiencies of international human rights law is defective because it overlooks what I have called the reciprocal legitimation of international institutions and states and, more generally, the ecological nature of institutional legitimacy. States enhance the legitimacy of international law by performing much of the work of specifying and adjudicating abstract norms of international human rights law, thus compensating for the lack of an international legislature and judiciary. At the same time, the constraints on sovereignty that international human rights law provides enhances the legitimacy of states, in part by requiring states to take seriously the interests of foreigners and in part by providing citizens with assurance that the state will not be the ultimate arbiter of complaints about its own human rights performance. Just as important, the fact that international law enhances the legitimacy of states enhances its own legitimacy. One important function of international human rights law is that it facilitates this relationship of reciprocal legitimation. Through ratifying international human rights conventions, states assume legal obligations that compensate for the legitimacy-compromising deficiencies of international institutions and

which at the same time contribute to their own legitimacy. Recip-rocal legitimation is best understood if we employ the idea of the Extended Legal-Institutional Order, on analogy with the Extended Mind. The basic idea is that legitimacy assessments should be made on the basis of the functions of institutions and that law can enable institutions to benefit from a division of labor. Just as it would be a mistake to say that international law has no enforcement mecha-nisms, thereby overlooking the fact that states enforce international human rights laws in their own jurisdictions, so it is equally mis-taken to say that international law is primitive and incomplete because it lacks a hierarchy of courts with compulsory jurisdiction, thereby overlooking the fact that international law recruits domes-tic courts to perform adjudicative functions. From a functional standpoint—and it is largely function that is crucial for legitimacy—the boundaries of institutions and of legal systems are much more encompassing than critics of the primitiveness and incompleteness of international law assume. Given the relationships of reciprocal legitimation that exist between states and international legal human rights institutions, the "democratic deficit" of the latter will di-minish if the trend toward democratization of states continues.

(16) Although the legitimacy of international legal human rights in-stitutions depends in significant part on their close connection with state institutions and NGOs, they exhibit a high degree of modu-larity vis-à-vis one another. Consequently, legitimacy deficits in one particular institution, such as the Security Council, need not under-mine the legitimacy of the international legal human rights system as a whole.

(17) Once the role that international human rights institutions play in helping to legitimate states is appreciated, the worry that asser-tions of the supremacy of international human rights law are a threat to state sovereignty is mitigated. Nonetheless, whether acknowl-edging the supremacy of international human rights law is compat-ible with proper respect for sovereignty and for the values of constitutionalism depends on two factors: the quality of interna-tional legal human rights norms and the nature of the processes by which domestic legal systems incorporate international human rights law. When international human rights law impacts constitutional

arrangements the method of incorporation ought to be robustly democratic, but in many cases it is not.

(18) There are at least three cogent justifications for an international legal human rights system similar to the existing one: an argument from the benefits that such a system provides, an argument for the conclusion that the existing international legal order is unjustifiable without such a system, and an argument for the conclusion that states and the governments that are their agents have a special obligation to establish an international legal human rights system or to support it if it already exists, because they are the chief beneficiaries of and exert the most control over an international order that is unjustifiable without such a system.

(19) Although the benefits of having an international legal human rights system will vary across states, all states, including those that have especially good domestic legal systems, have an obligation not only to support but also to participate in a supranational system of legal human rights.

(20) Having an international legal human rights system, instead of relying only on regional legal human rights systems, is valuable from the standpoint of the fundamental idea of the human rights enterprise, that of making the behavior of states toward those under their jurisdiction a subject of international concern, because an international legal human rights system empowers the widest range of legitimate actors to hold states legally accountable.

# INDEX